Sculpting In Clay With Dale Power

Text written with and photography by Jeffrey B. Snyder

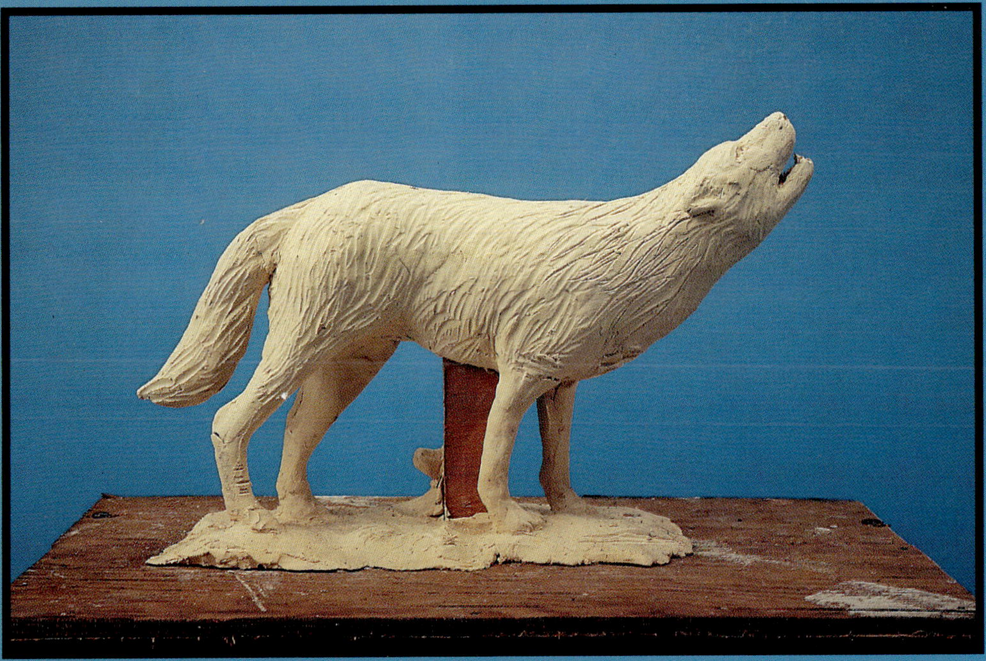

Schiffer Publishing Ltd
4880 Lower Valley Road, Atglen, PA 19310 USA

Acknowledgments

I would like to thank my friends at Sculpture House (100 Kamp Meeting Avenue, Skillman, NJ 08558).

Contents

Library of Congress Catalog Card Number: 97-80127

Book Design by: Laurie A. Smucker

ISBN: 0-7643-0113-6
Printed in China

Published by Schiffer Publishing Ltd.
4880 Lower Valley Road
Atglen, PA 19310
Phone: (610) 593-1777; Fax: (610) 593-2002
E-mail: Schifferbk@aol.com
Please write for a free catalog.
This book may be purchased from the publisher.
Please include $3.95 for shipping.
Try your bookstore first.

We are interested in hearing from authors with book ideas on related subjects.

Introduction

Clay is one of the quickest mediums in which to work out your ideas. It works especially well when you can only find a single view of an object you intend to create or when there is a special stance or position you wish to create for your figure. It is a simple matter to construct and move an armature into that particular pose.

Oil based clay is used here (named Roma Italian Plastilina, to be specific) instead of water based clay. Oil based clay doesn't harden up on you and has a longer working life. No special care is required to keep oil based clays from hardening.

Three projects will be completed here to detail the various techniques required to create human and animal figures in clay. The three projects are:

1) an elderly gentleman;
2) a bearded man;
3) an impala.

I hope you enjoy these projects. Best of luck with all of your artistic endeavors!

—Dale Power

Tools

The photograph and caption illustrate and list all of the tools you will need to successfully complete these projects.

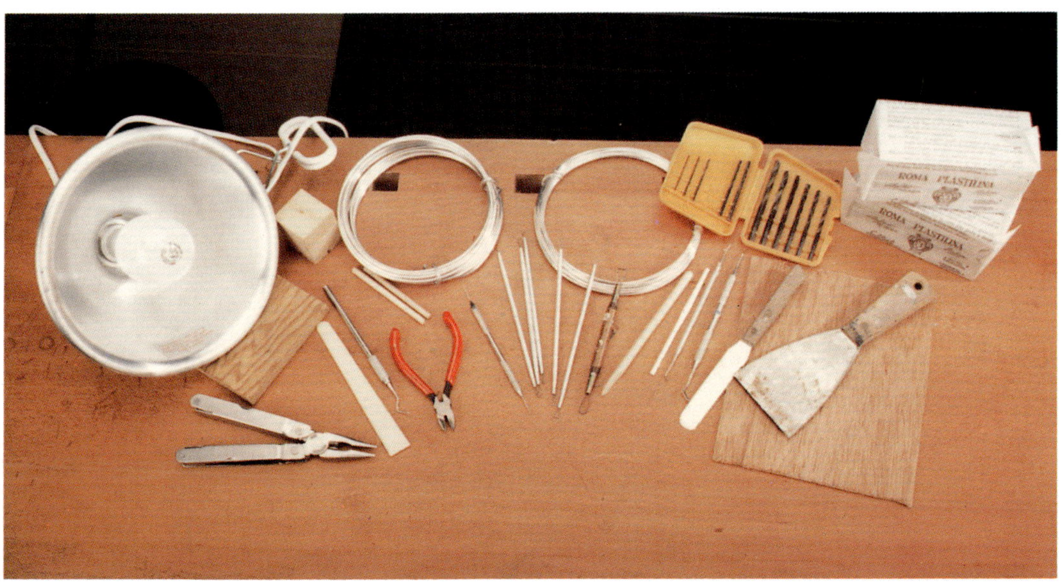

The tools we are going to need for clay sculpting include: needle nosed pliers, small wire cutters, an assortment of clay sculpturing tools, some dental picks, a light with a reflector, a couple of different sizes of putty knives, some twist bits, blocks of wood for mounting armatures, 1/8" and 1/16" aluminum wire, 1/8" plywood, and plastilina clay.

Projects

Clay Preparation

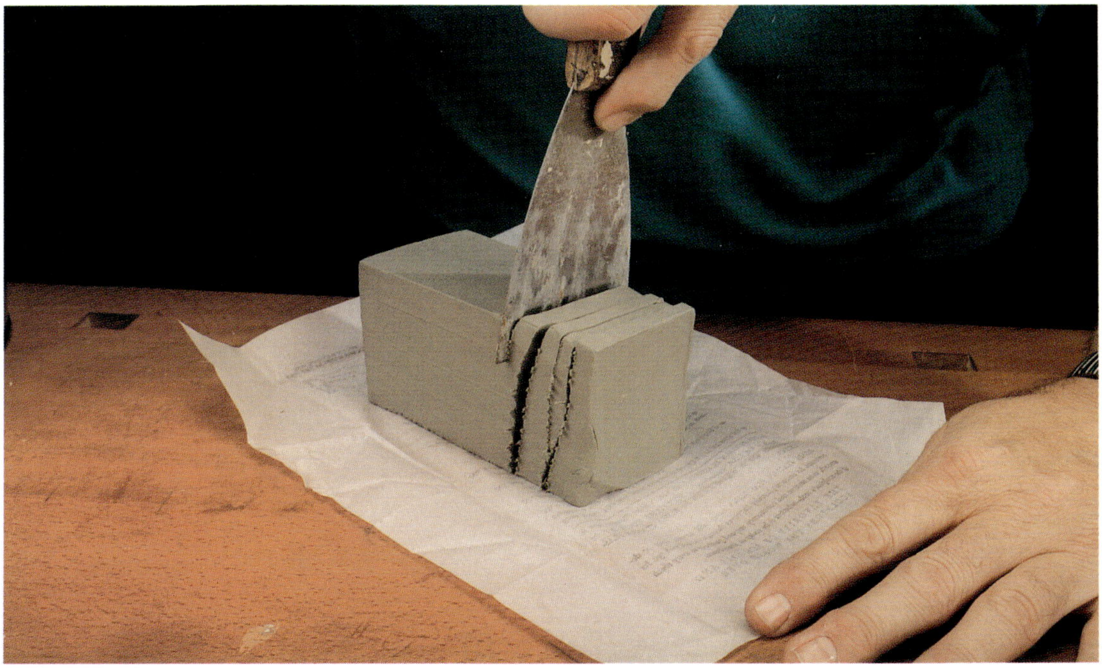

Start preparing the clay by cutting it into slabs, using a putty knife or other large instrument. Each clay slab should measure between 1/4" and 3/8" thick

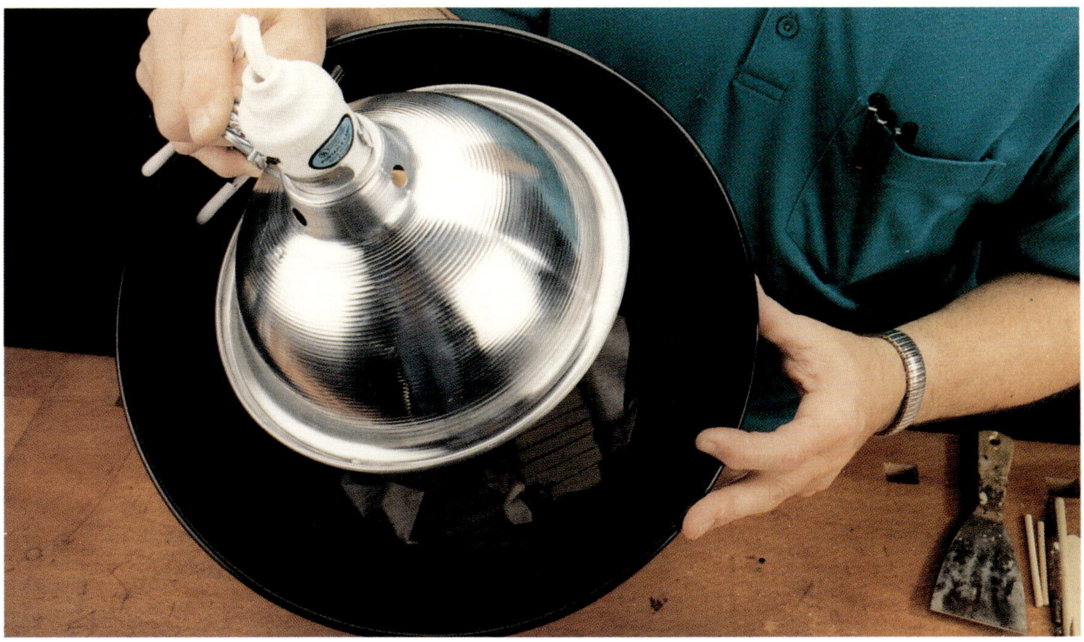

To make the clay easier to work with, place it into a metal waste paper basket and suspend your light over it. The light will soften the clay and make it more enjoyable to work with.

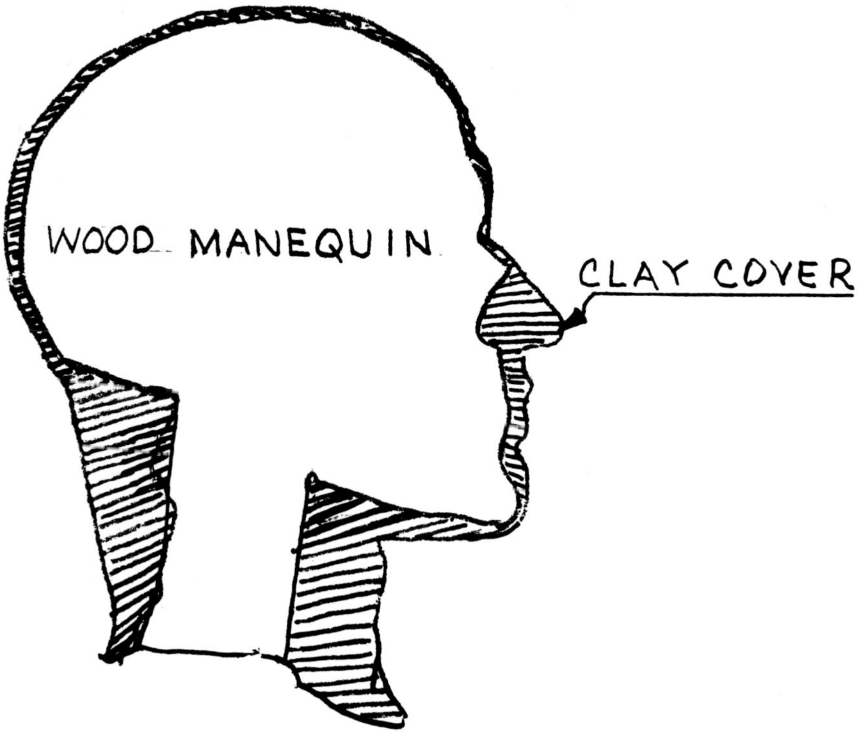

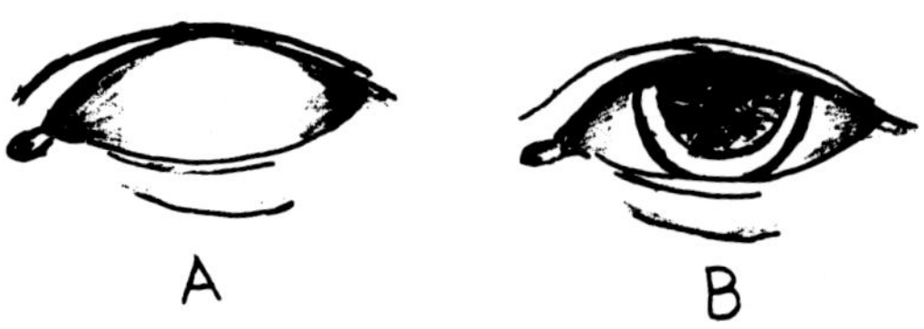

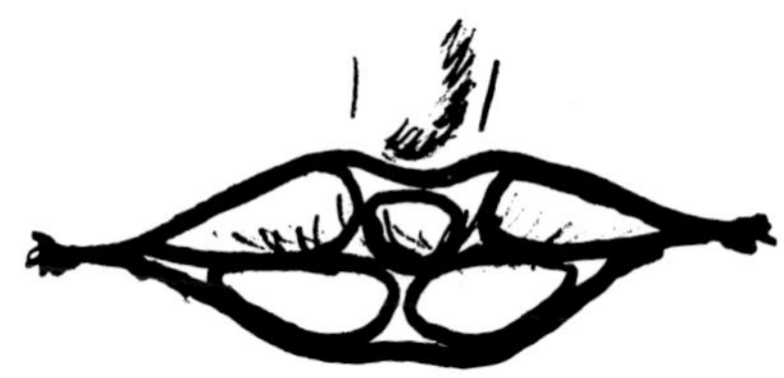

The upper lip consists of (3) three sections and the lower lip has only(2) two.

A This type of eye was used on Roman sculpture. It gives a blank look to the eye.

B This type of eye while giving a more real look, also gives a hard look with little life in it.

C This is a Greek type of eye used by sculpters to give more life to the eye, making it much more appealing.

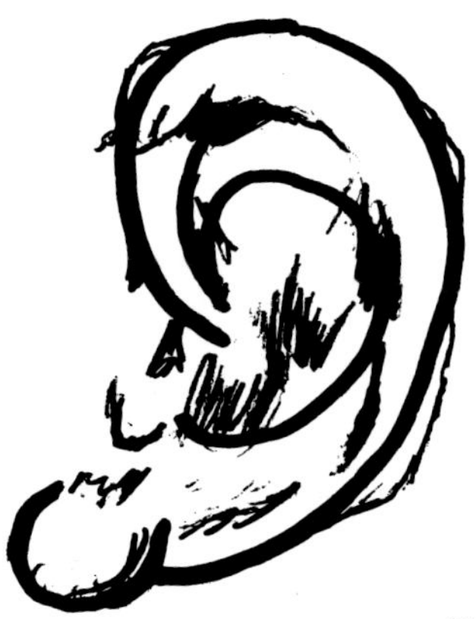

The ear is generally a C shape as shown here.

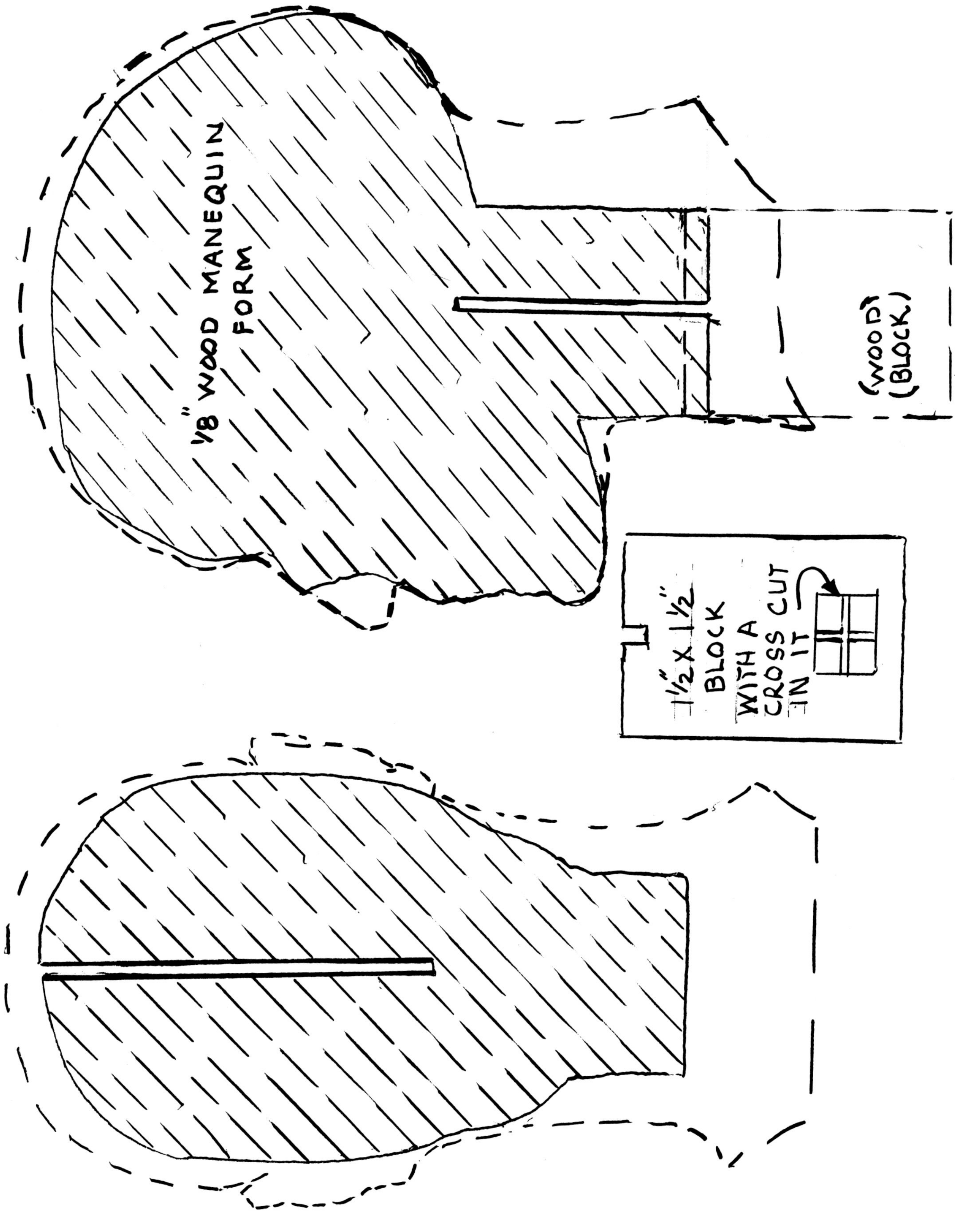
1/8" WOOD MANEQUIN FORM
(WOOD) (BLOCK)
1 1/2" X 1 1/2 BLOCK WITH A CROSS CUT IN IT

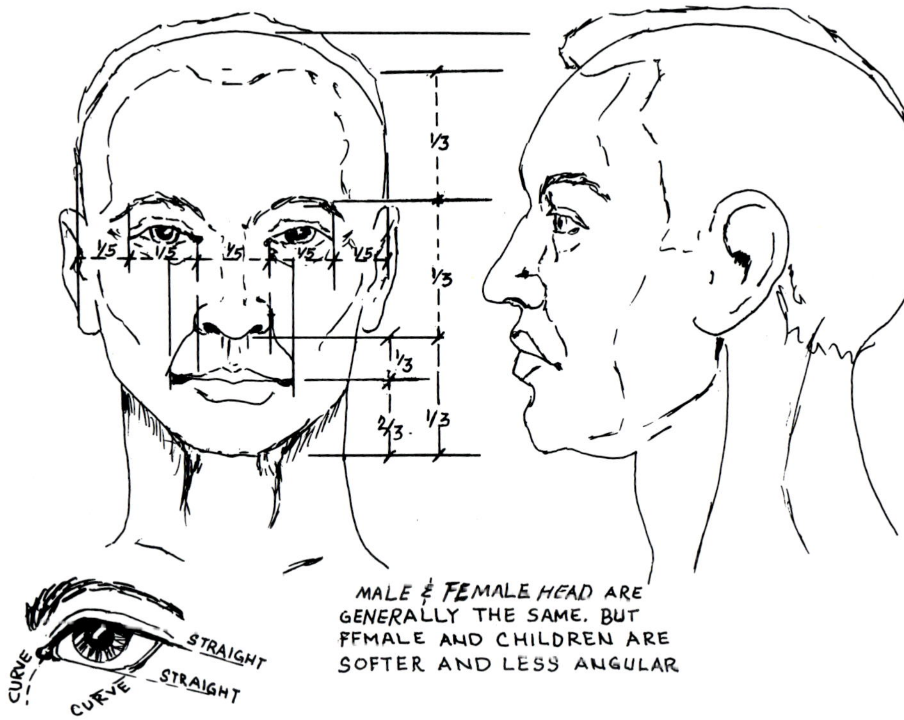

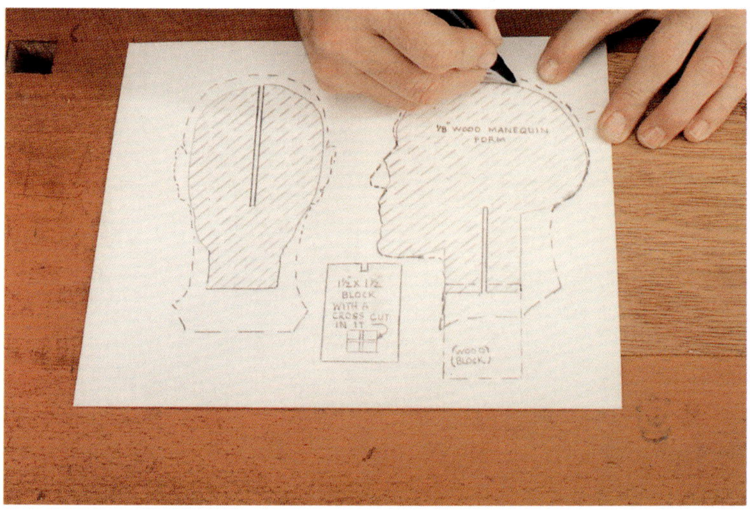

Transfer the drawing of the armature onto 1/8" thick wood.

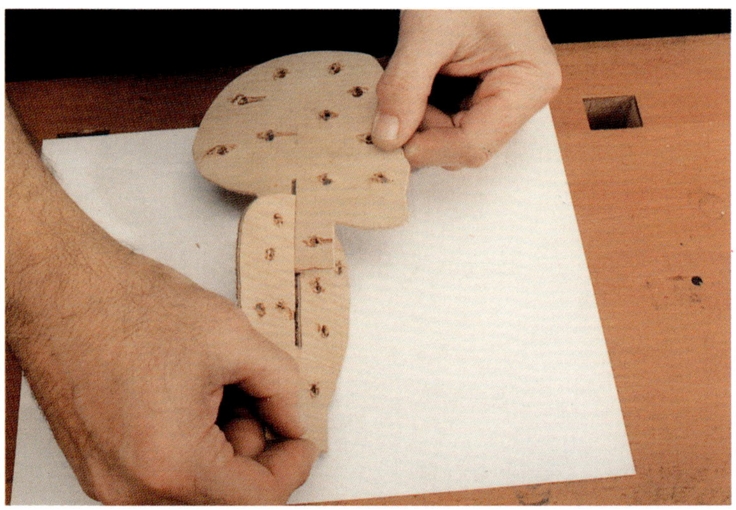

Sliding the armature together.

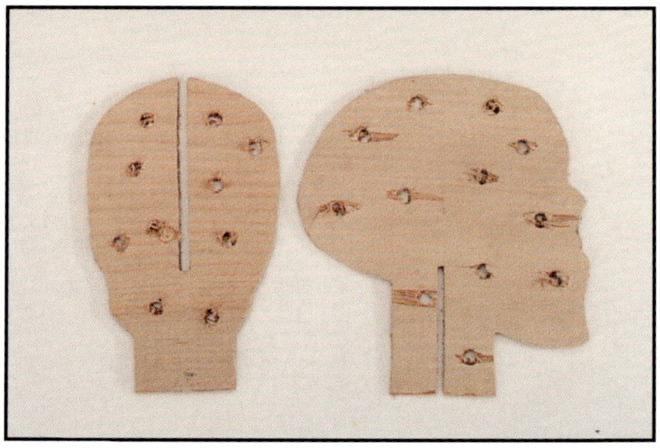

After cutting out the plywood armature and drilling randomly spaced 1/8" holes, you are ready to start the assembly by sliding the two together.

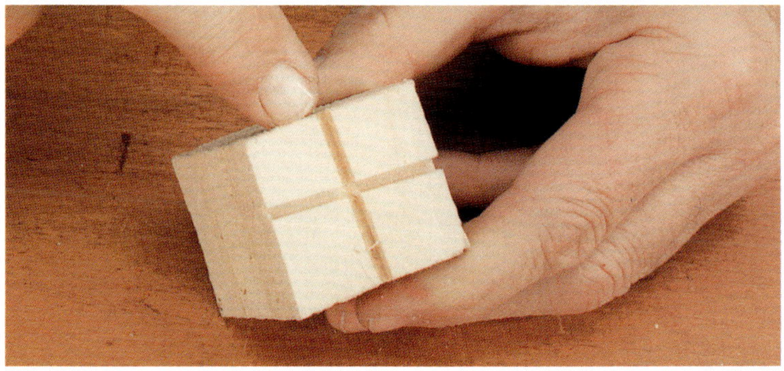

Prepare a base to hold the armature. The base is made of a 1 1/2" x 1 1/2" block of wood. This block may be of any height you want, but it needs to have an X cut into the top. The X must be large enough to receive the 1/8" wood.

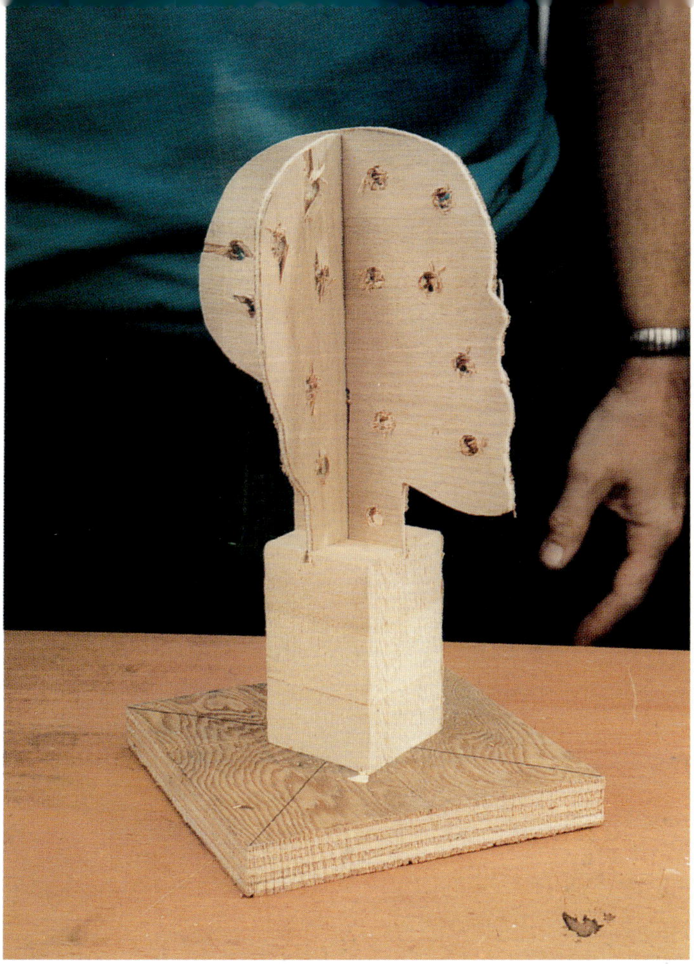

Attach the block to a plywood base. Assemble the armature on top of the block.

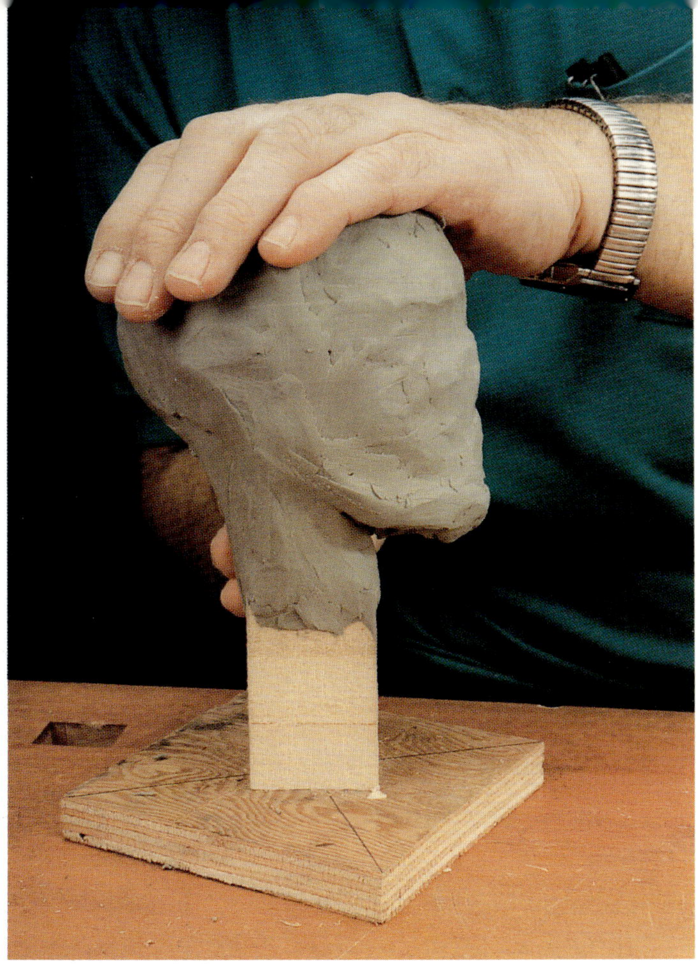

Keep applying the clay until you have it close to the proper general shape for a head. This is the way the head will be roughed out before adding the finer details.

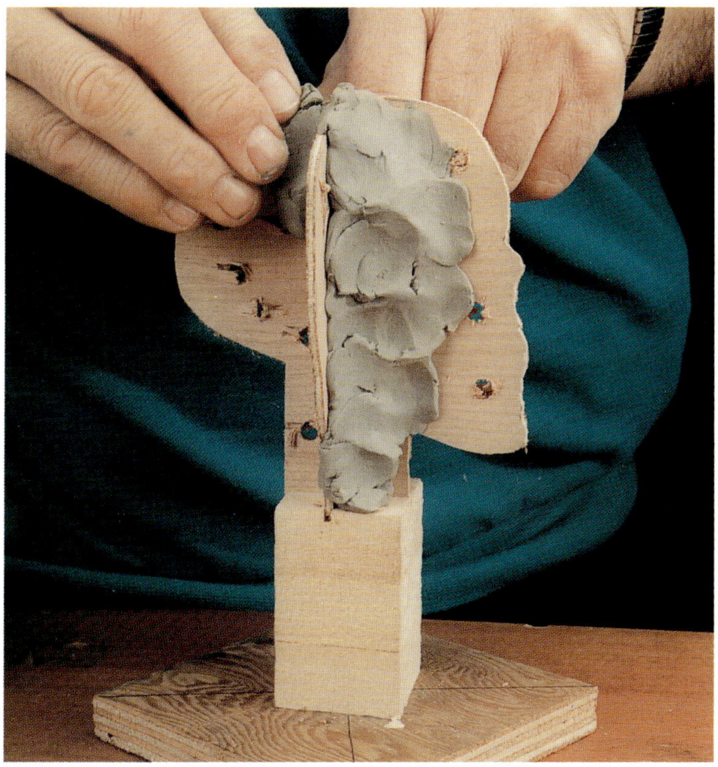

To begin creating the elderly gentleman, adding a roll of clay to the armature, pressing it to make sure that it is worked into the predrilled holes.

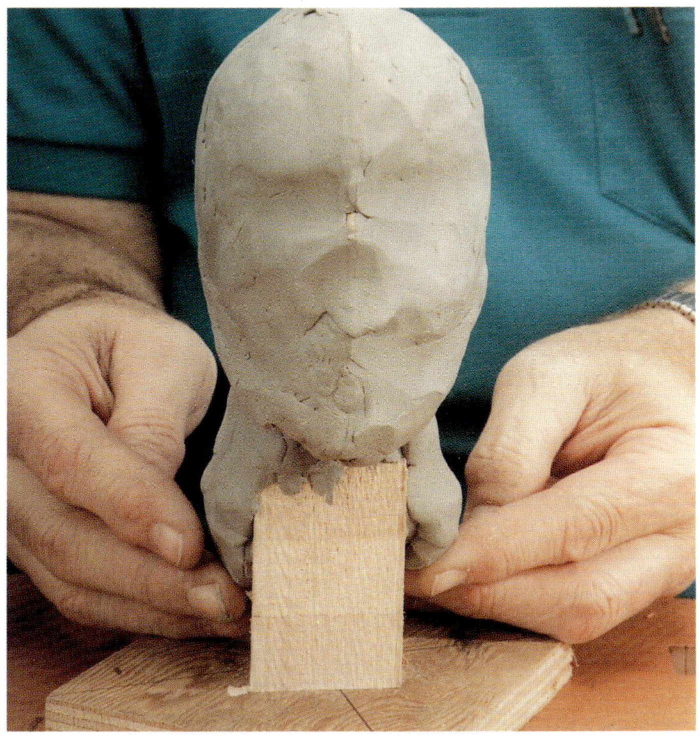

Start to fill out down onto the neck and shoulders to support the head.

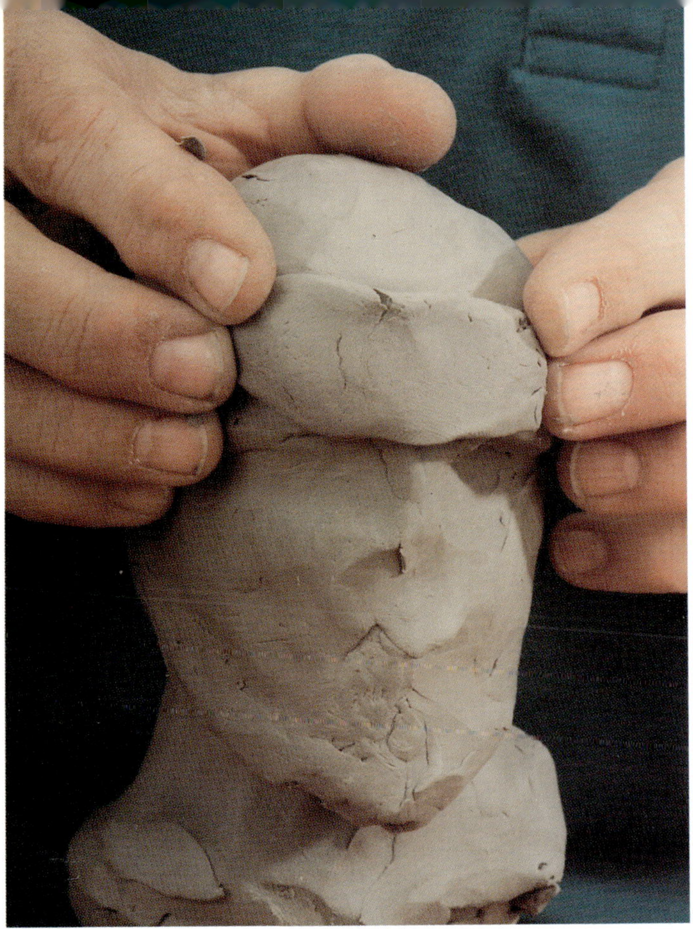

Start adding on the features of the face by laying a flat strip across the forehead to begin forming the brow line.

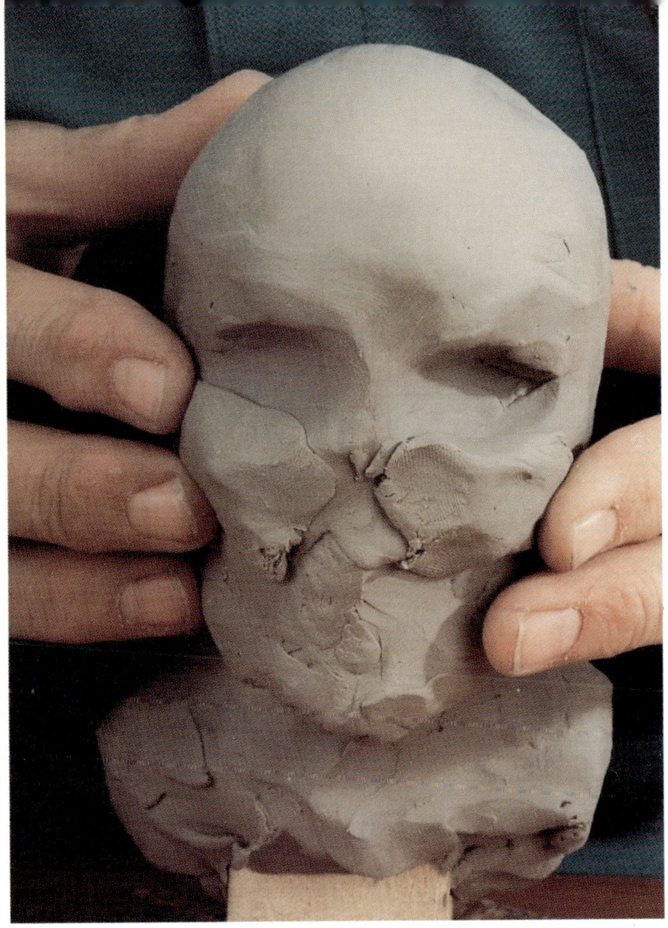

Make up strips of clay and lay them on for the cheek bones.

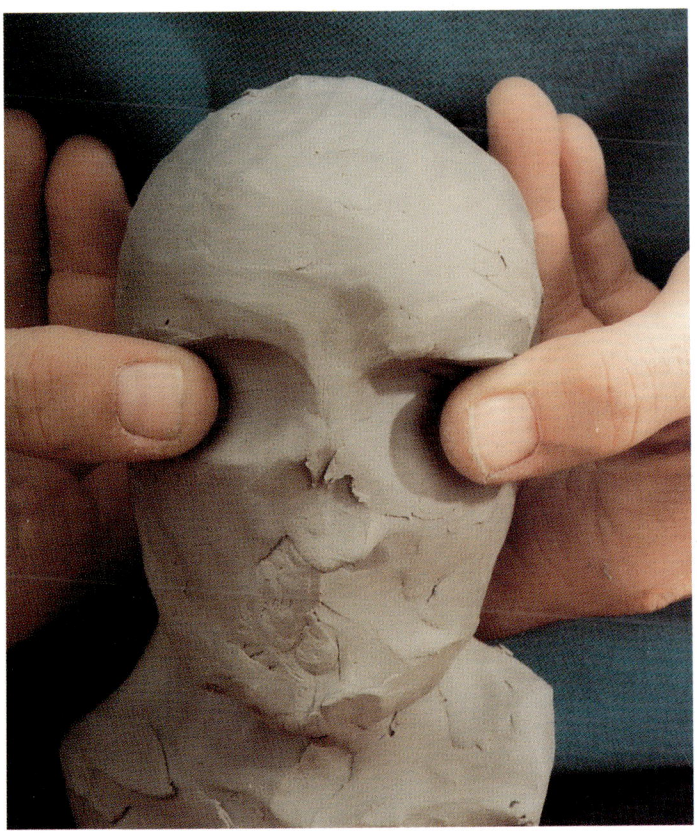

Taking your thumbs, press into the clay to form eye sockets.

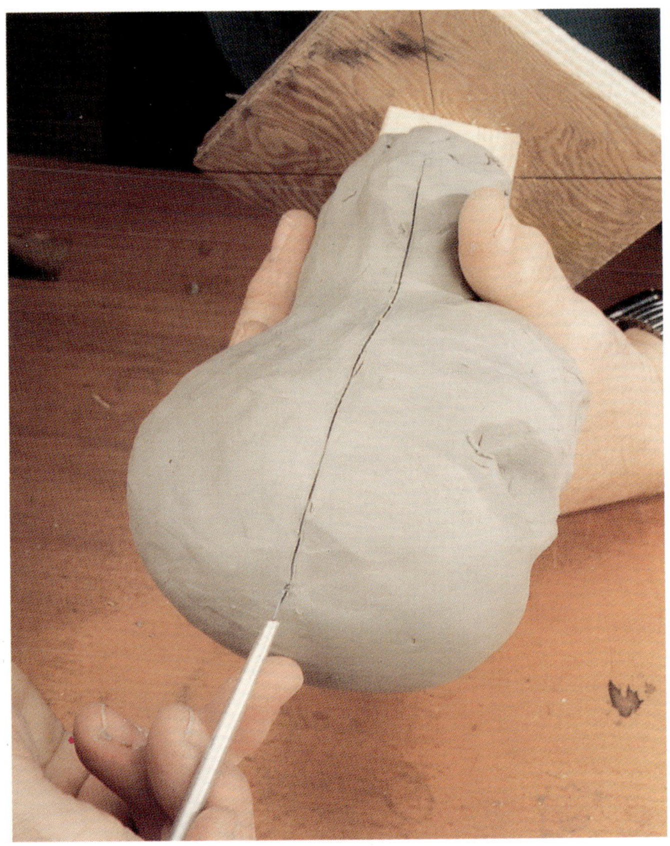

Using a fine sculpture tool, draw in a line indicating the half way point from front to back on the side of the head.

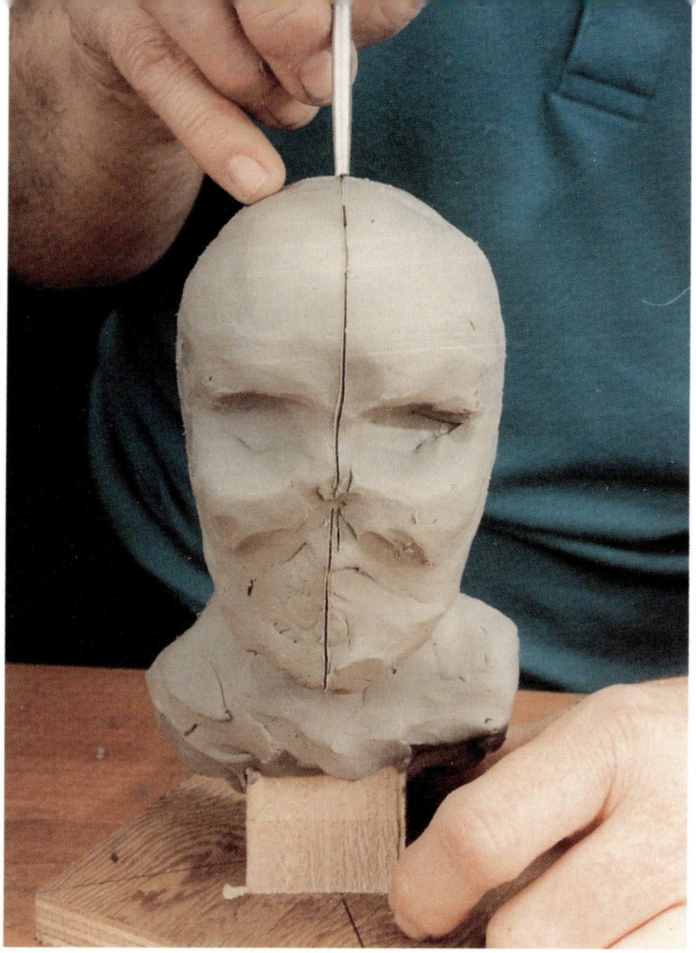

Repeat this process to get the centerline down the front of the face.

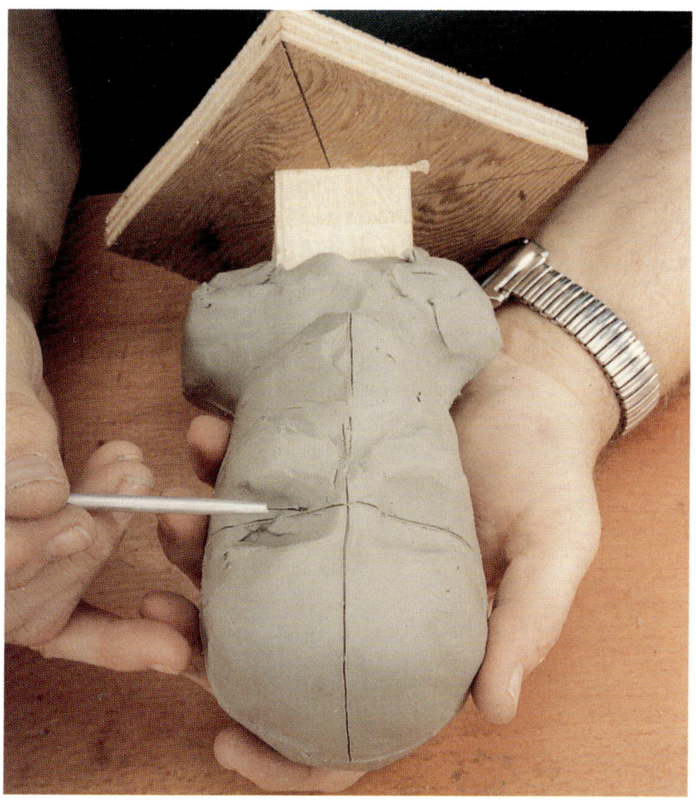

Draw a line at the half way point between the top of the head and the chin. This will be the line that indicates the location of the bottom lid of the eye.

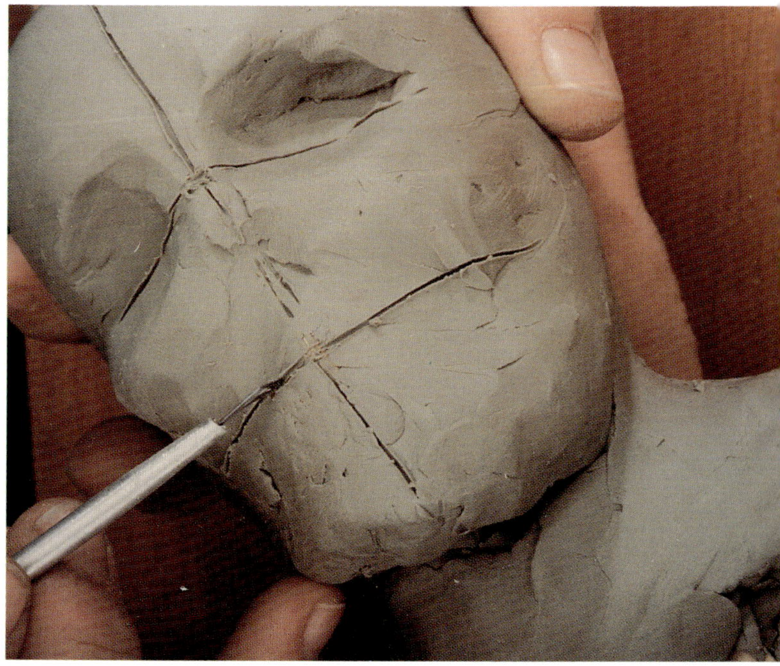

Halfway between the line for the bottom of the eyes and the chin, draw a line for the bottom of the nose.

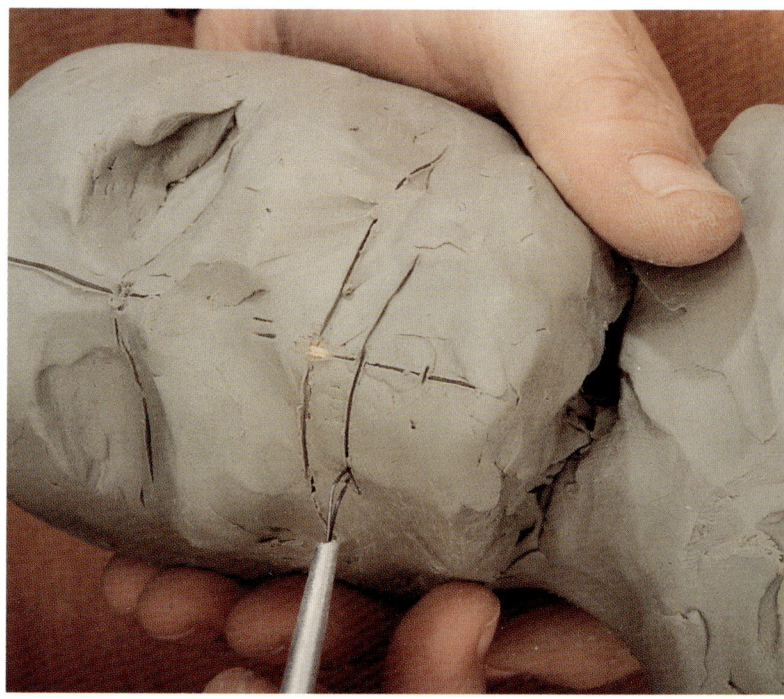

Divide the space between the bottom of the nose and the chin into three equal parts. The top lip will fall on the line 2/3 of the way up from the chin.

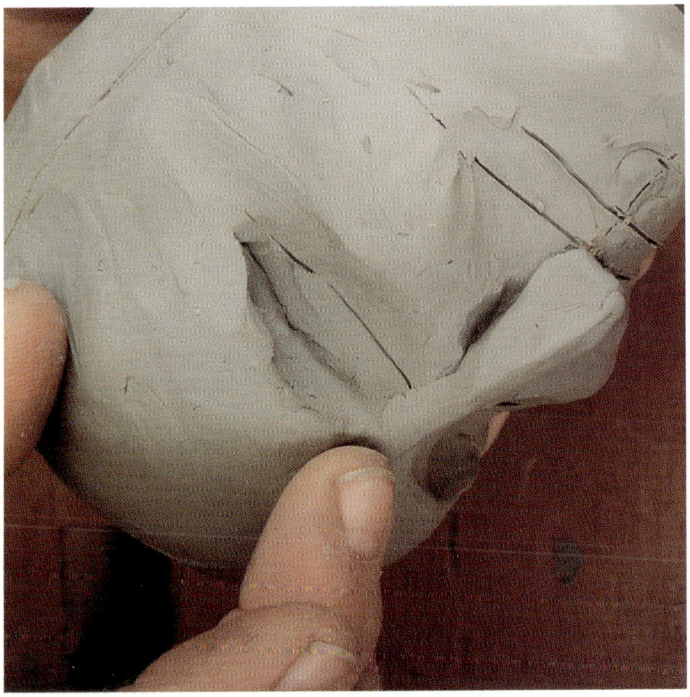

Add a piece of clay and flatten it to start to build up the bridge and center section of the nose.

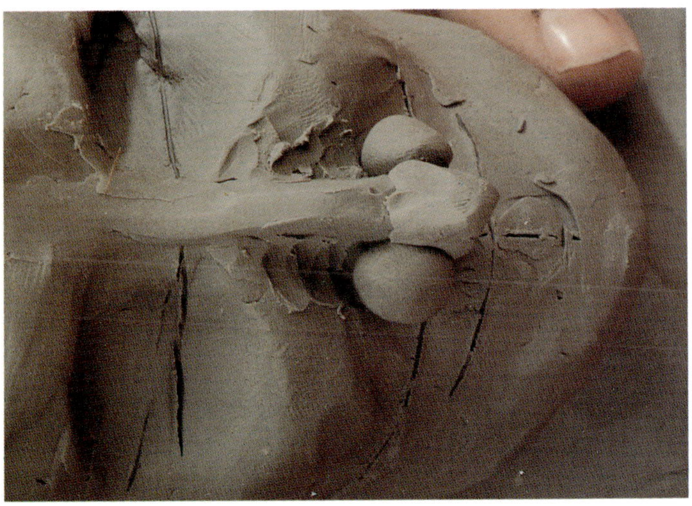

Add three balls of clay (of roughly the same size) to the nose — one in the center and one on either side for the ball of the nose and the nostrils.

Add a small roll of clay on either side of the bridge of the nose.

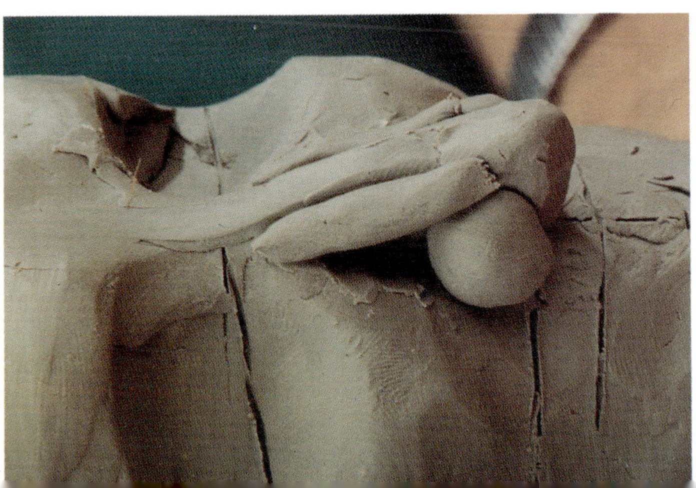

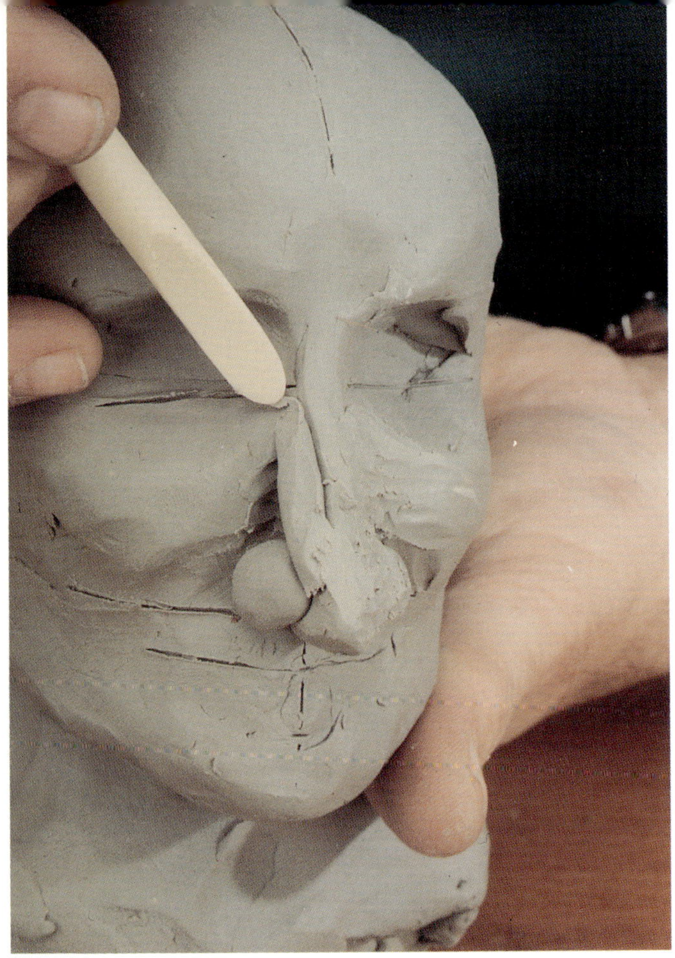

Blend the two rolls of clay into the nose to start forming the bulk of the nose. Blend them out onto the cheek. Also blend the three balls of clay together over the nostrils. Use a sculpturing tool for this.

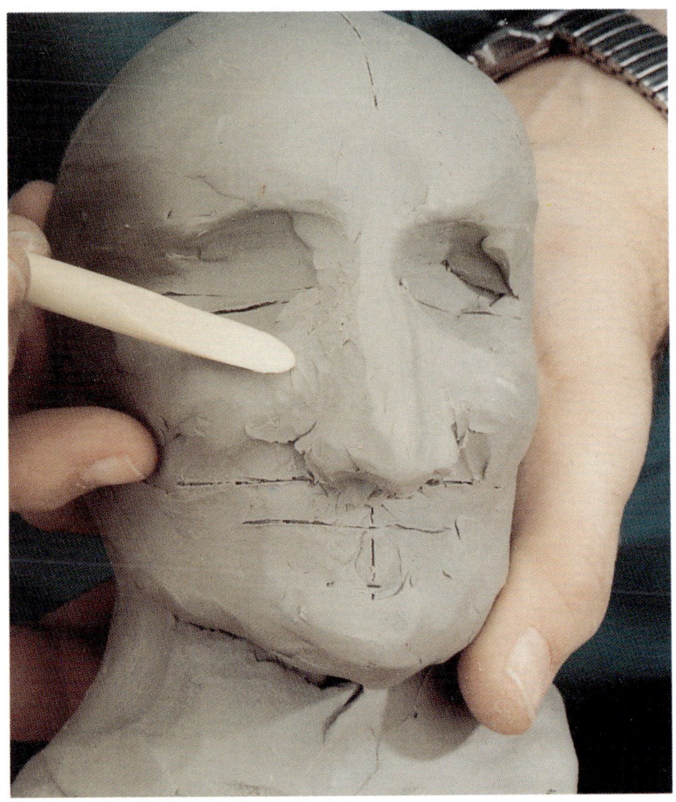

The nose starts to take shape.

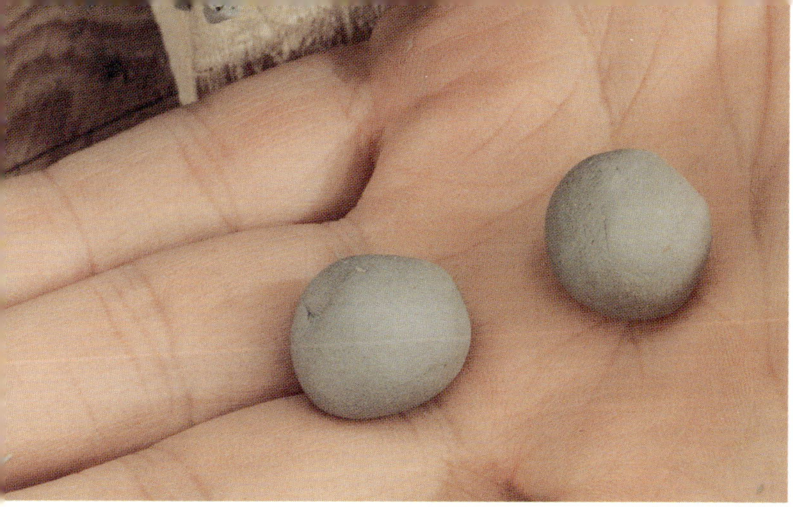

Make two balls of clay of approximately the same size that will fit comfortably into the eye sockets you have left in your face. These will be the eyeballs.

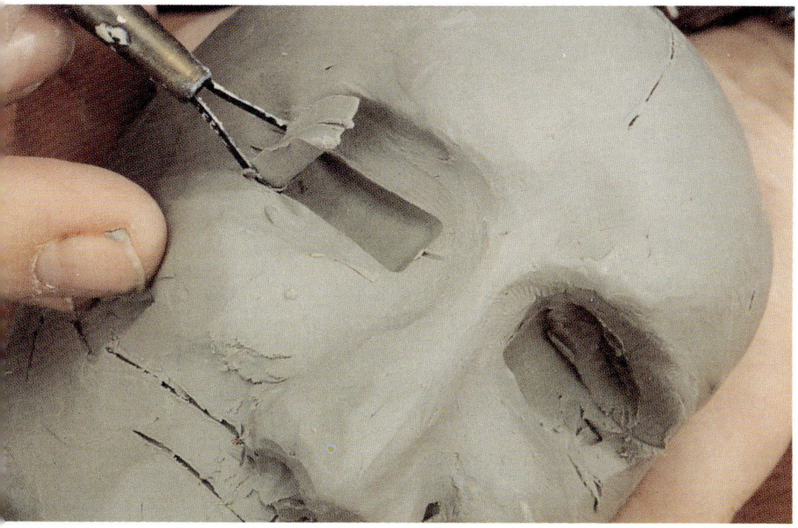

Cut in and remove some of the clay in the eye socket using a sculpturing tool so that you can place the eyeballs in. Remember not to remove clay below the line that you have drawn for the lower eye lid.

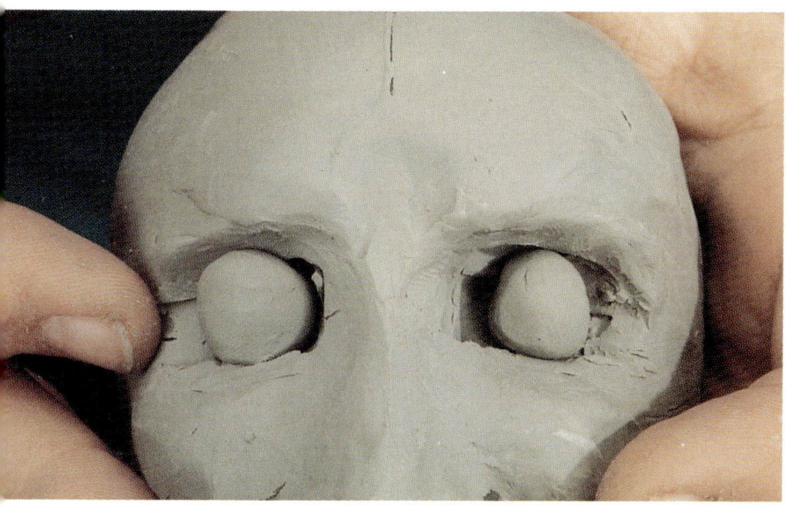

Place the eyeballs in the sockets.

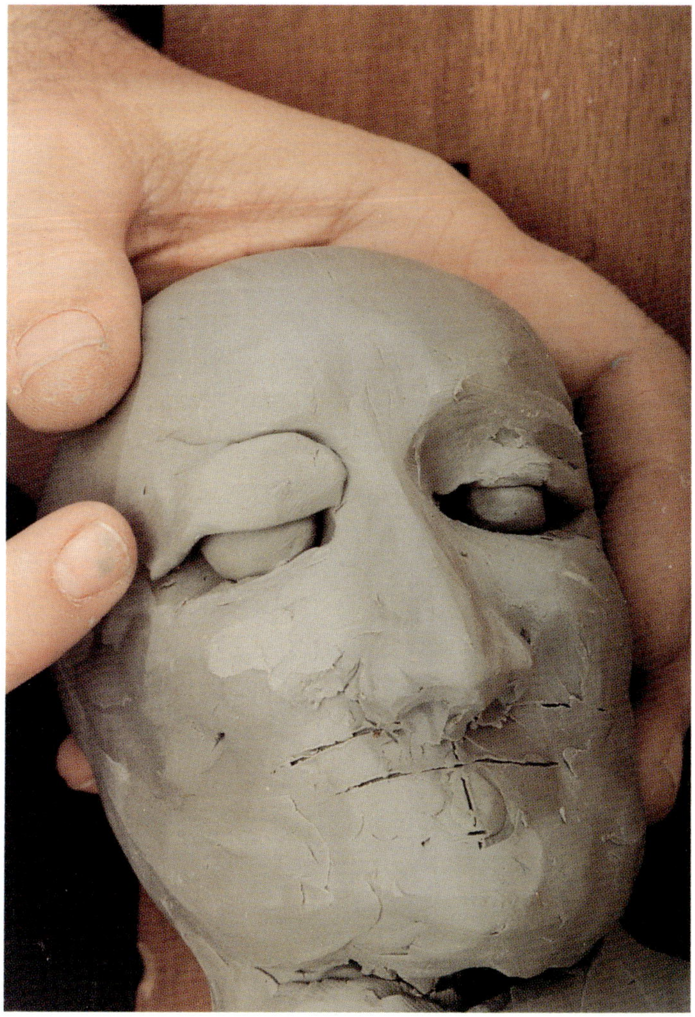

Make a small wafer of clay and lay it in over the upper half of the eyeball to produce the top eye lid.

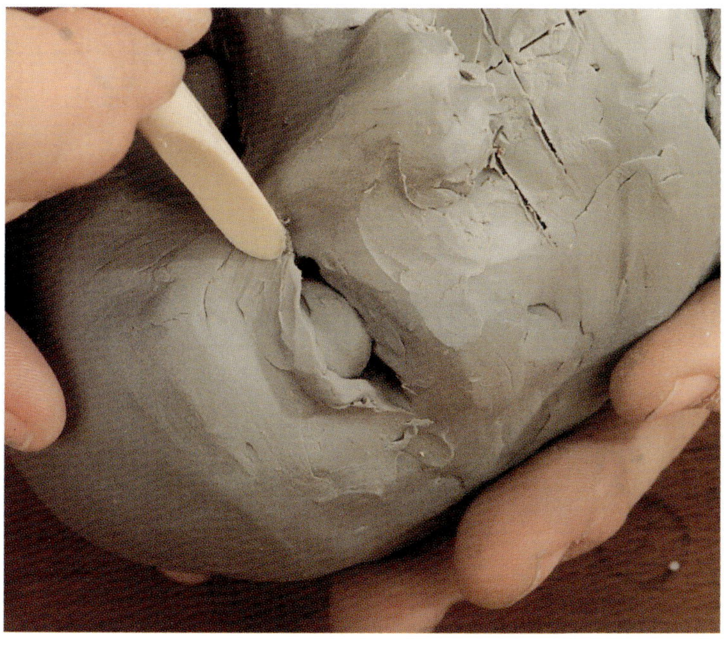

Shape the eye lid in place over the eyeball, remembering that the inside of the eye closest to the nose is deeper than the outside.

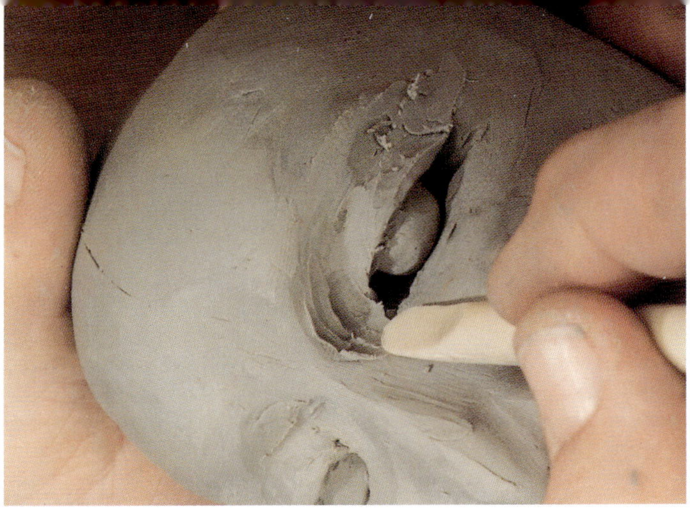

The deeper set inside corner of the eye.

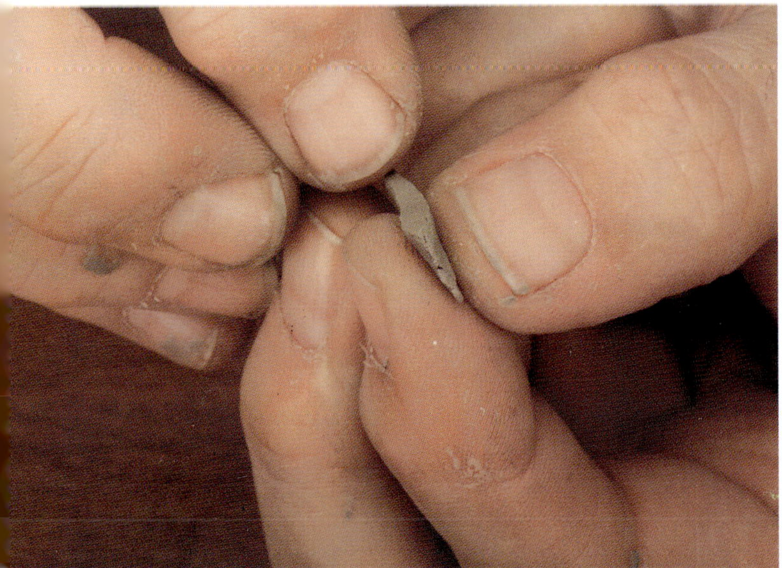

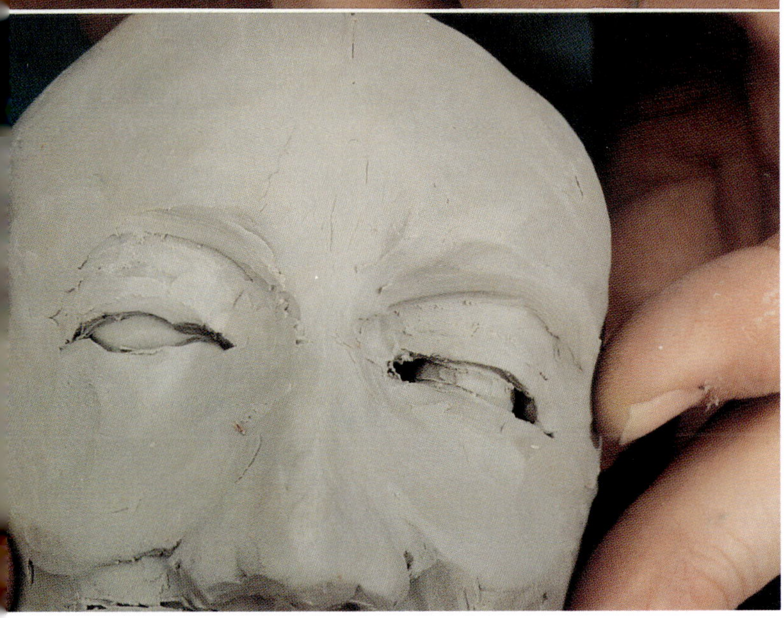

Take a thin sheet of clay, flatten it along the top edge, and make it very thin along the bottom edge. Lay it in against the eye to form the bottom lid. Line the bottom lid up with the line indicating the placement of the bottom lid. Both eyes are in place.

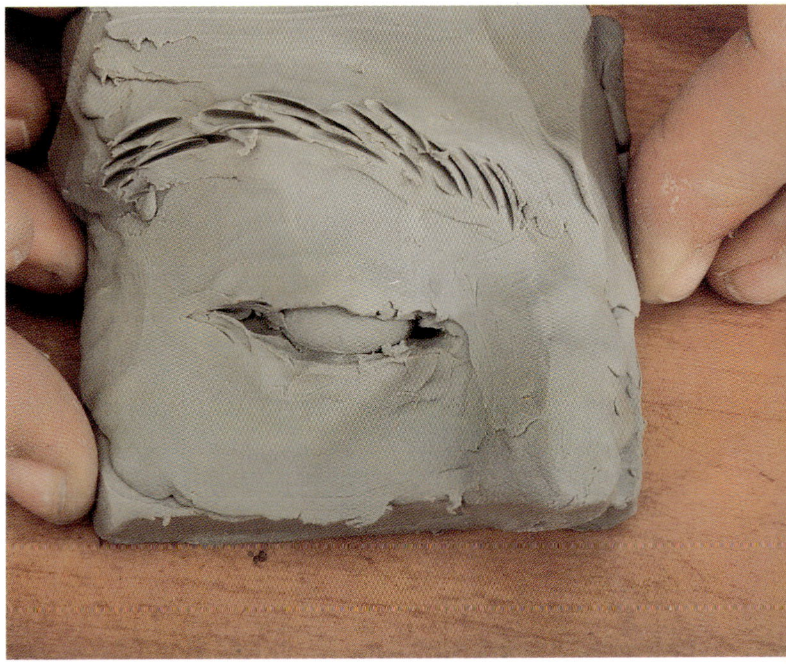

This is a sample eye, a little larger sized so that you can see how the top and bottom eye lids are laid in. I will also show you how to lay in the features of the eye itself. Right now you have a "Roman" eye. The Romans painted their eyes onto their sculptures using the blank eyeball as their "canvas."

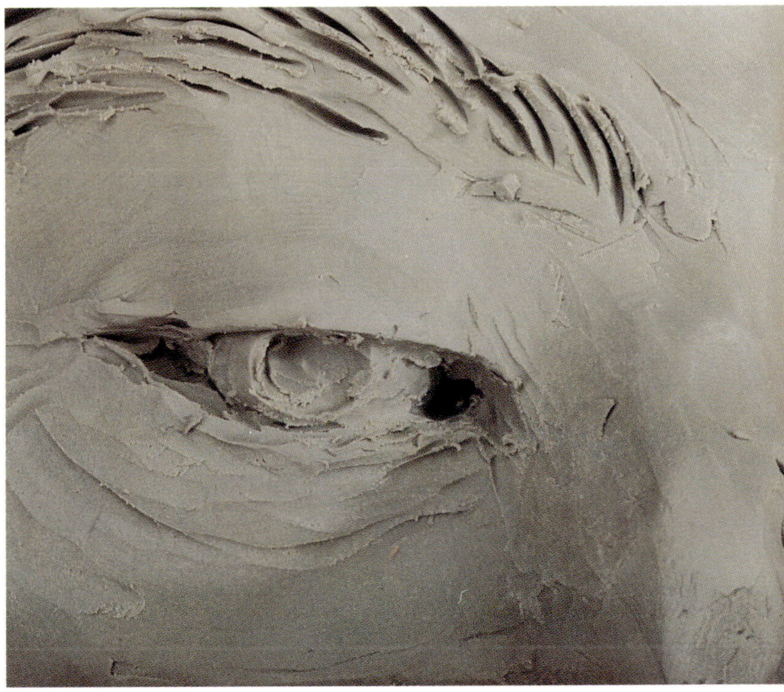

This style of eye (while providing a more realistic look) gives a much harder look to the eye. To make this eye just cut a small dish shaped center out of the eye.

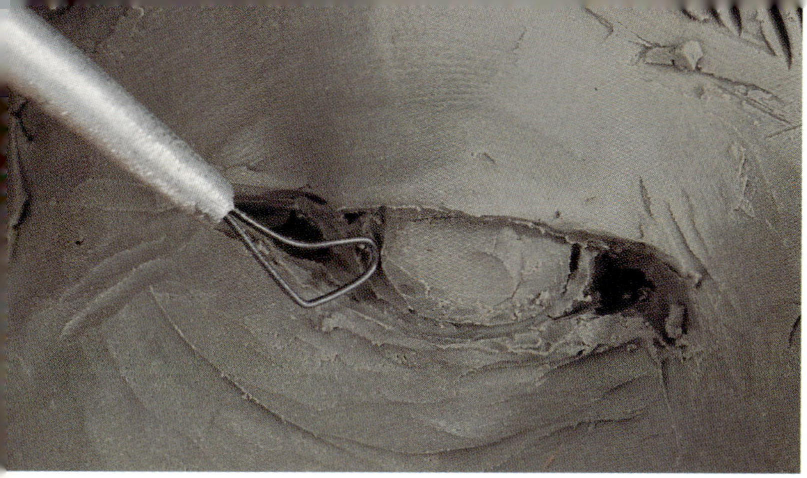

The last eye style is called a "Greek" eye. It is made in three stages. The first stage is to draw the iris onto the eye.

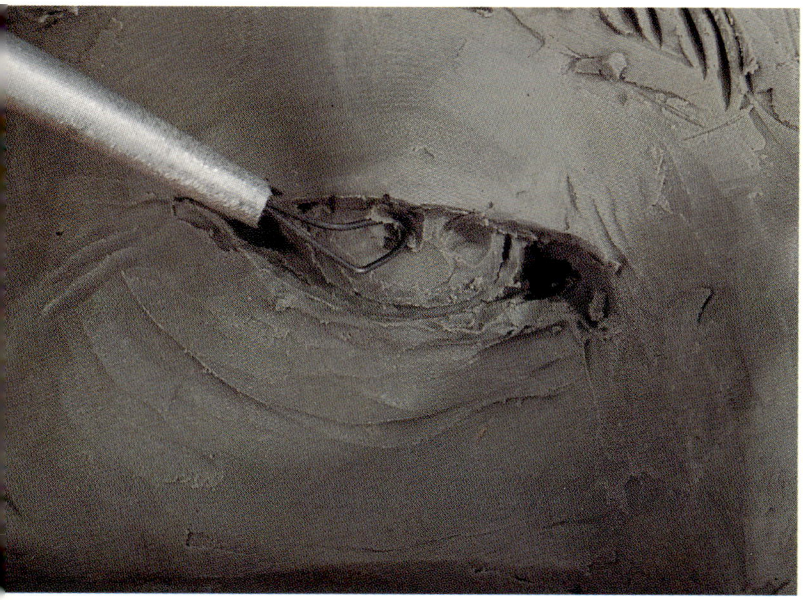

The second stage is to cut two small circles near the top lid of the eye.

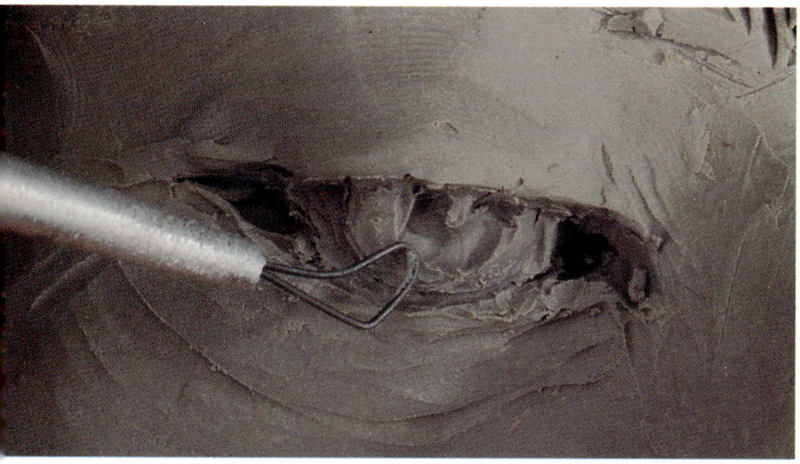

The third stage is to connect the two circles with a crescent moon shape, leaving the center untouched. This gives you a much more realistic eye by appearing to add a highlight to the eye.

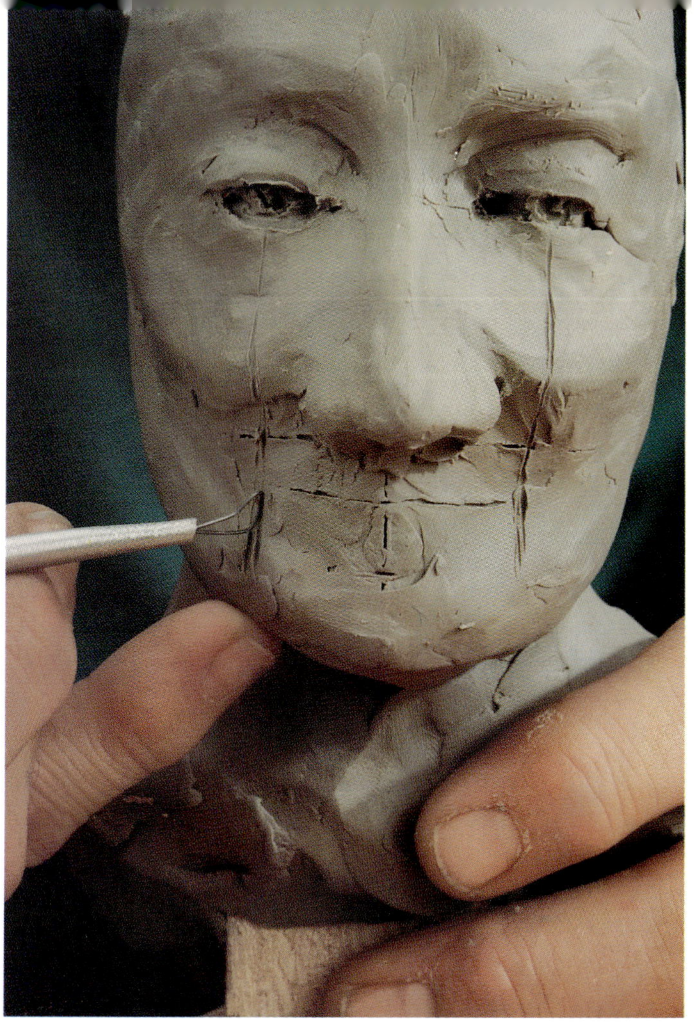

The eyes are detailed. To locate the corners of the mouth, draw a line straight down from the center of each pupil.

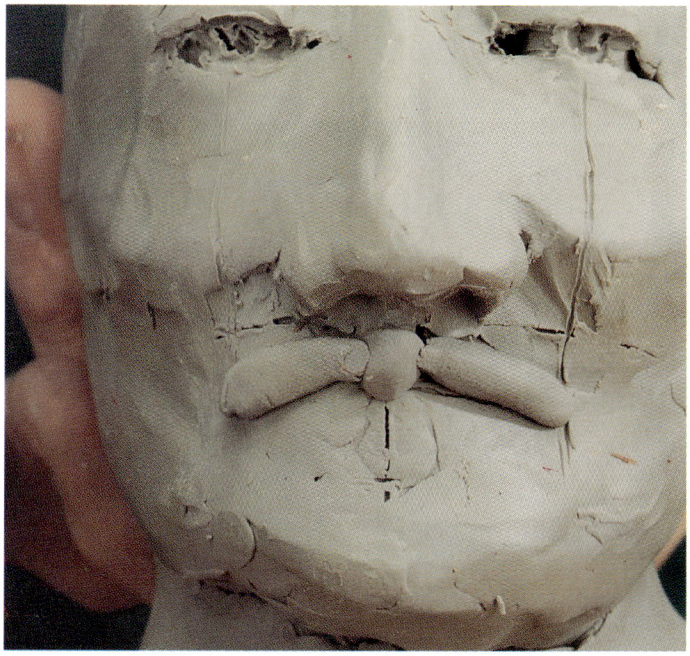

The lips are made in five parts. The first part is the center lobe of the upper lip. This is made with a small ball of clay. The second and third parts are the coils that go on either side of the center of the upper lip.

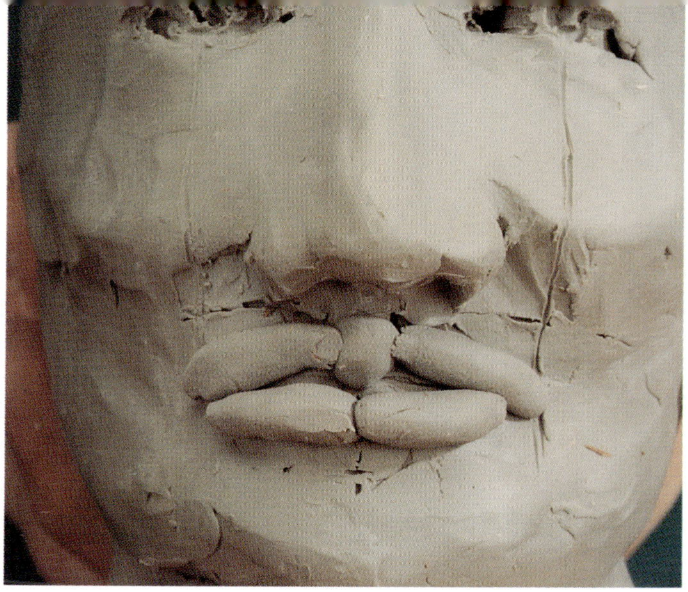

The last two parts are the two coils that form the bottom lip.

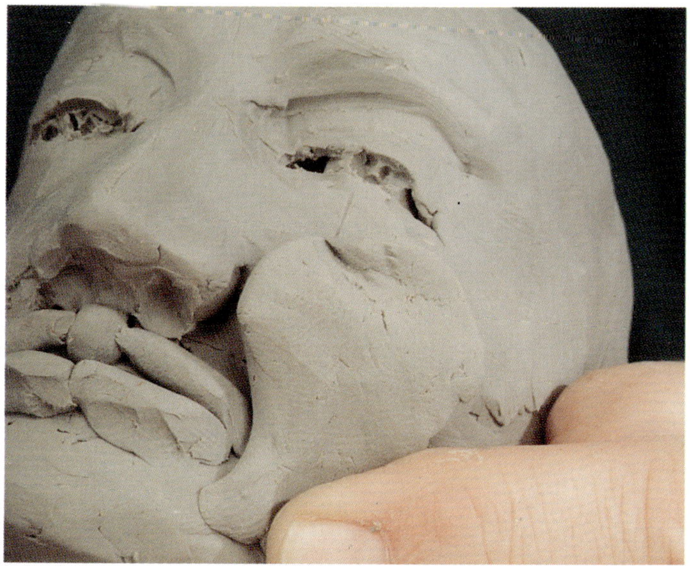

Lay in the muscles forming the lower cheek, using large roughly apostrophe-shaped slabs of clay for these muscles.

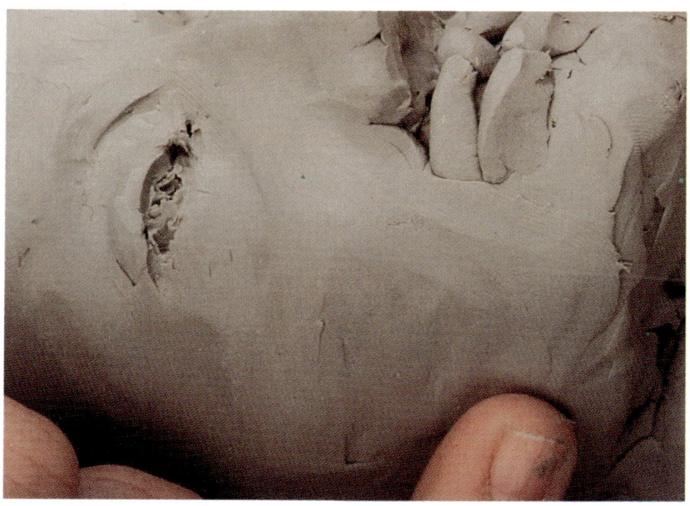

Blend in the cheek muscles.

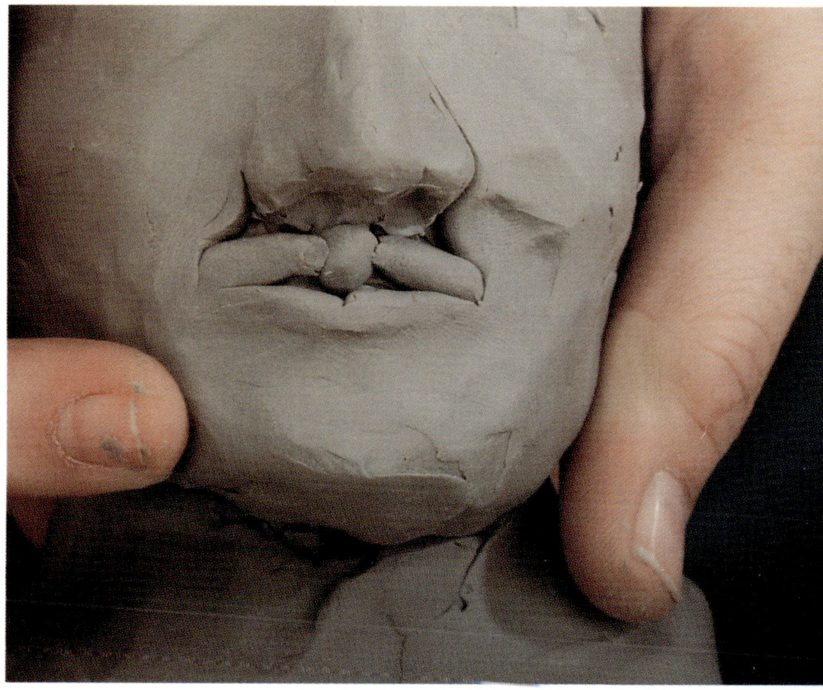

Blend in the bottom lip.

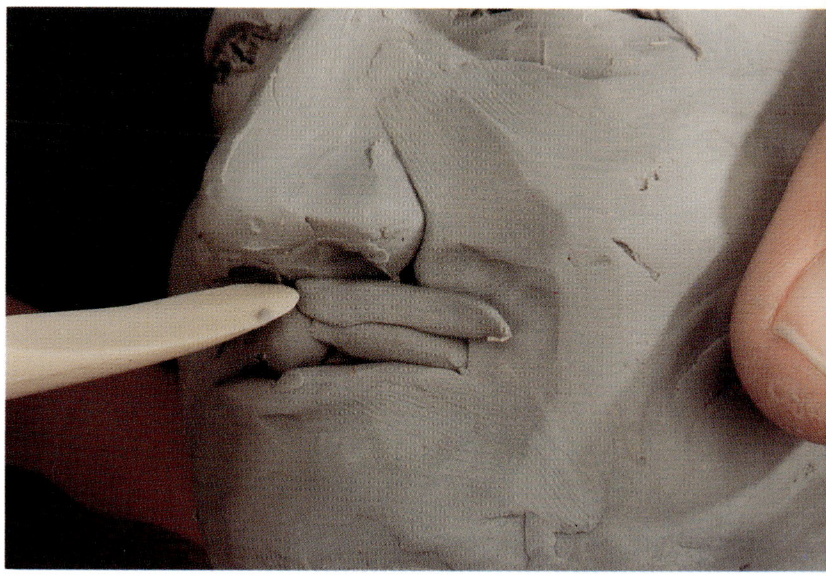

Form the top lip by first laying in another small coil above each of the two segments of the lip and then by blending them in.

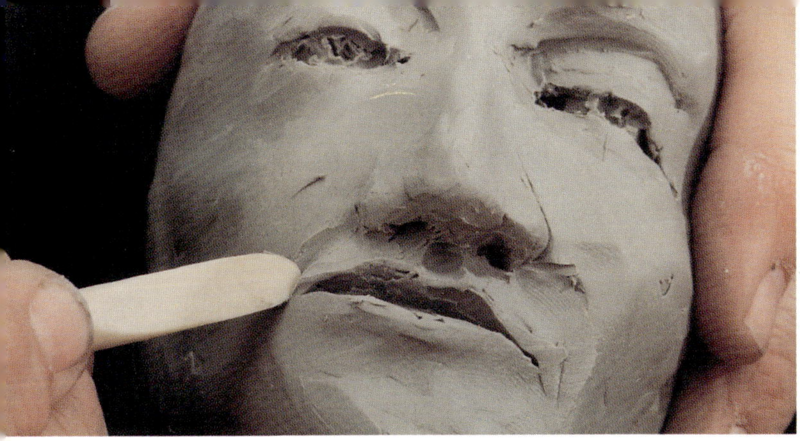

Form the top lip by first laying in another small coil above each of the two segments of the lip and then by blending them in.

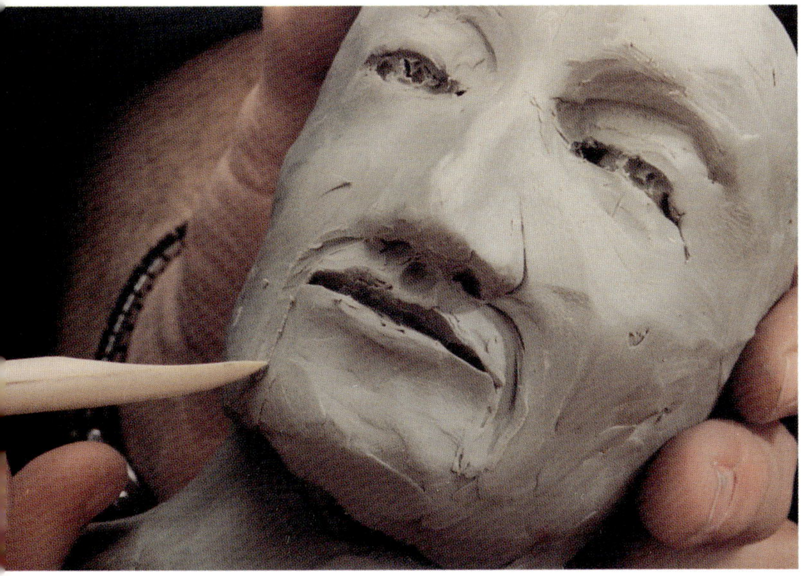

Put in the "smile lines," the line of the muscles of the lower cheek, Be careful not to pull down the corners of the mouth while placing these lines or your figure will appear to be frowning.

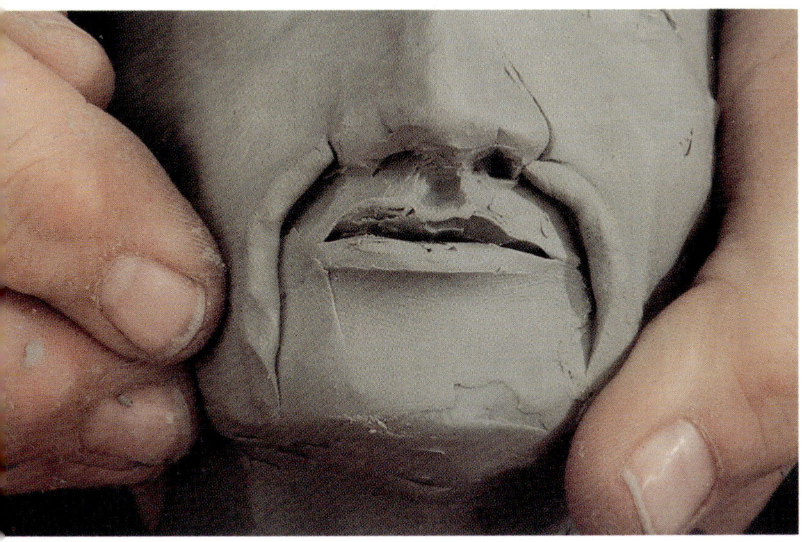

To emphasize the smile lines, place two small rolls down each side of the face, following the smile lines.

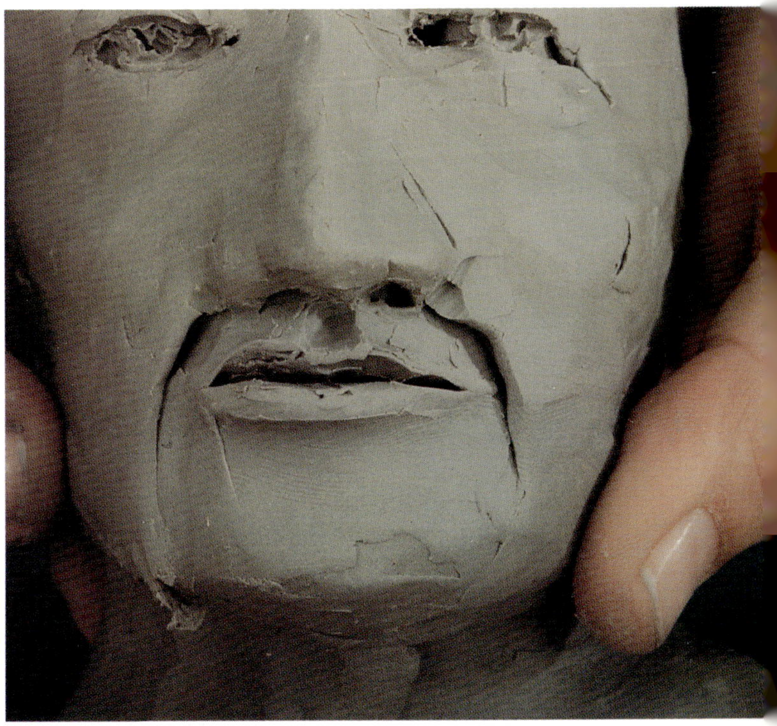

Blend the rolls in, pulling them back into the sides of the face.

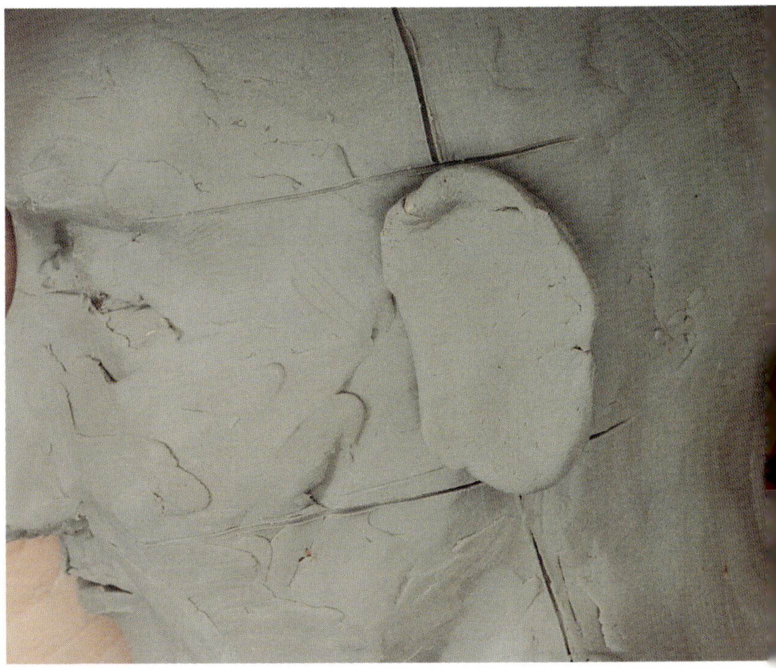

Refer back to the center lines we drew on the sides of the head. If you project a line from the eyebrows to that centerline and a second line from the bottom of the nose to the centerline, the ears will fall between these lines. To start sculpting the ear, begin by forming a piece of clay roughly shaped into a C. This "ear" is laid directly on the centerline and blended in.

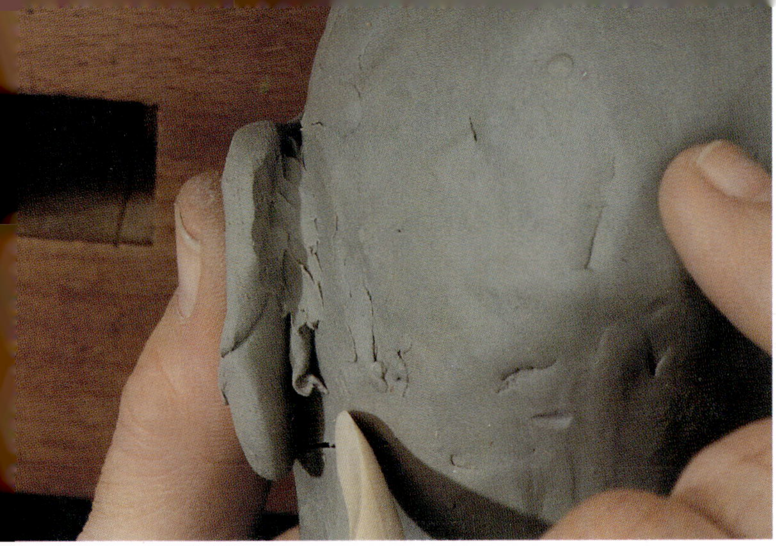

Place a small coil of clay in back of the ear and blend it in to form the connection between the ear and the head.

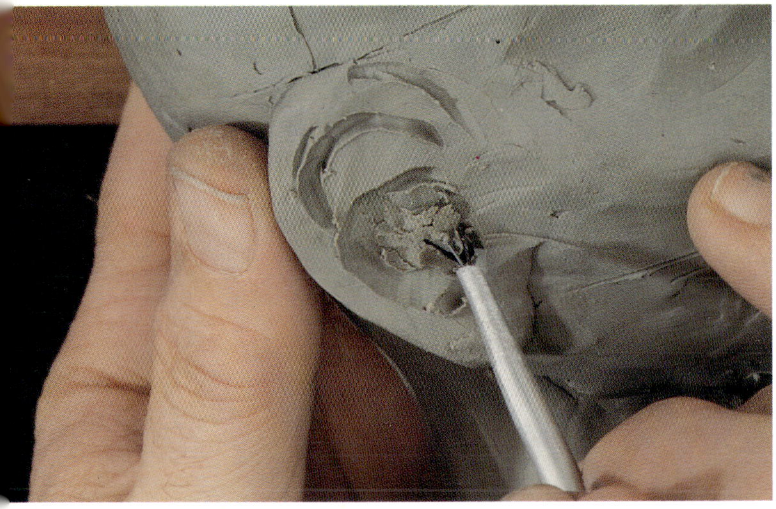

Roughly lay out the shape of the inside of the ear. Since most people don't know what ears look like, pay close attention to the ears around you. The ears don't have any sharp angles in them. They are smooth forms. Once shaped, take a finger or a tool and round the edges of the inner workings of the ear to make them smooth.

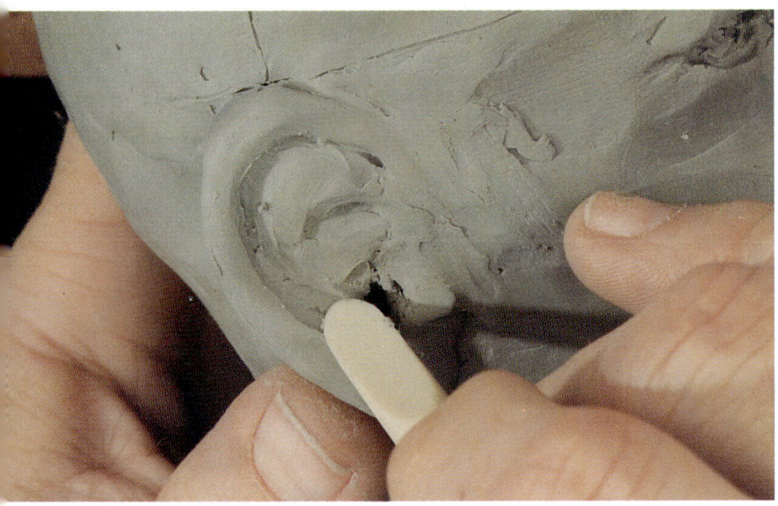

Like this.

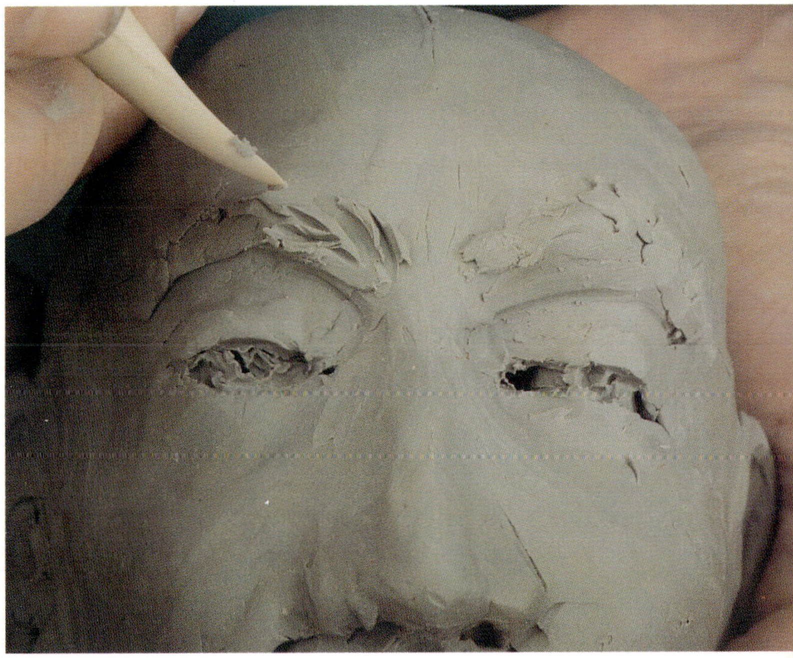

To add some age to your sculpture, start by sculpting heavier, shaggier eyebrows. Lay in some patches of clay on the eyebrows and then, using a tool, add unkempt hair lines.

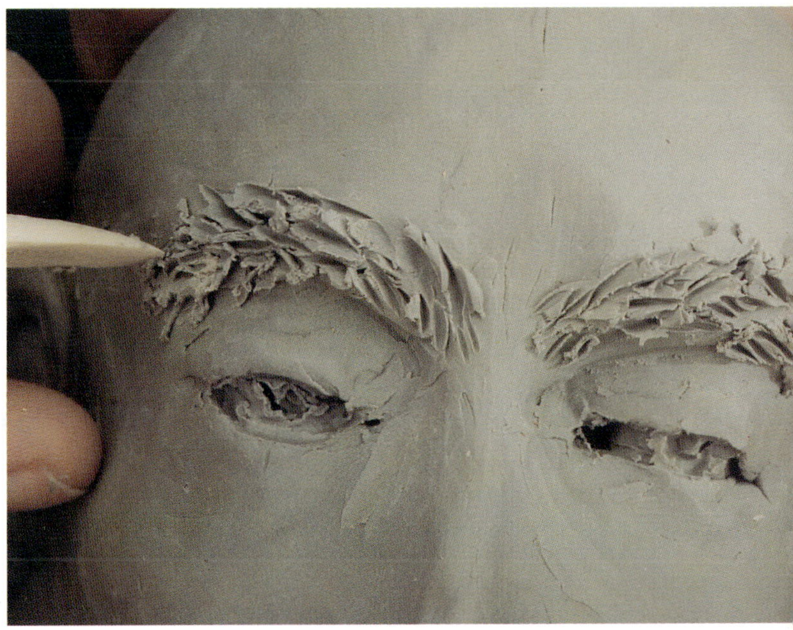

The bushy eyebrows are in place.

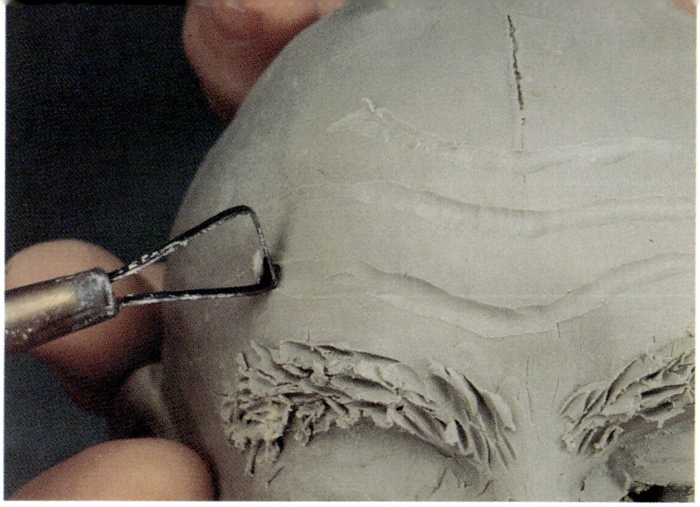

Add wrinkles to in the forehead, two or three are normal.

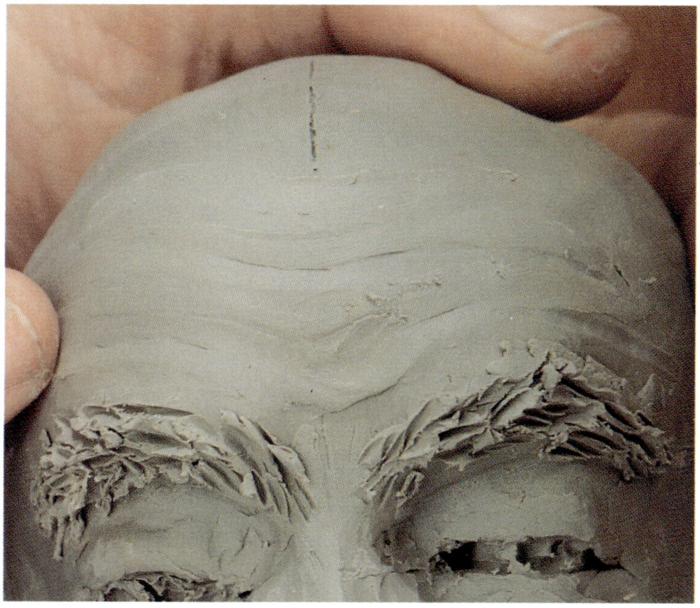

Blend these wrinkles in with your finger so that they also have no hard edges.

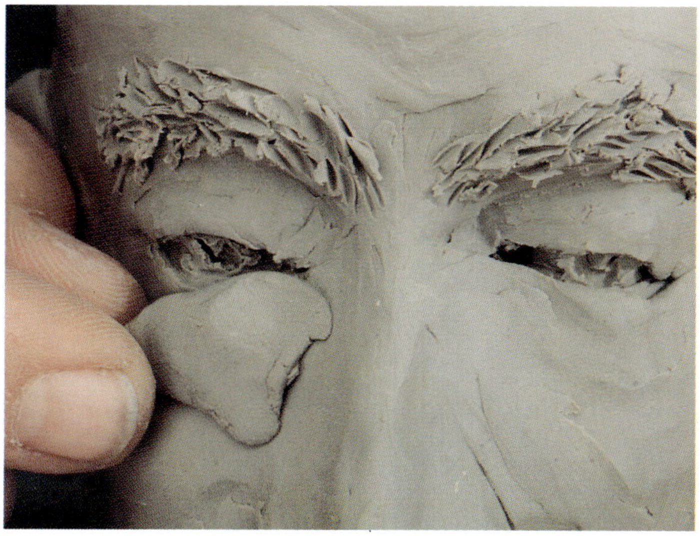

You can add a lot more tissue under the eyes as well. Lay a slab of clay underneath each eye and form excess tissue to create bags.

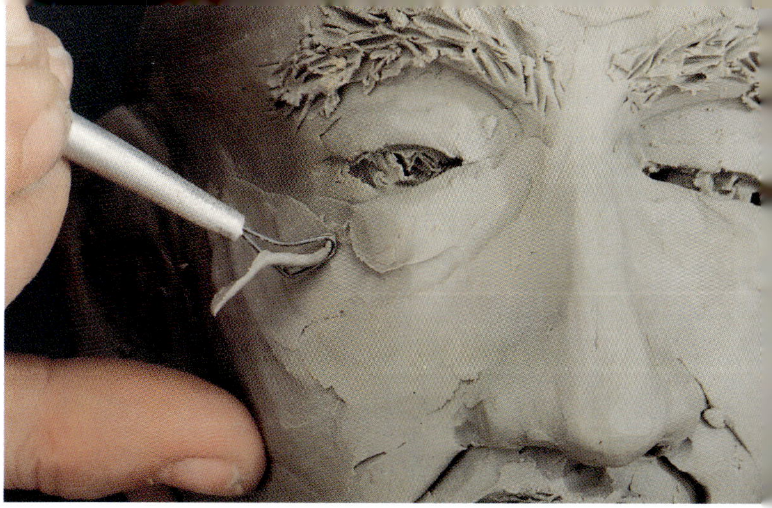

Blend in the bags with the edge of your finger or with a tool.

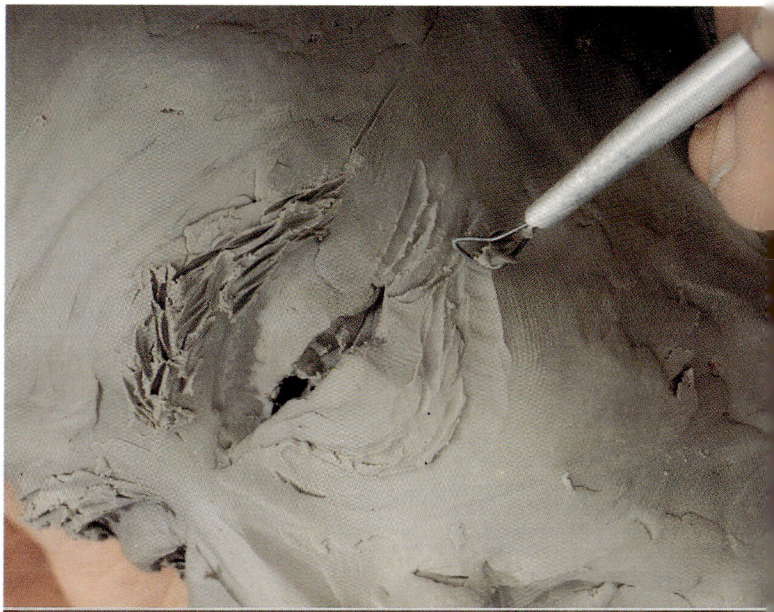

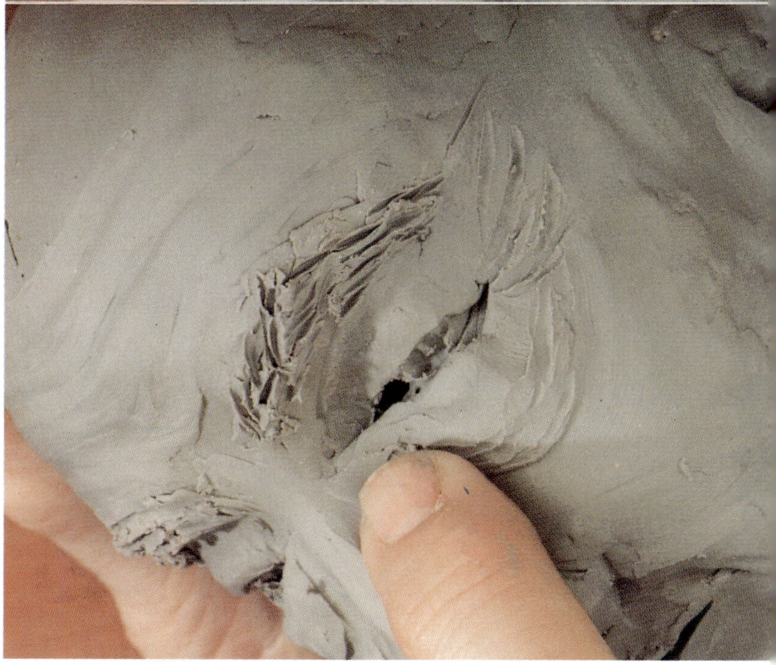

Using a sculpting tool to put in bag lines and crows feet around the eyes. Blend them in with your finger.

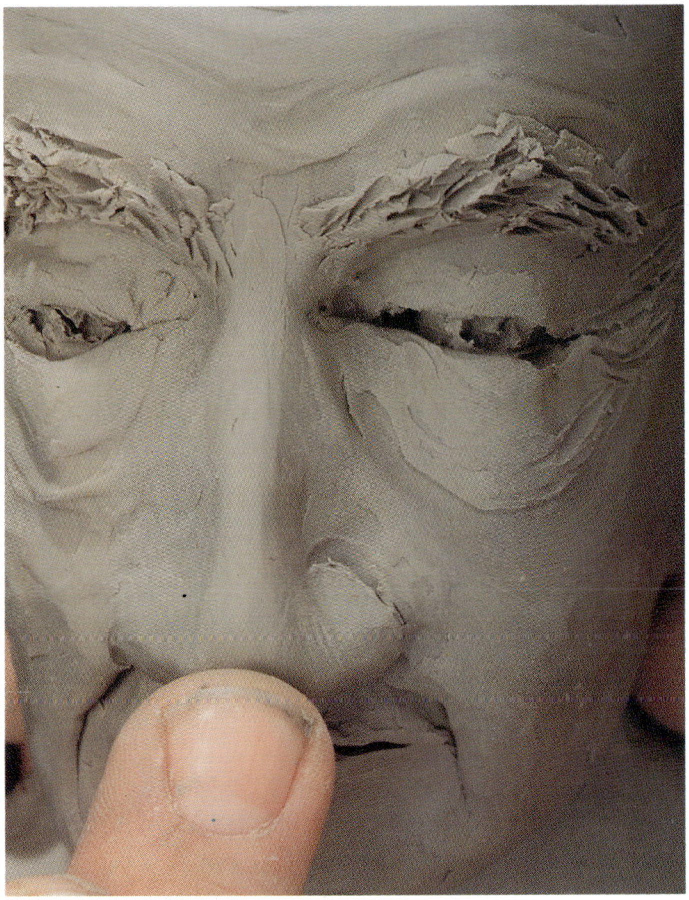

Flatten the nose a bit. With age, cartilage in the nose breaks down. The nose get flatter and wider. Gently press in on the end of the nose.

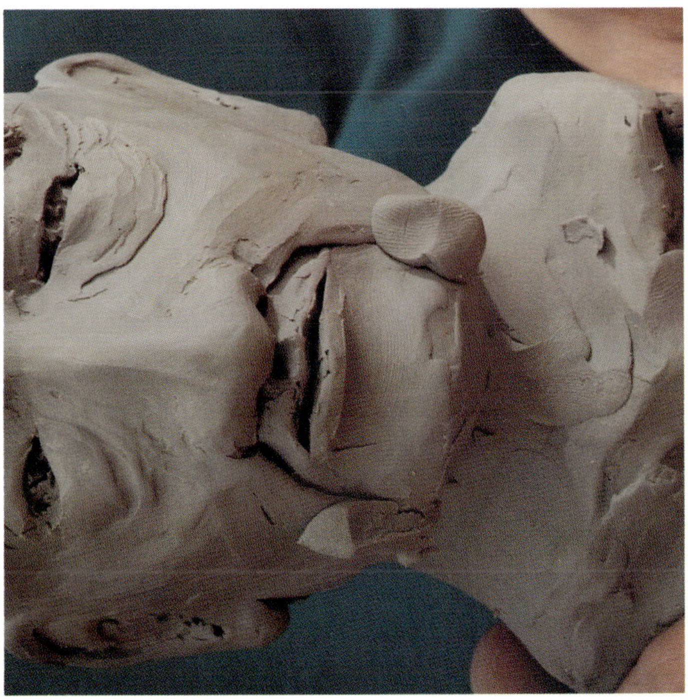

To add a little more age to the face, add blobs of clay and blend them in to create sagging jowls.

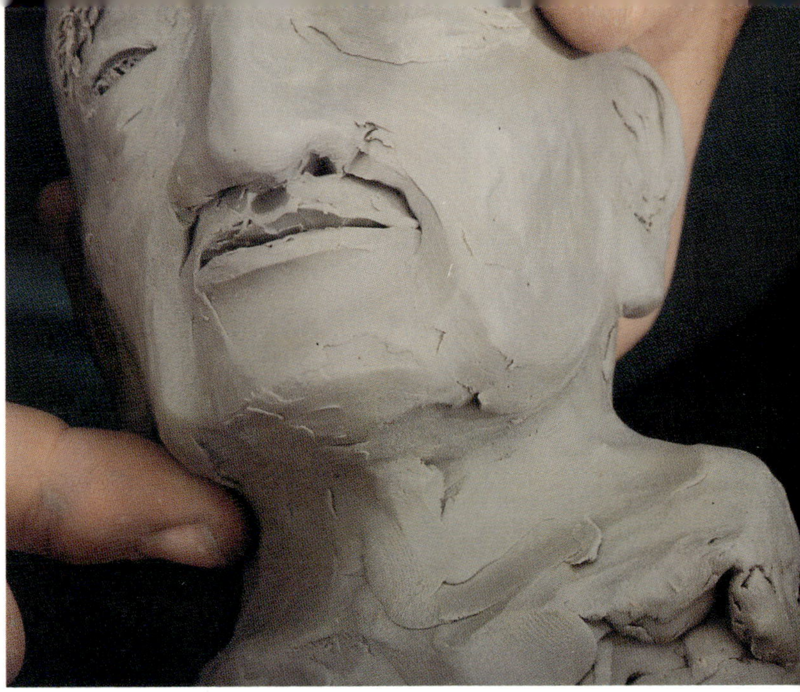

The blended jowls.

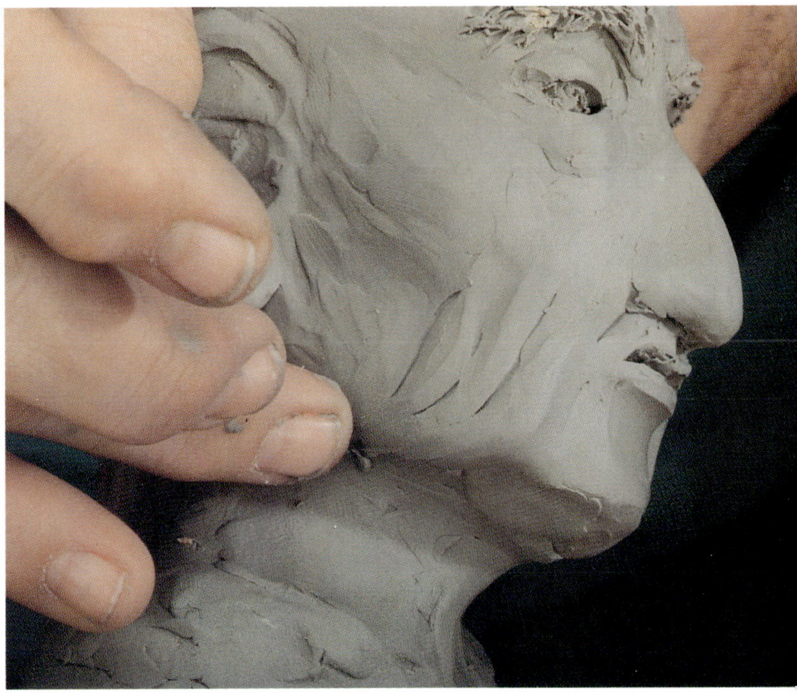

Add more wrinkles to the lower face. Cut them in with a sculpting tool and blend them in with your finger.

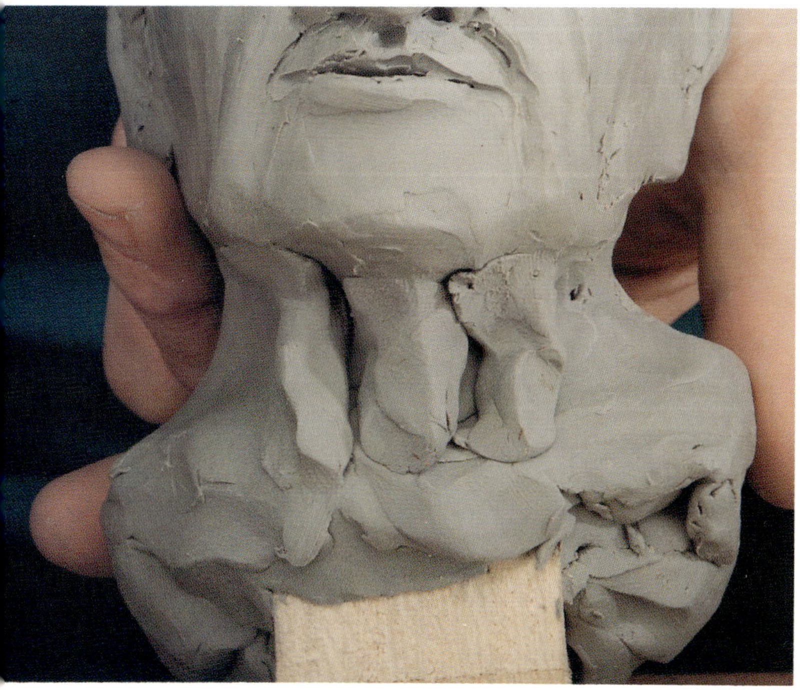

Now we'll add drooping wattles to the neck. First add three coils of clay to the neck.

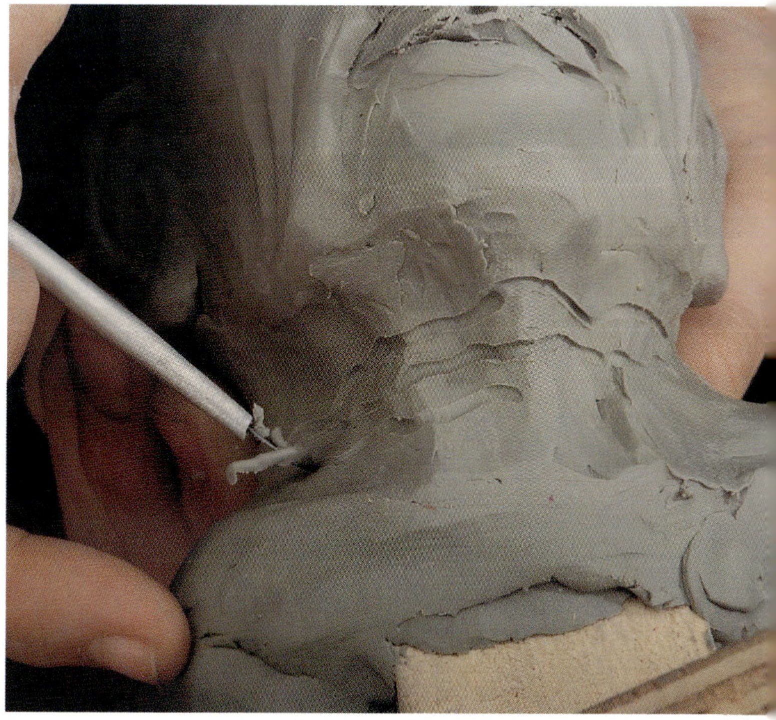

Add some wrinkles in the wattles. Allow the lines to squiggle their way across the neck. Blend these in just a bit.

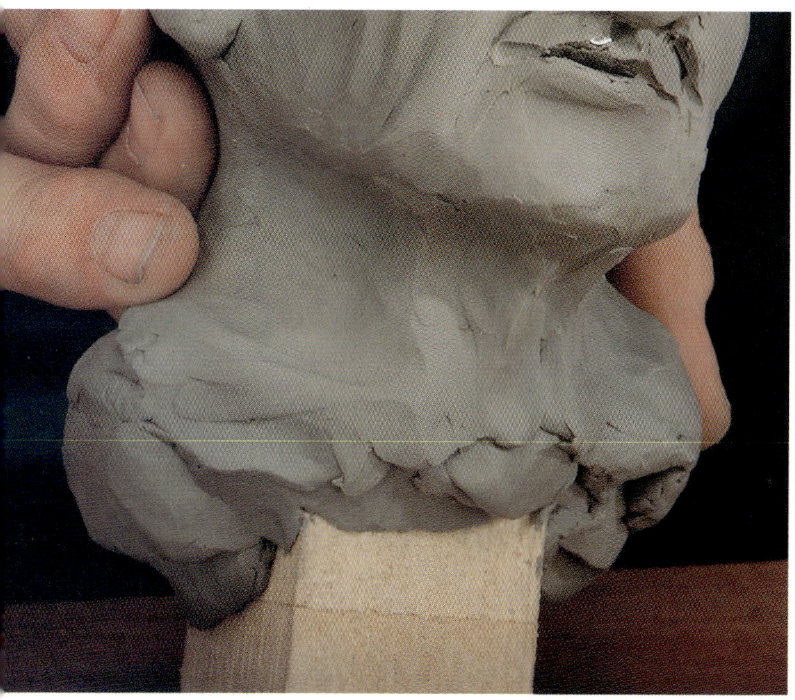

Blend these in to form the loose skin on either side of the Adam's apple and the Adam's apple itself. When blending them in, form the collar bone at the same time.

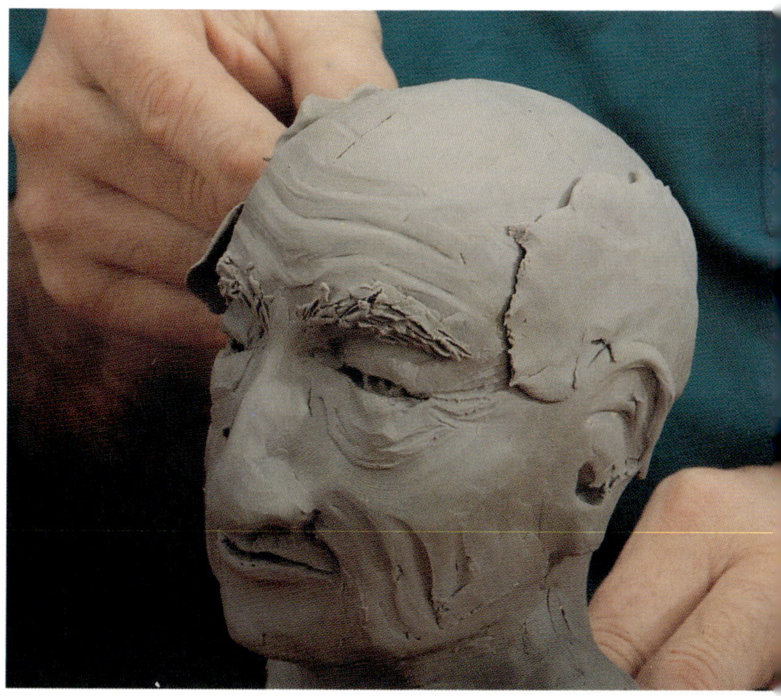

His hair can be laid on in a flat sheet. Old as he is, we'll make this gent bald on top.

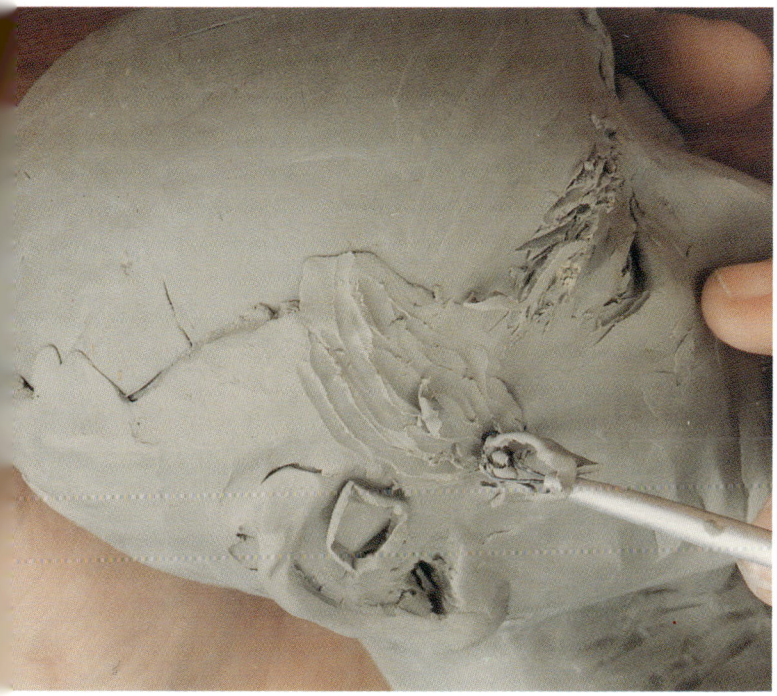

Start his hair out by cutting in uneven lines to indicate masses of hair rather than single hairs.

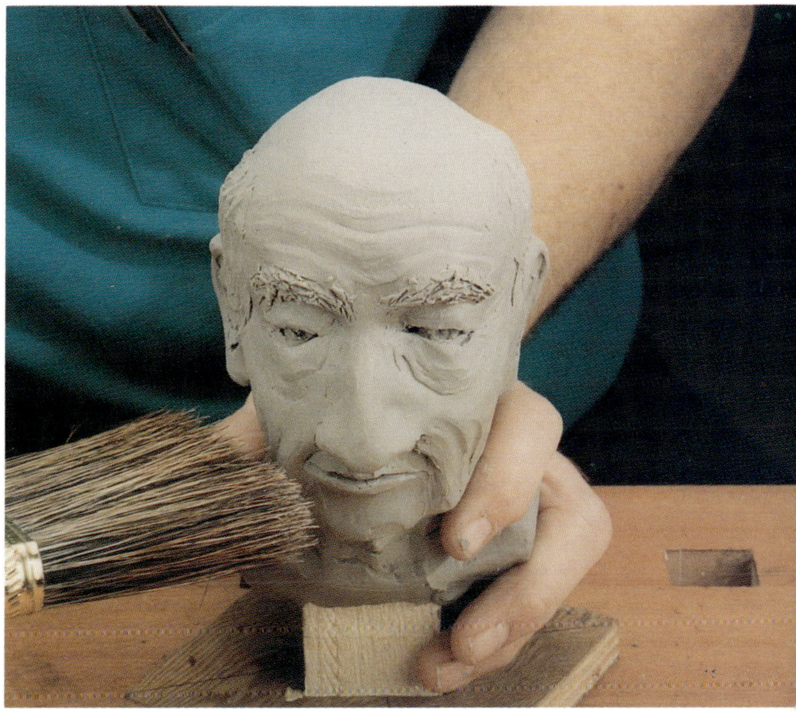

To give a more realistic texture to the clay, lightly tap the surface of the clay with the bristles of the brush.

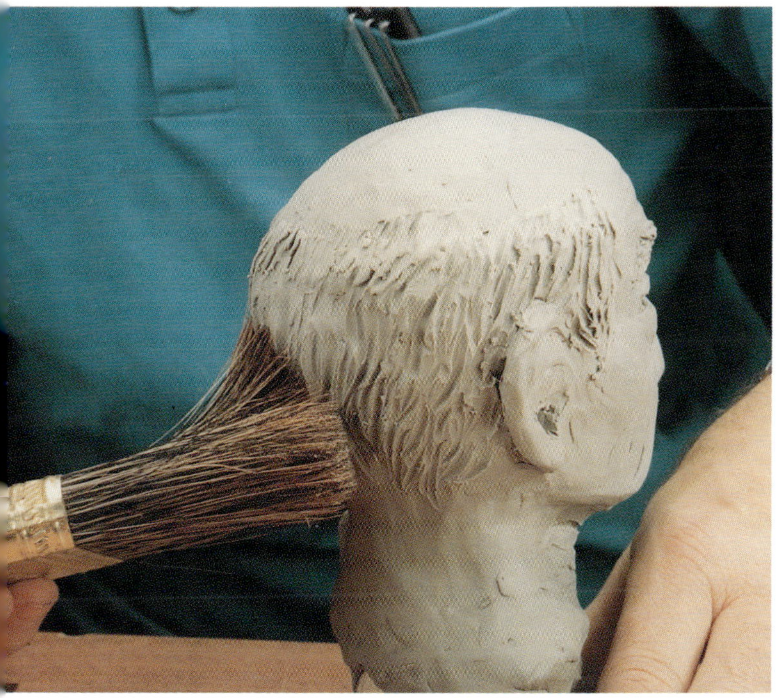

The masses of hair cut into place. By using a large paint brush and brushing the hair, you remove loose particles of clay and add a slight texture to indicate individual hairs.

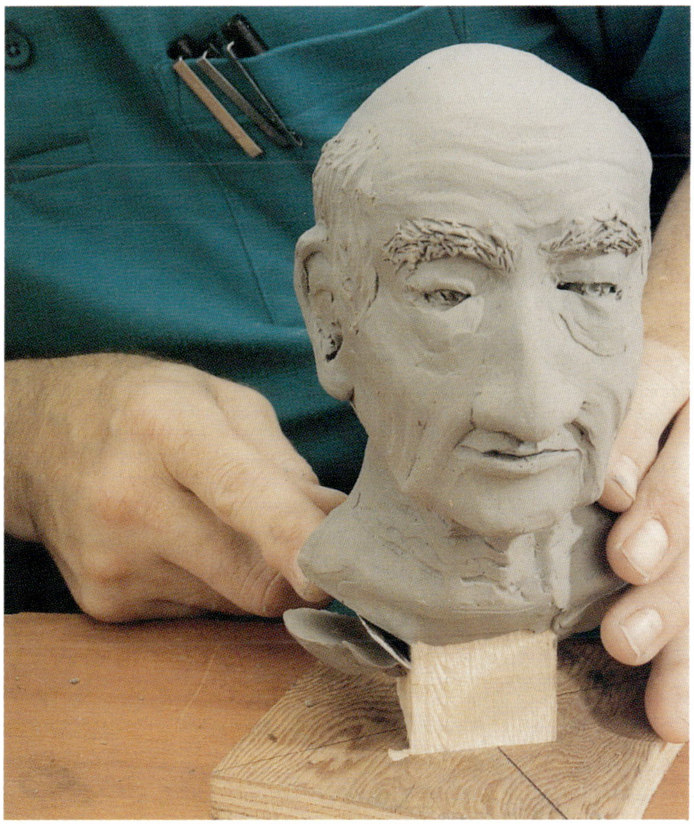

Finally shape the shoulders as a finishing touch.

The finished head.

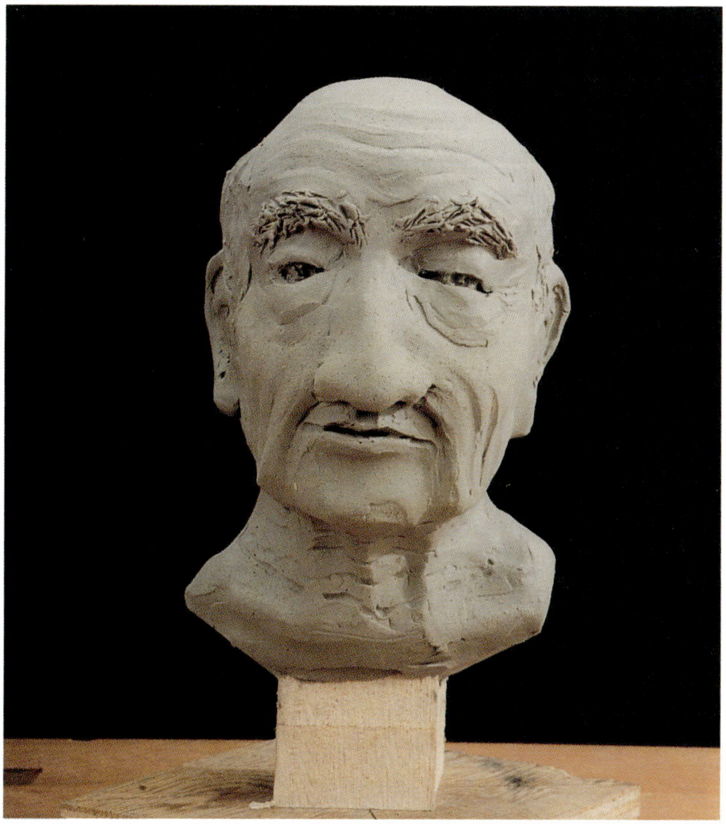

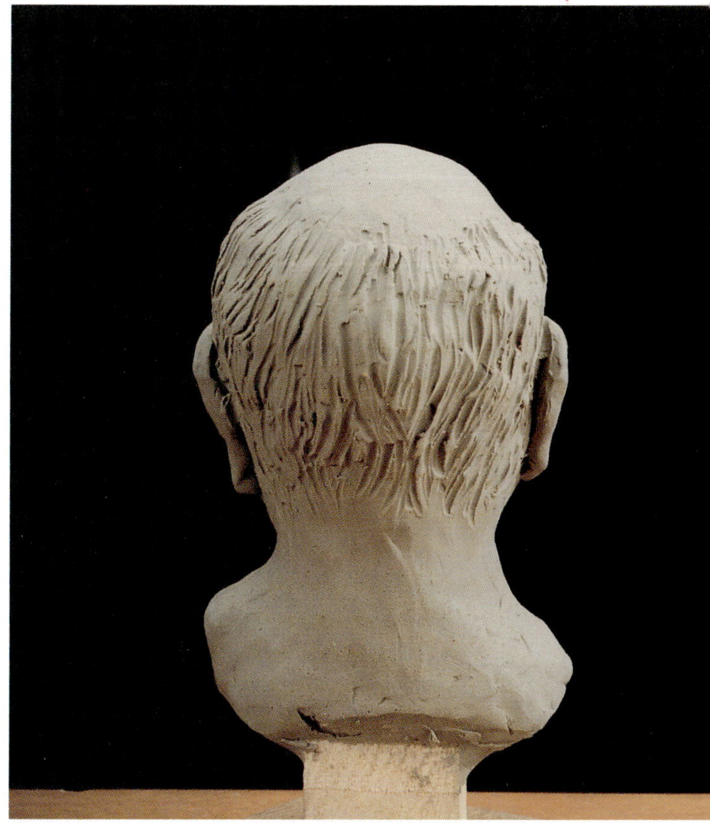

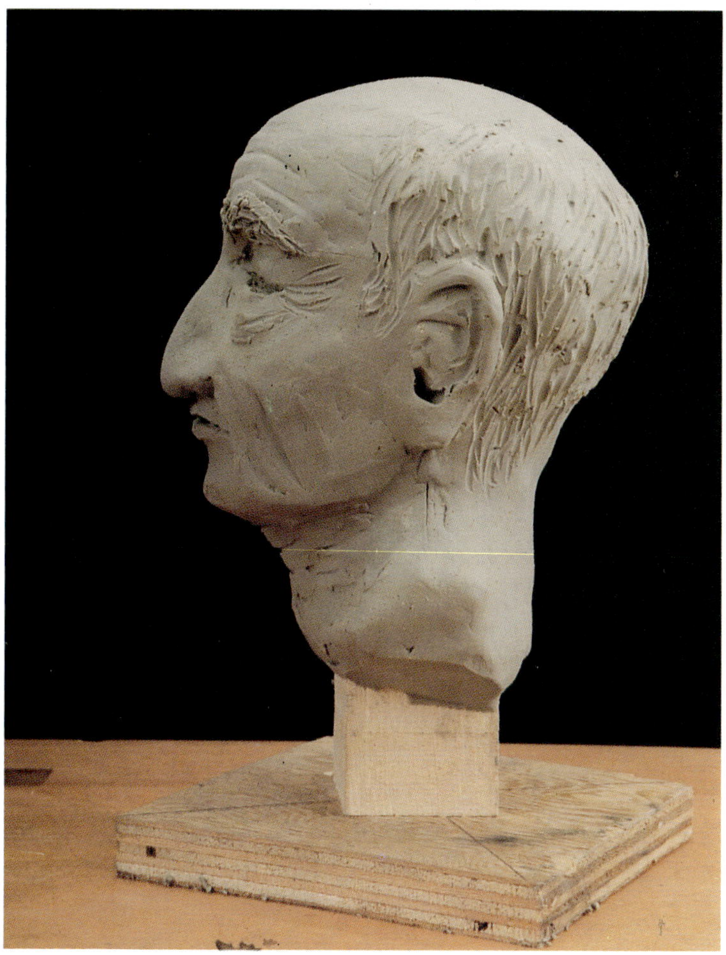

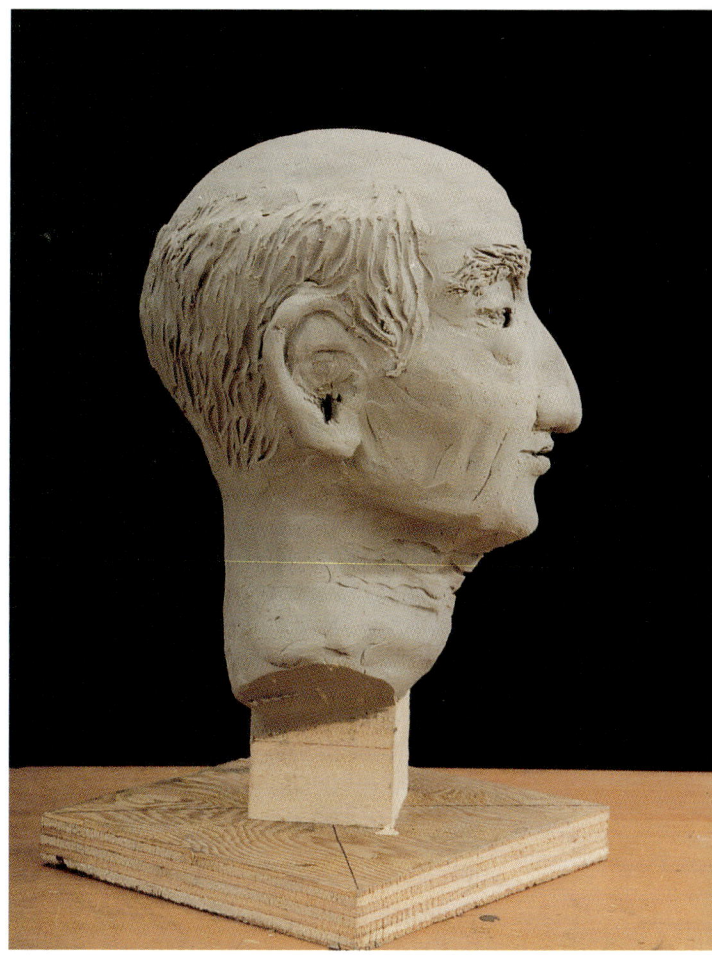

The Second Project, The Bearded Man

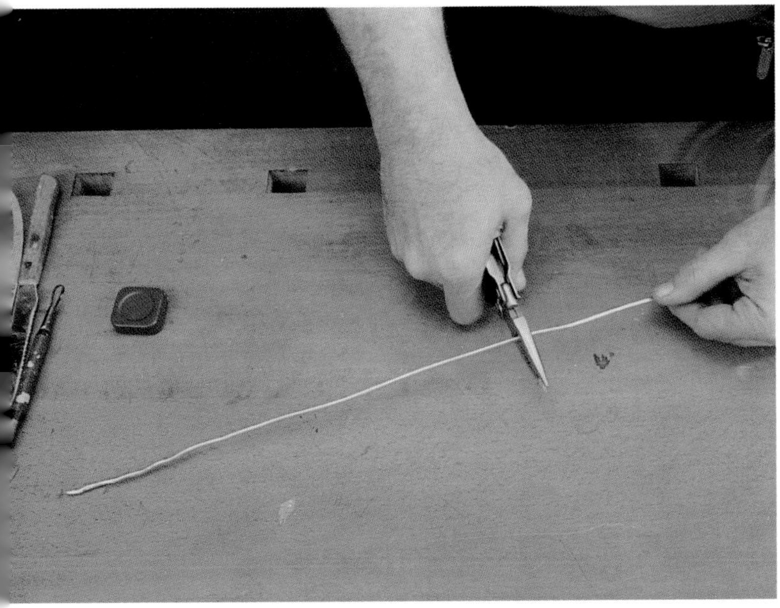

Starting with 1/8" aluminum armature wire, snip off two twelve inch long pieces. Use the cutter that comes as part of the needle nose pliers to complete this task.

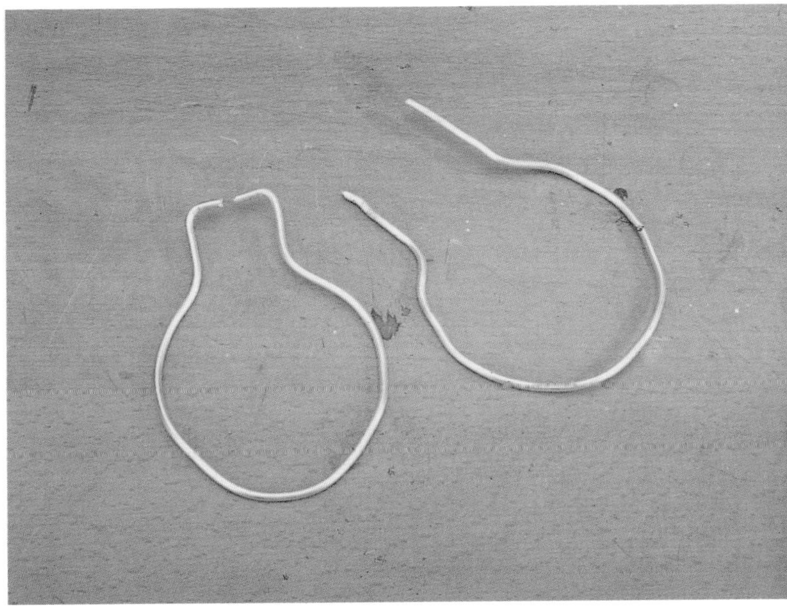

With both pieces roughly keyhole shaped, bend the last 3/8" of wire in toward the center on either side.

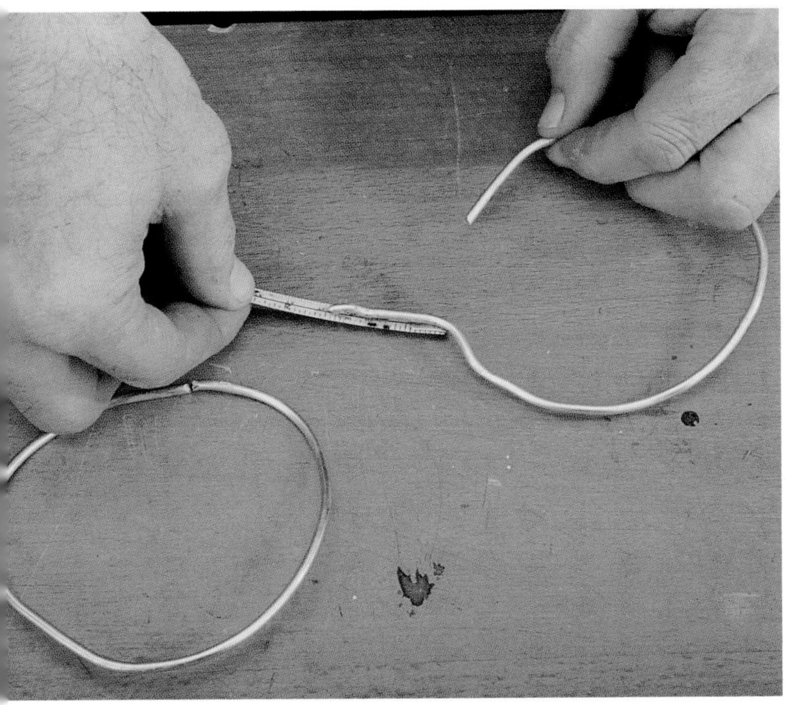

Roughly form two four inch circles with the wire. Measuring 1 1/2" out from either free end, bend both ends of the circle outward. Do this to both pieces.

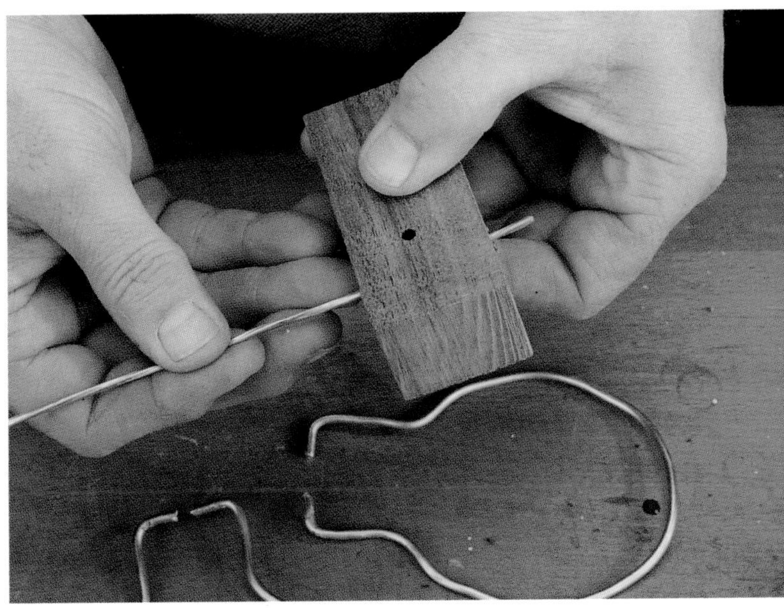

Take a wooden block 1/2" x 1/2" and drilling 1/8" holes straight through from both sides.

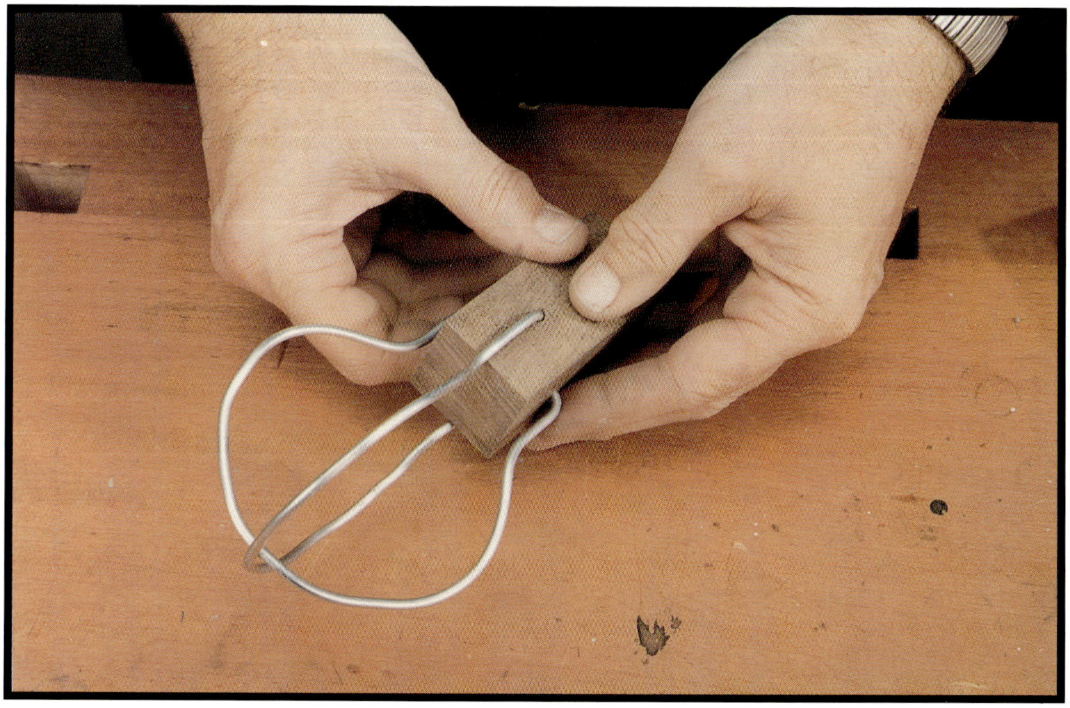

Take the wire armatures and place them into the two sets of holes.

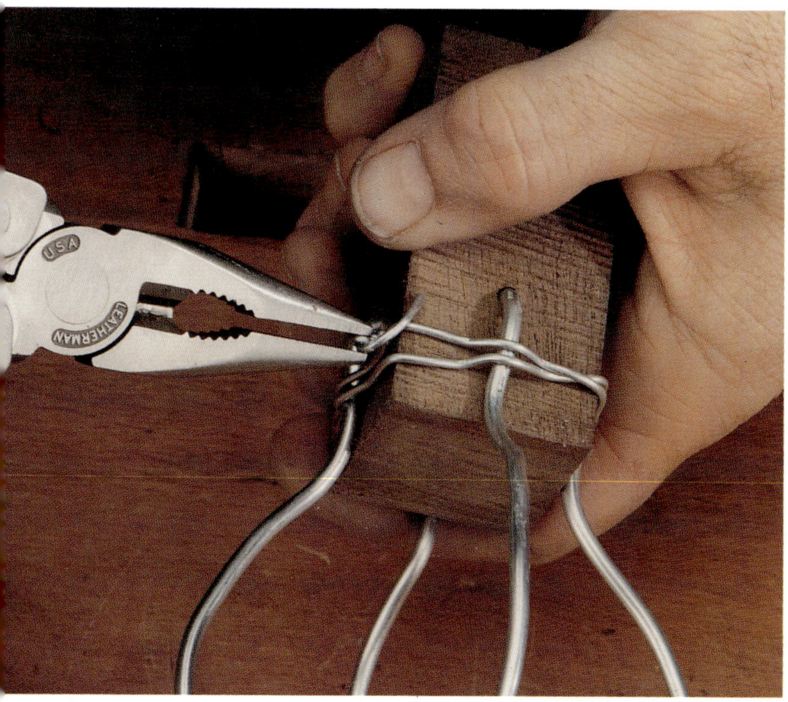

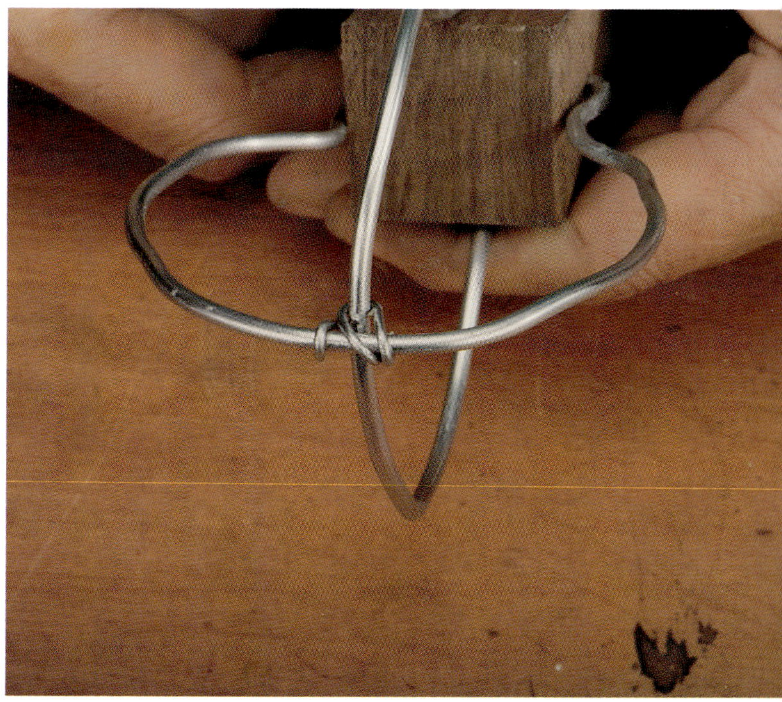

Secure the armatures by placing 1/16" wire around the joints both at the top and at the base. Twist the ends tight.

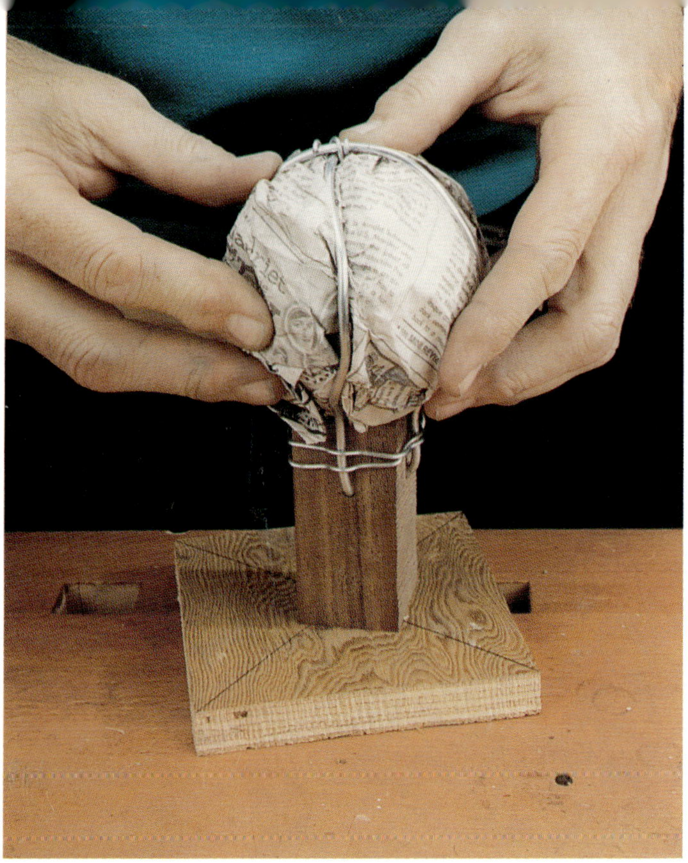

Secure the wood block to a plywood stand with a screw. Wad paper up to fill the void in the center of the armature. This reduces the amount of clay needed for the project.

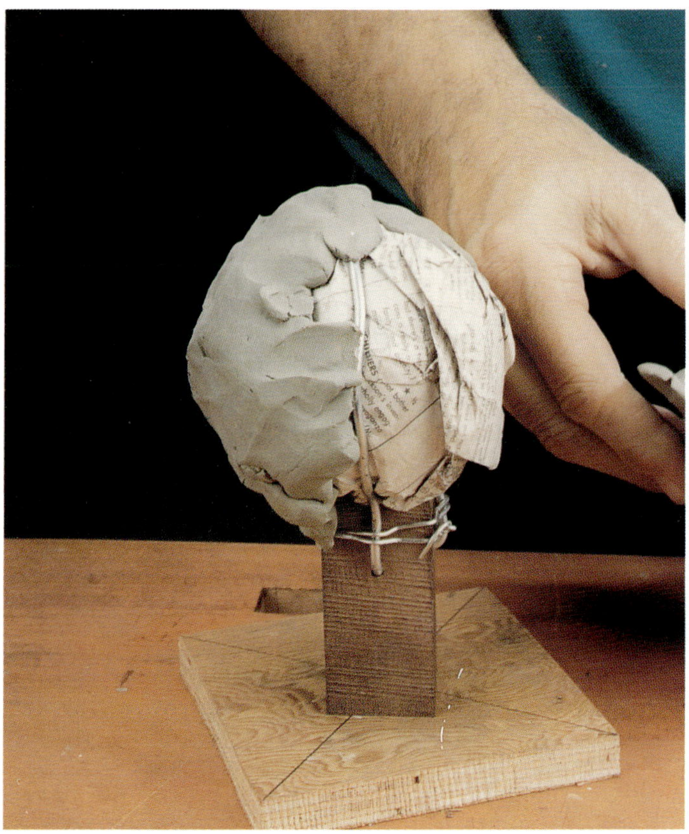

Lay sheets of clay over the armature to form a working surface. Features must be built up over this form of armature. You have no depth of clay to cut into.

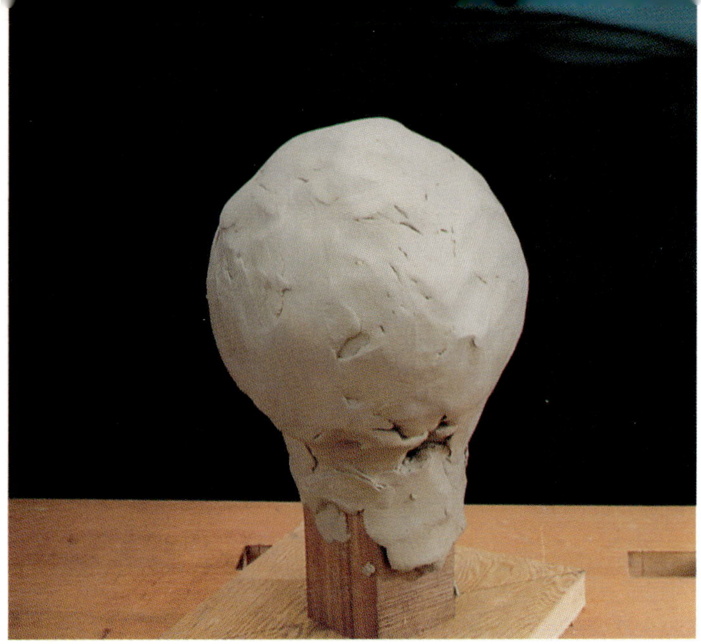

The clay sheets are in place.

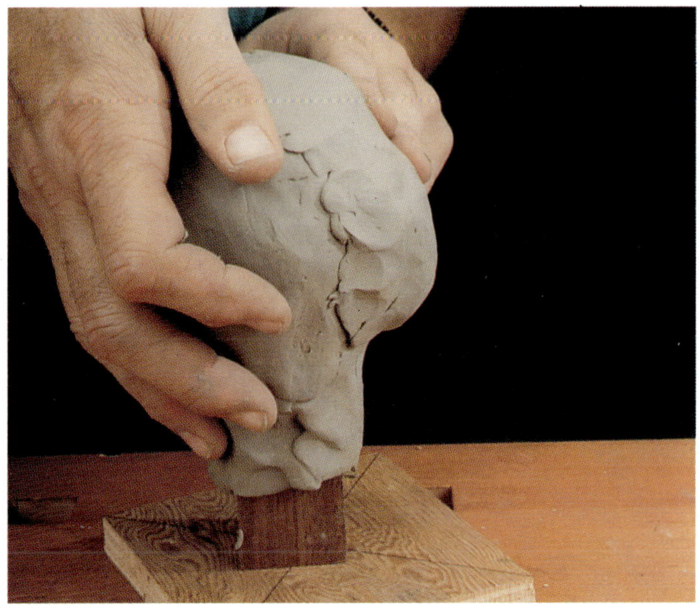

Lay a slab of clay on the side you decide is the front to start building the face out.

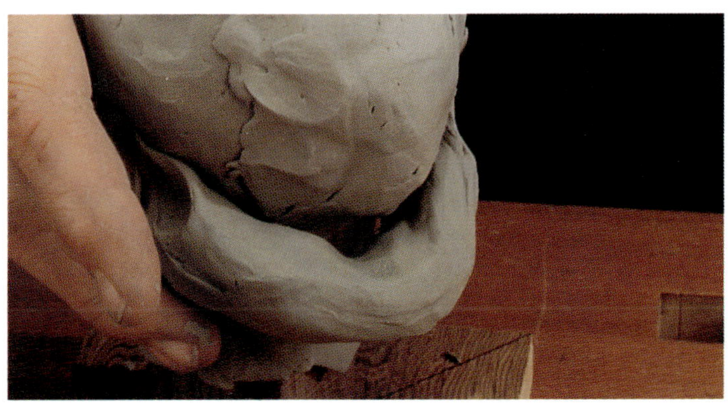

Attach a heavy coil of clay to the bottom to begin forming the lower jaw.

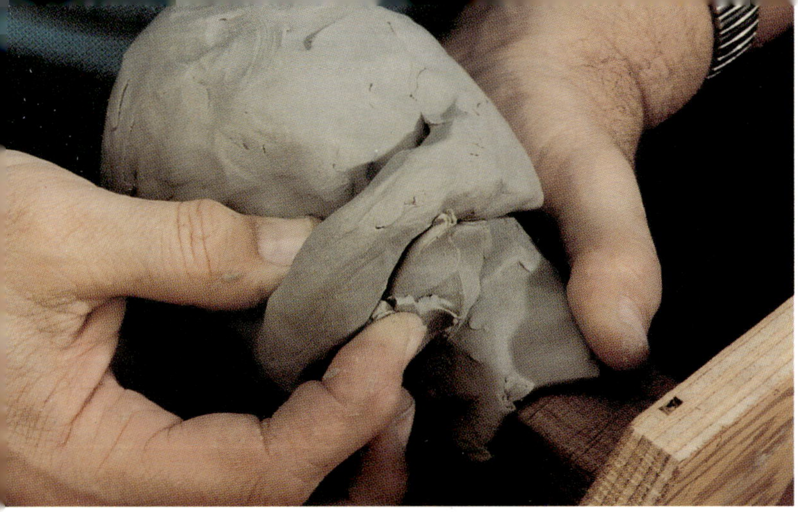

Fill in underneath the jaw coil to support it.

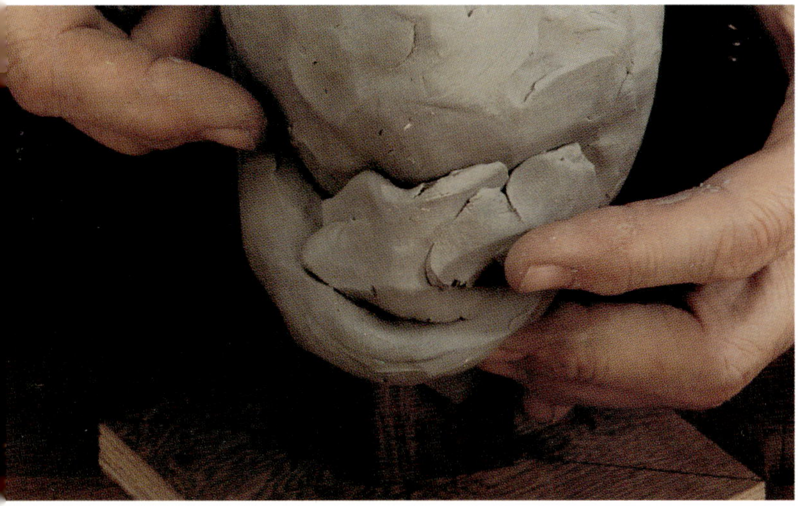

Fill in above the coil to start forming the upper jaw.

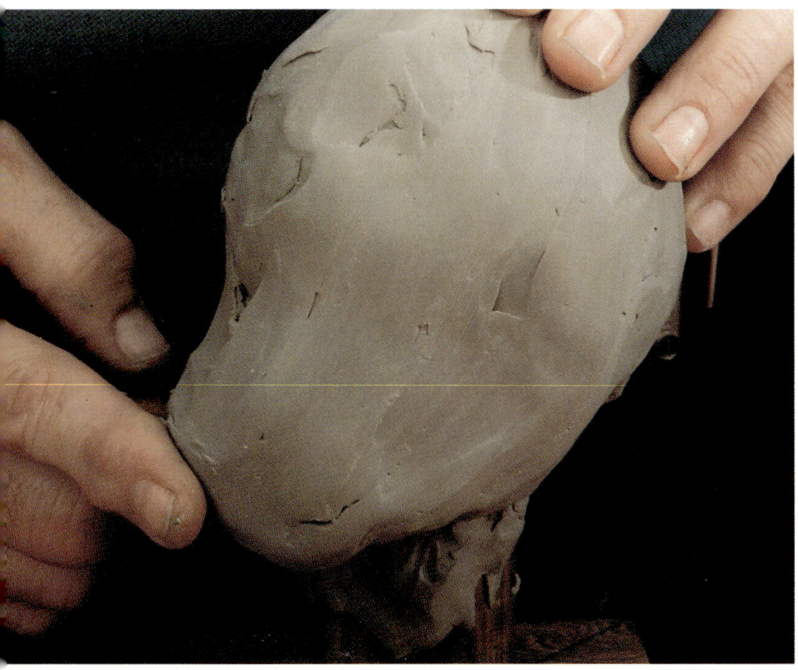

Start smoothing the clay of the upper jaw into the head to begin shaping the skull.

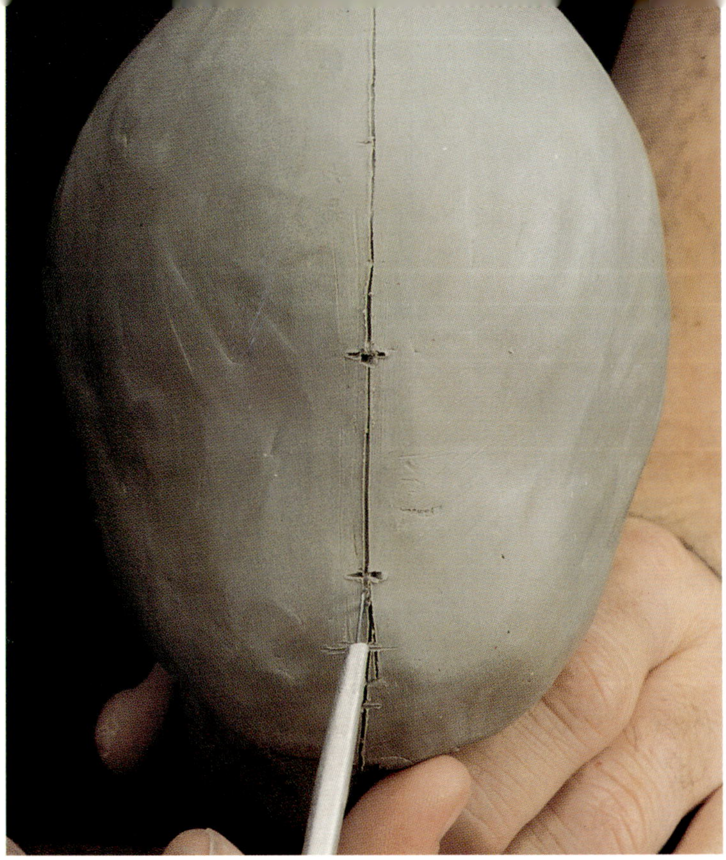

Once the skull is smoothed, start dividing the face up by establishing the centerline down the middle of the face.

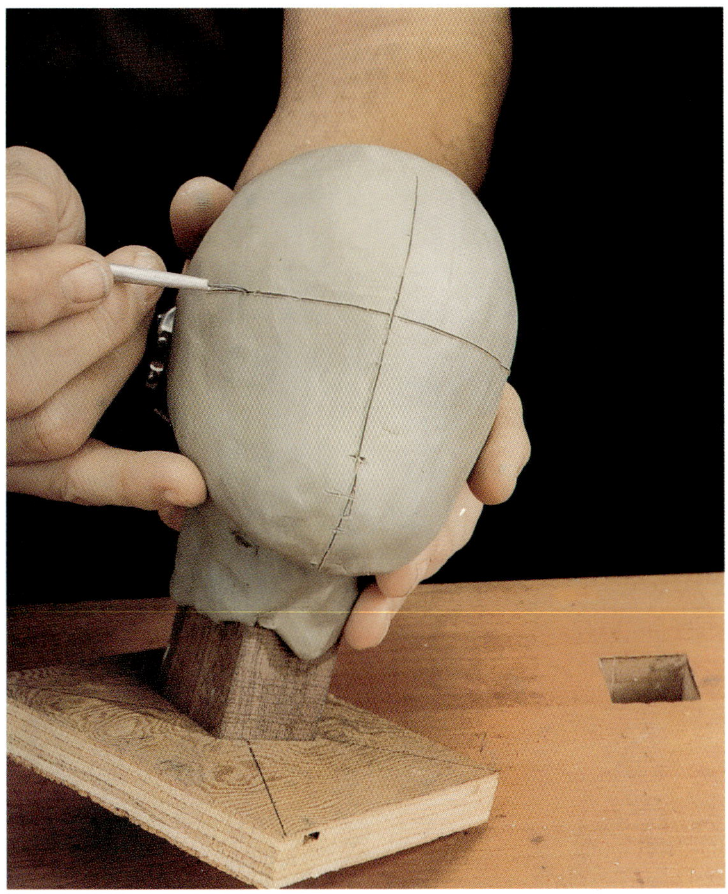

Divide the face in half between the top of the head to the chin to locate the top of the brow.

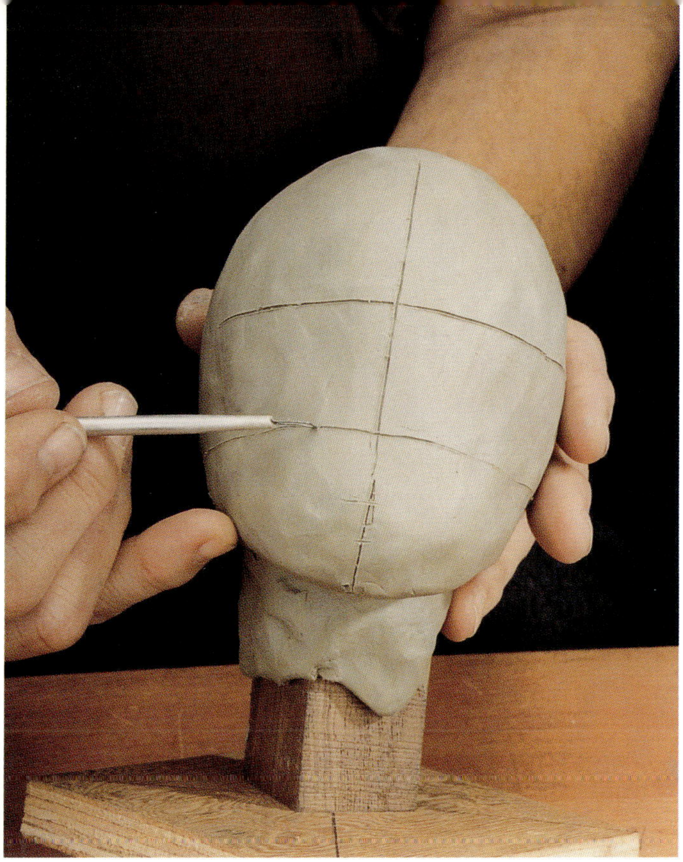

Divide the space between the brow line and the chin in half to indicate the location of the bottom of the nose.

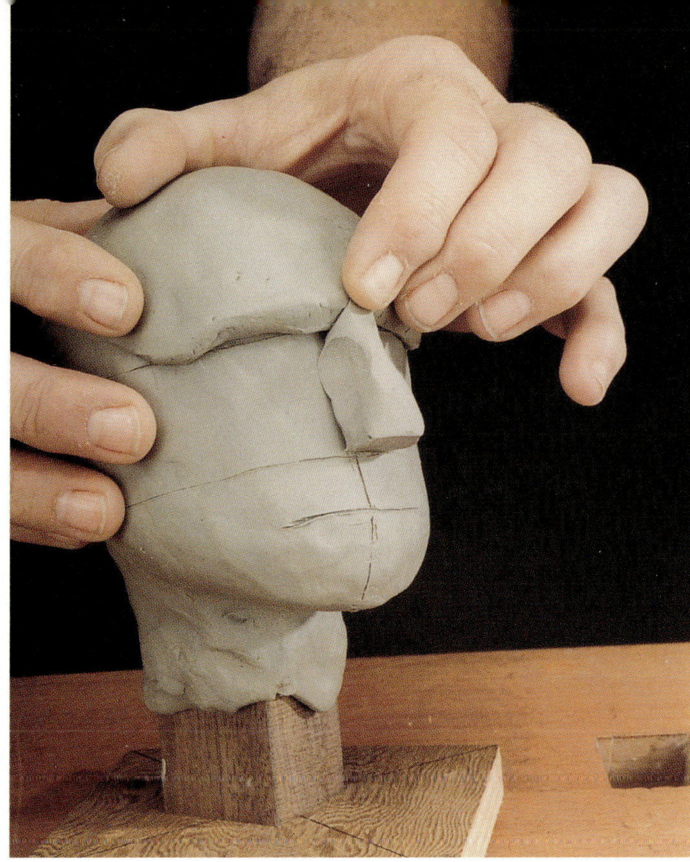

Place a slab on to build up the forehead. With this style of armature you have to build out more than with the first style of armature. Lay in a block of clay for the basic structure of the nose.

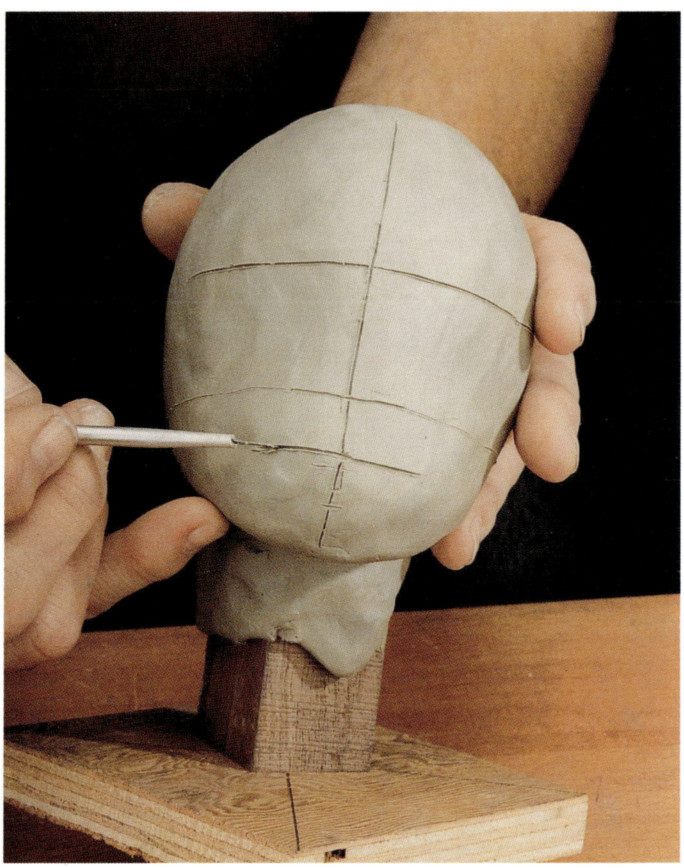

Divide the space between the bottom of the nose and the chin in thirds. The line two thirds of the way up from the chin will become the line of the mouth.

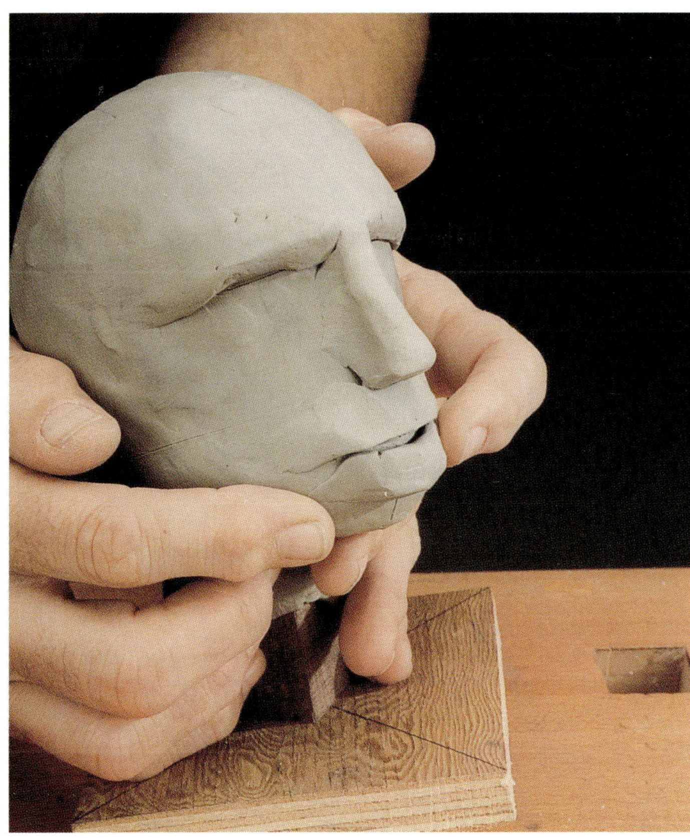

Lay in a sheet of clay for the upper lip and blend it in a bit. Lay in a sheet of clay roughly shaped for the lower lip as well, a little thicker than the upper lip.

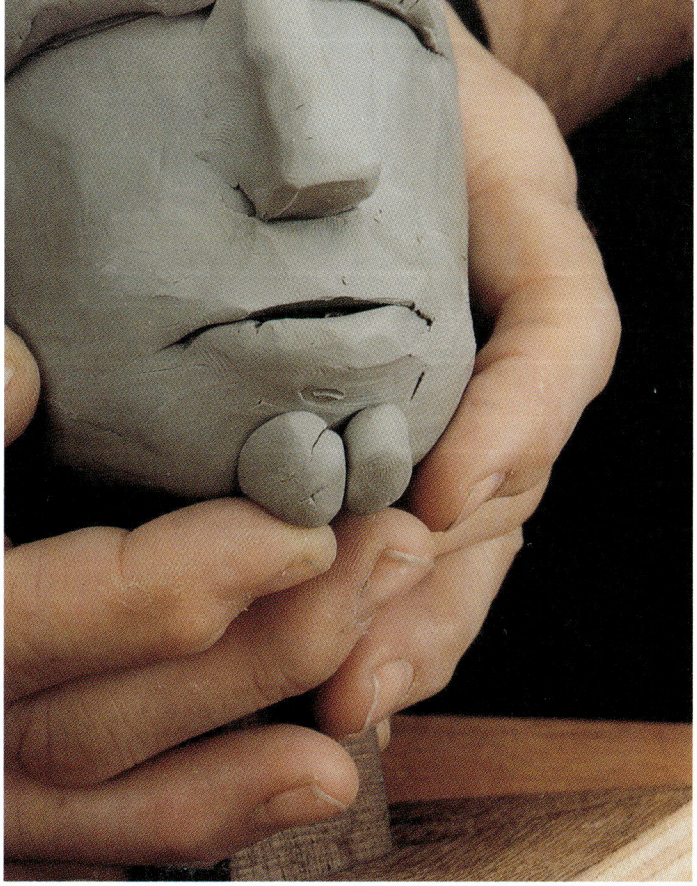

Roughly shape the lower lip into the head, smoothing the bottom edge out. Place two pea-sized balls on the chin to start forming the chin muscles.

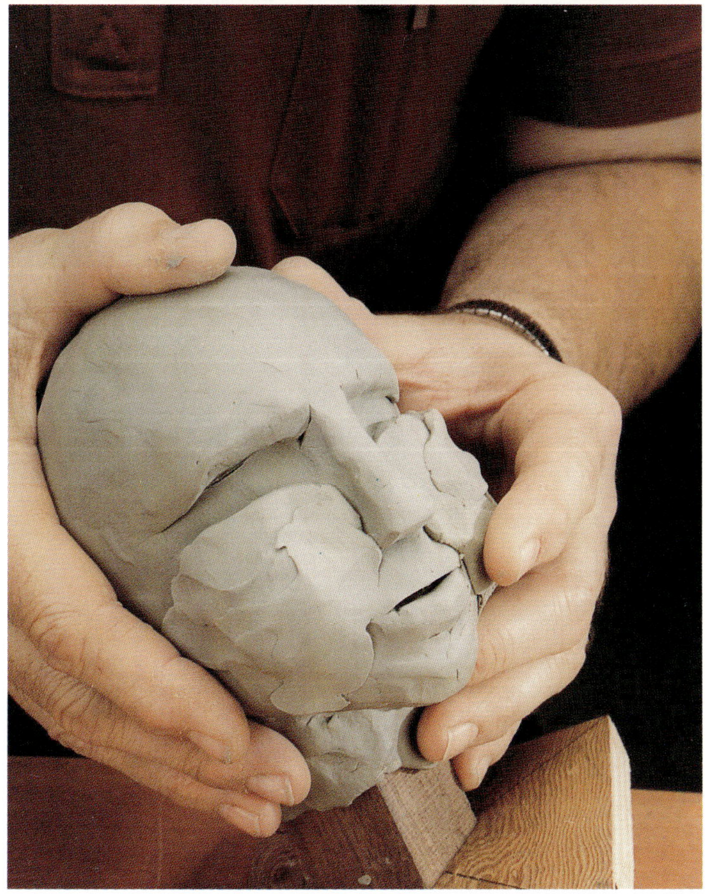

On either side of the head, lay in two more roughly cheek shaped pieces of clay.

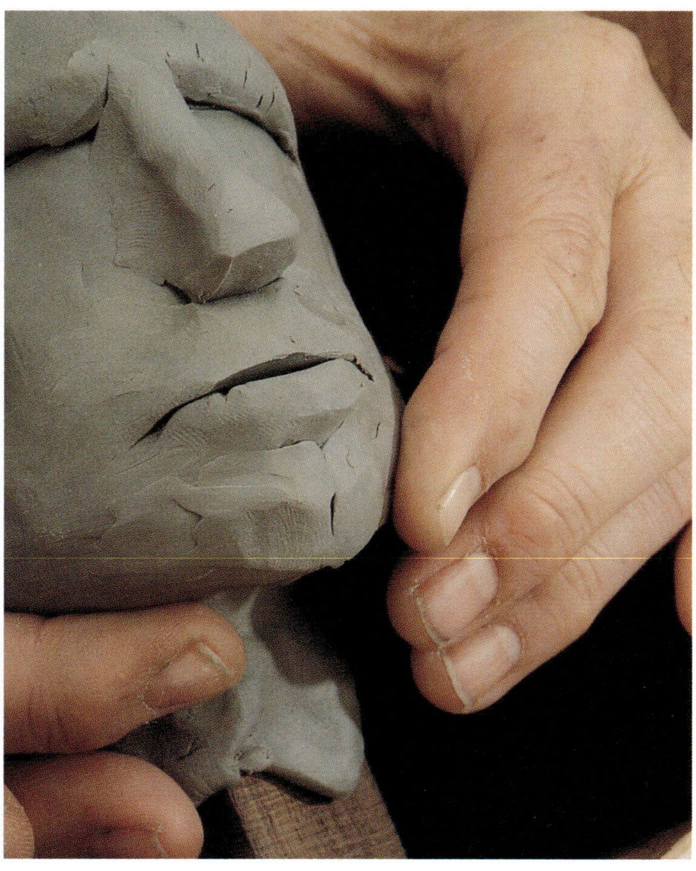

Smooth these balls in for the chin.

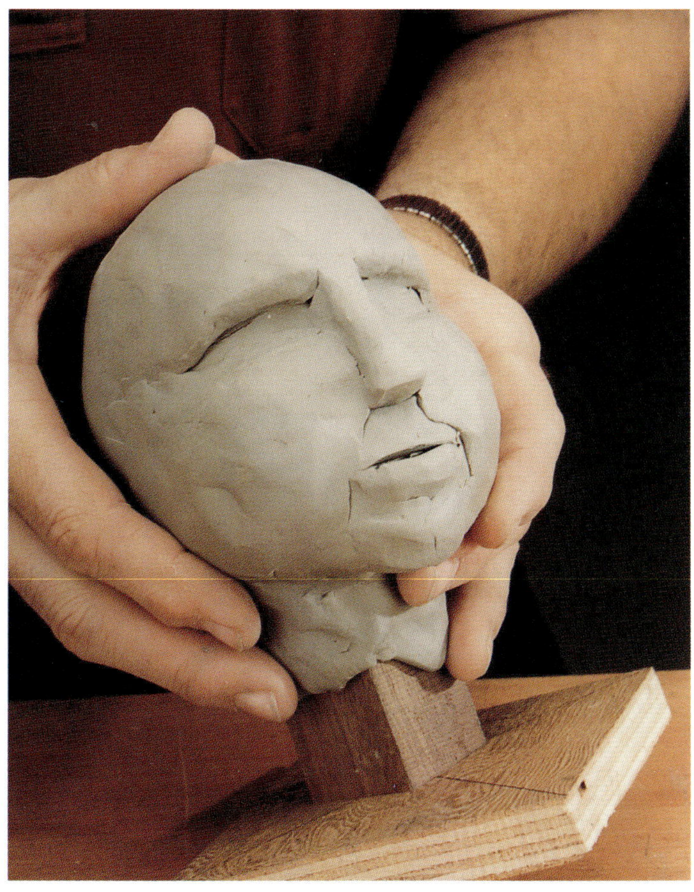

Smooth in the cheeks.

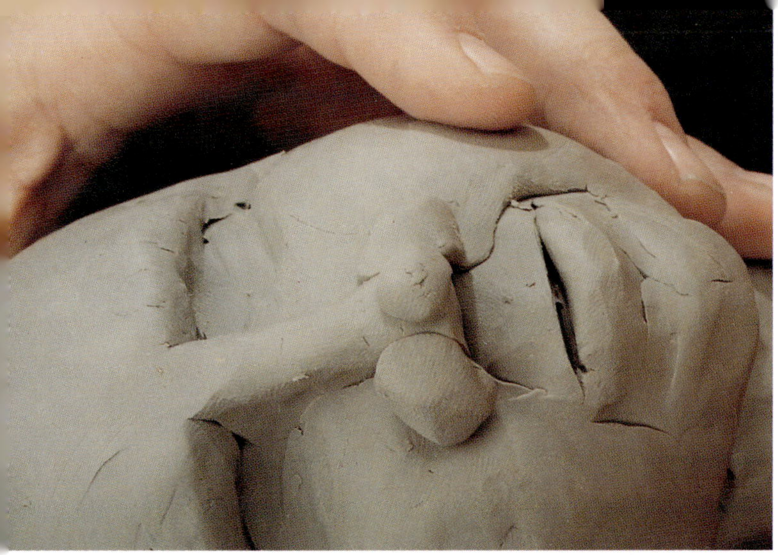

Make two more pea-sized balls of clay. Place them on either size of the nose to begin forming the nostrils. Use a third small ball to form the tip of the nose and blend it in.

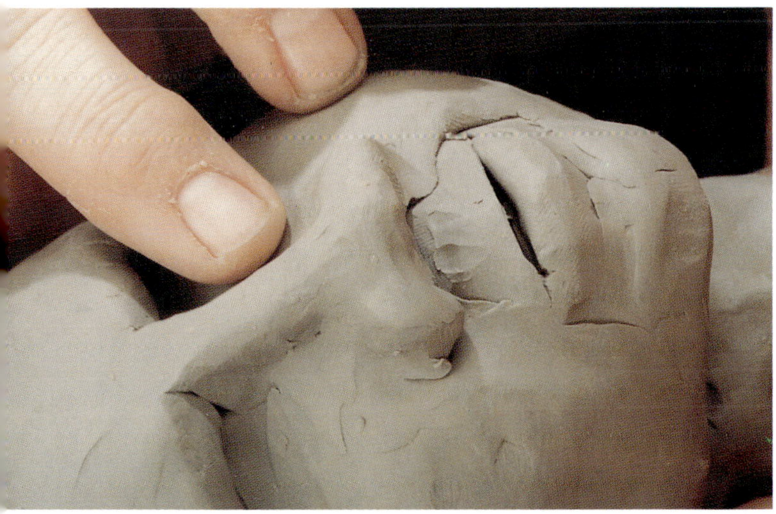

Blend in the nose.

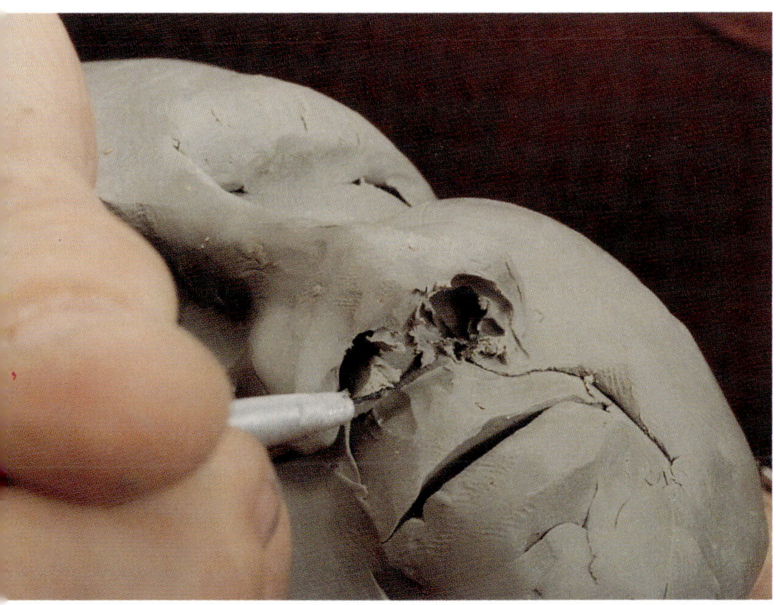

Remove clay for the nostrils underneath the nose.

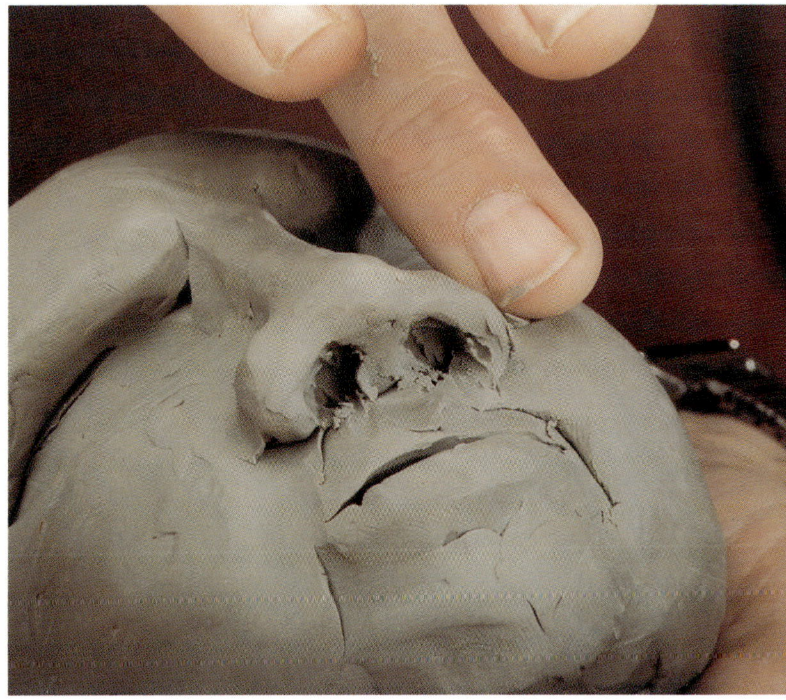

Since most people don't really know what their nostrils look like, spend some time looking in the mirror before sculpting these nostrils. Of course, you can always stand on a crowded corner and look up until others do the same and then check out their nostrils if you like.

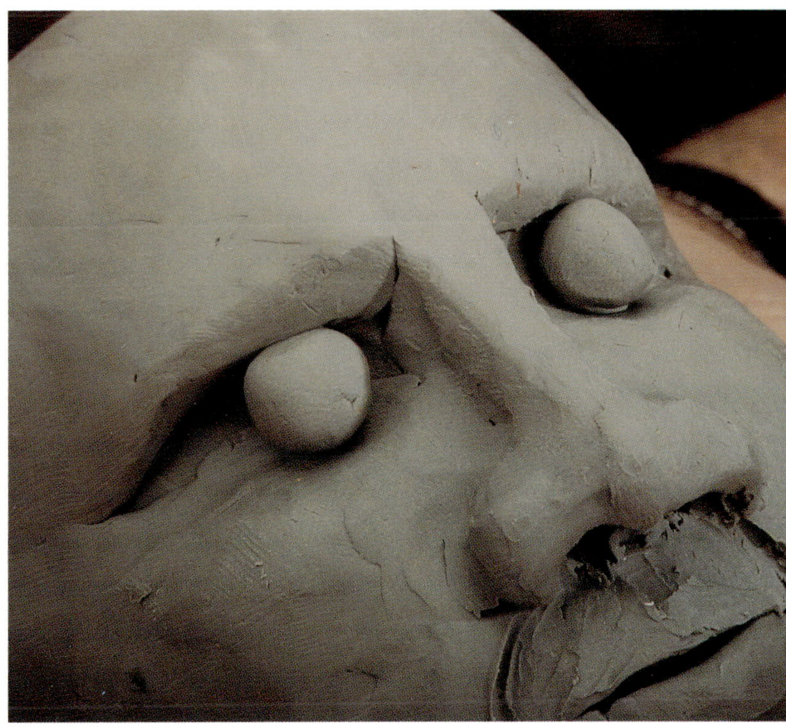

Begin the structures of the eyes by placing in two small elliptical balls of clay.

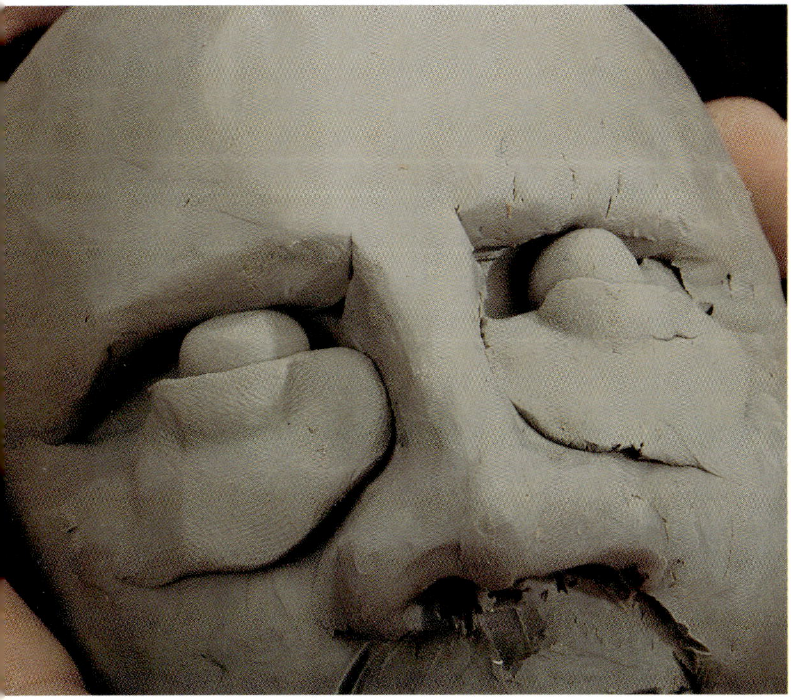

Lay in two slabs of clay underneath to start forming the lower eye lids.

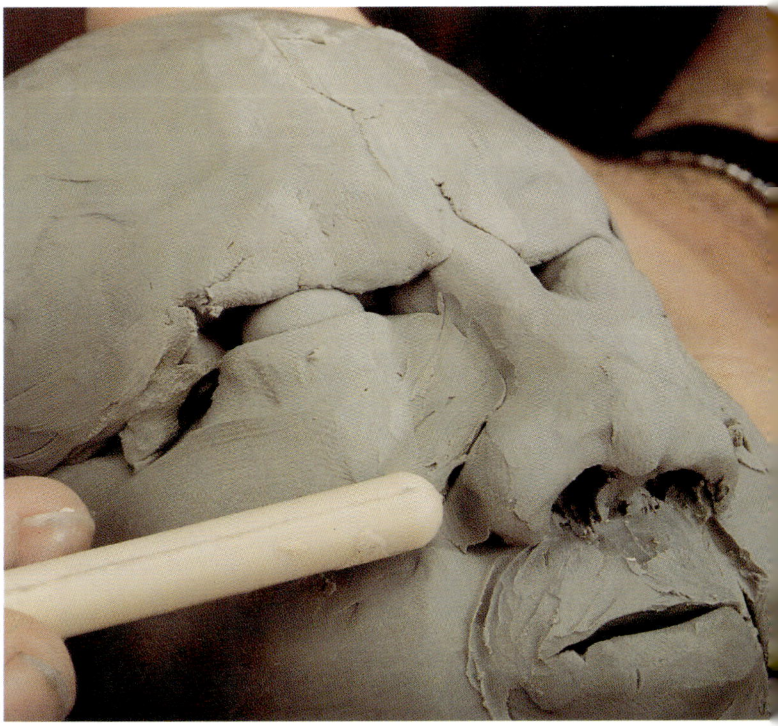

Blend in the upper and lower lids.

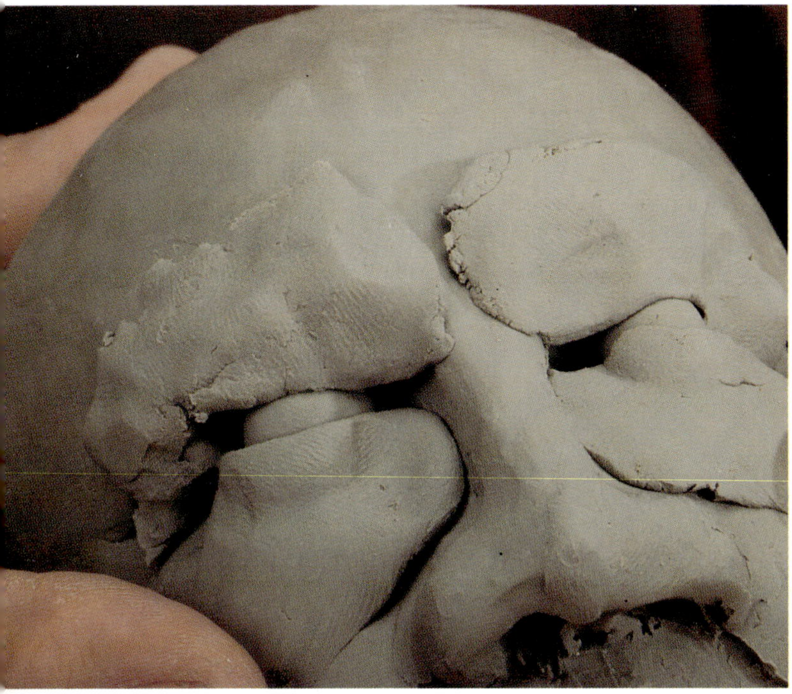

Place in two flat little slabs over the top to form the upper lids.

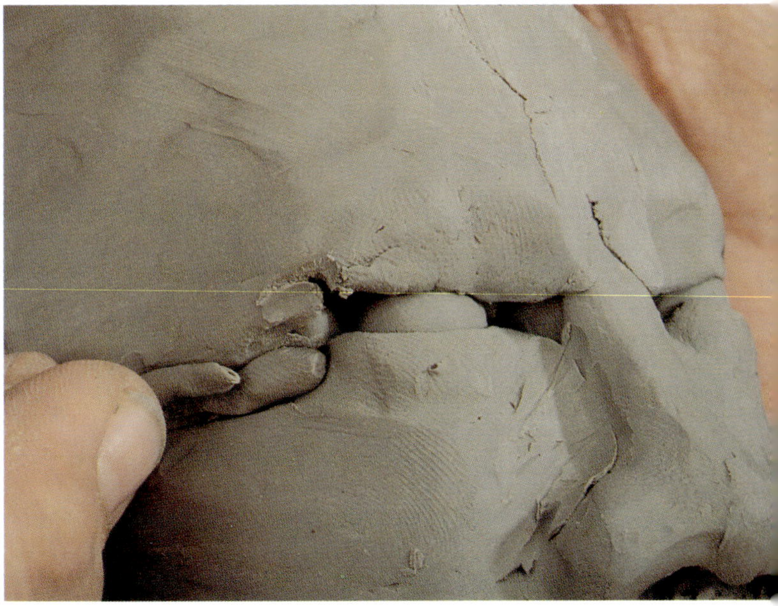

Add clay as needed to finish the structures of the eyes.

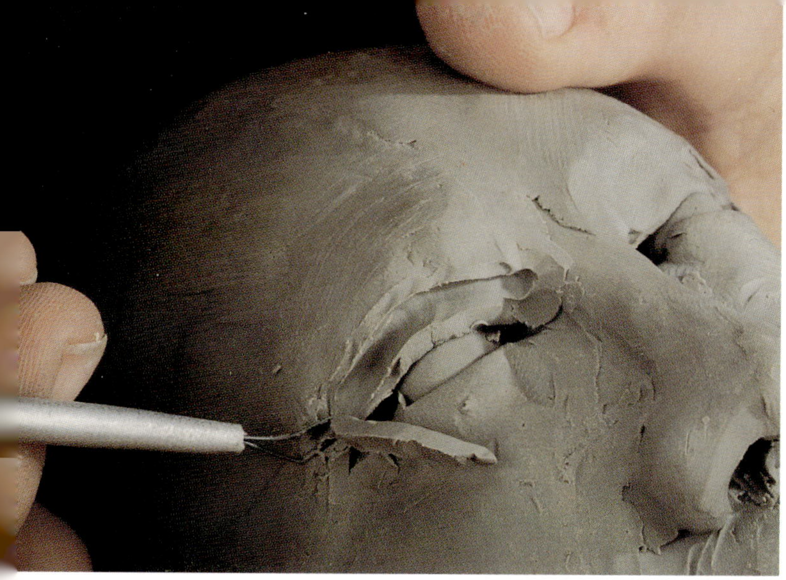

Cut away part of the clay over the eye to form the upper lid.

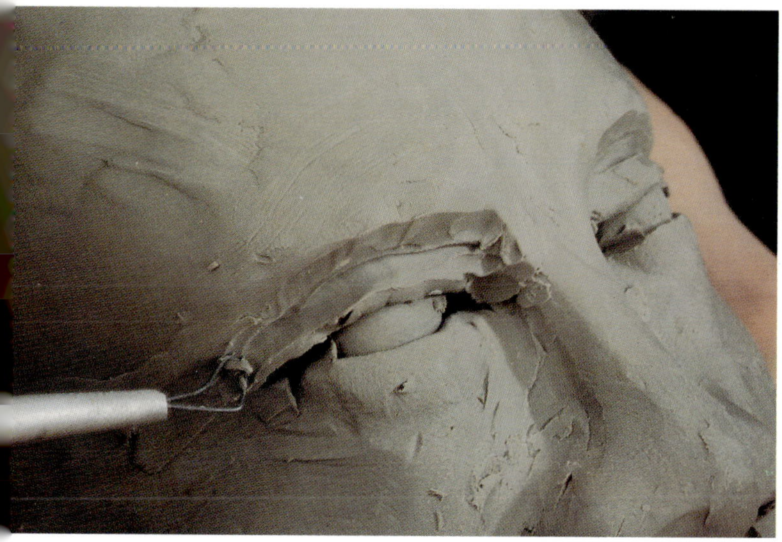

The upper lid is formed.

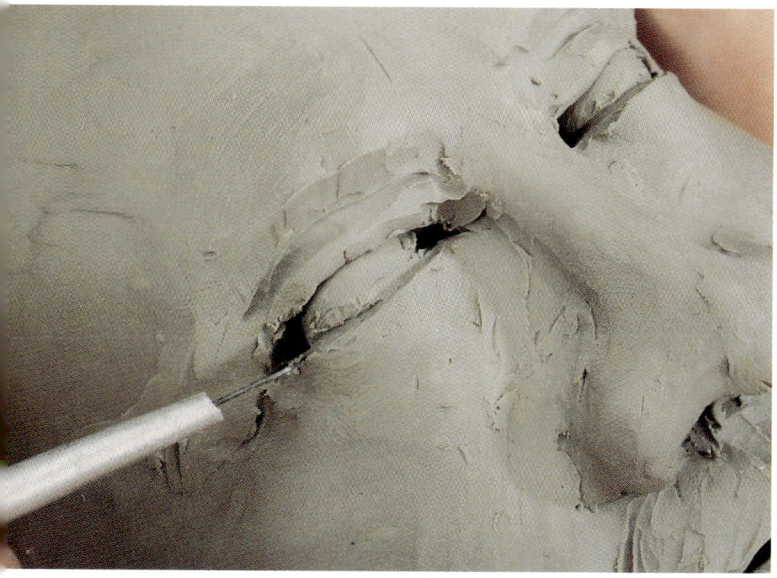

Square off the bottom lid on both sides. This opens his eye a little farther and forms more of a shadow to bring the eye to life.

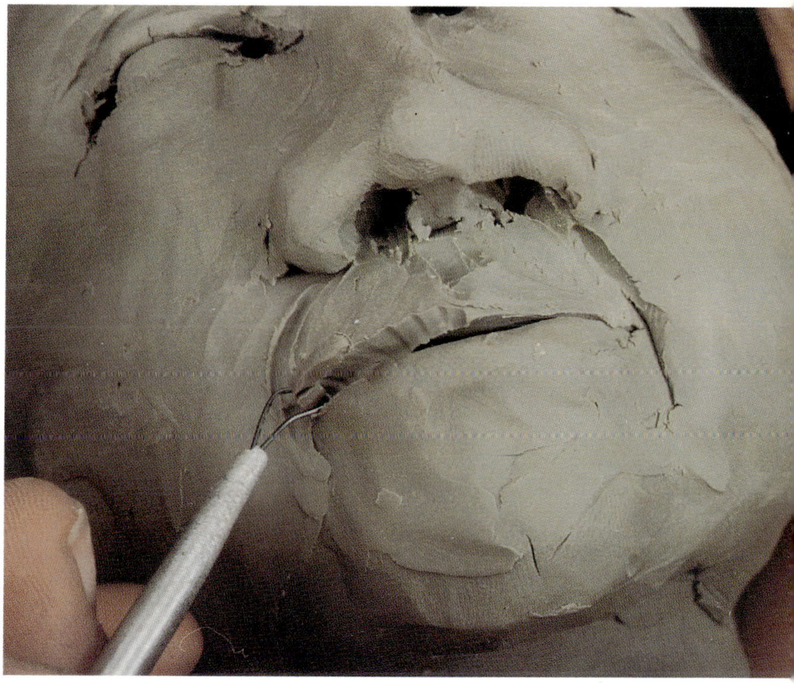

Cut away a slab along each side to form the upper lips.

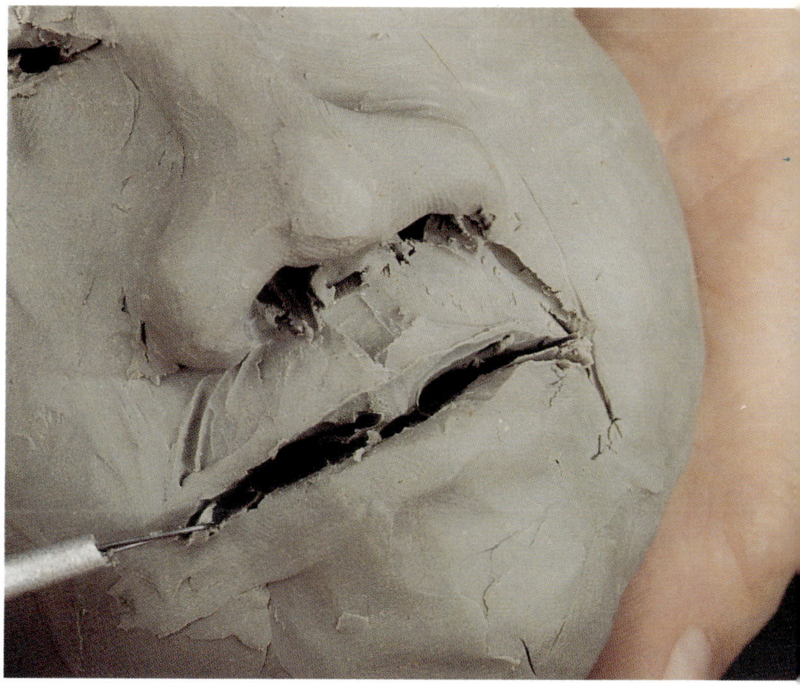

The upper lips in place.

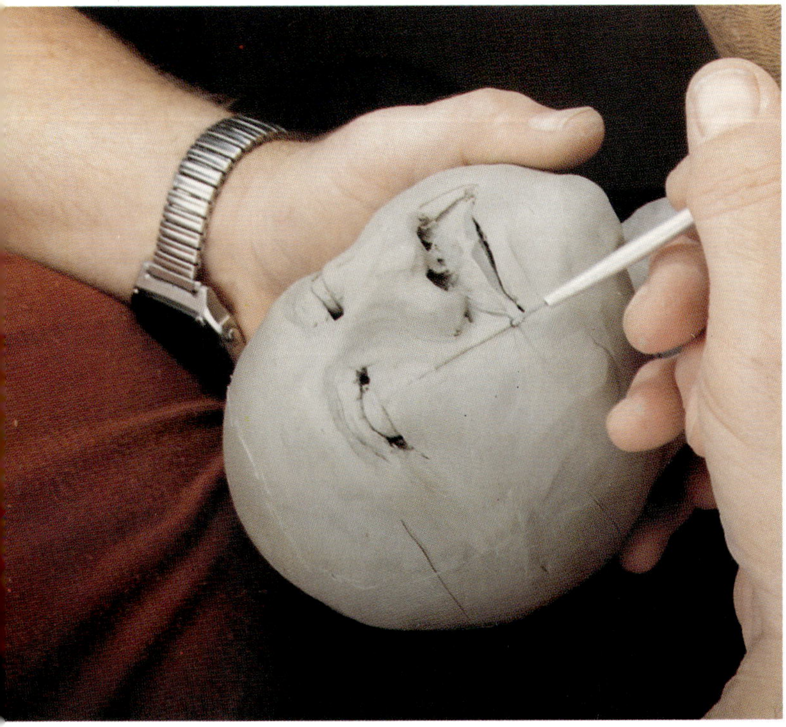

Check the width of the mouth now that the eyes are in. Bring down the lines from the center of the eyes and you will have the proper width for the mouth.

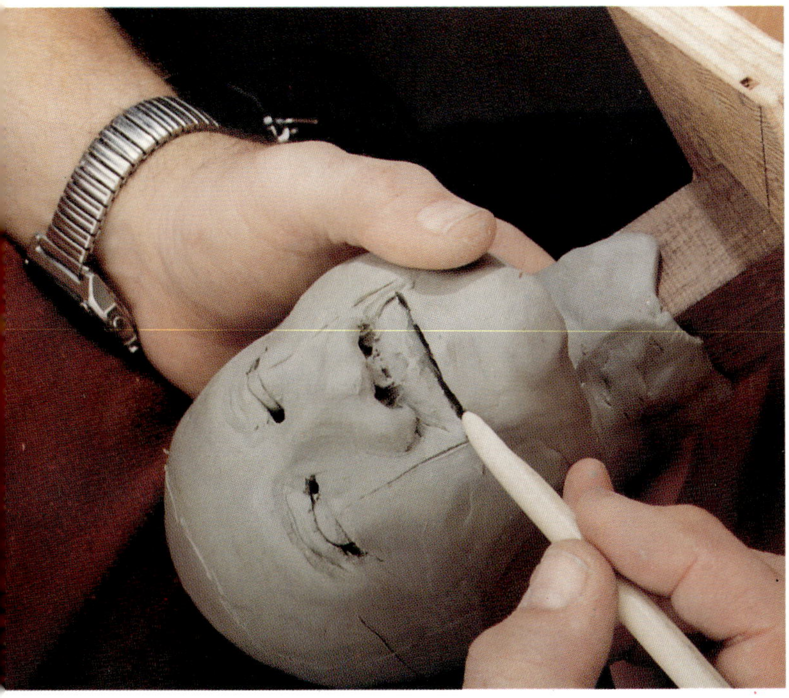

The corners of the mouth now meet the guide lines.

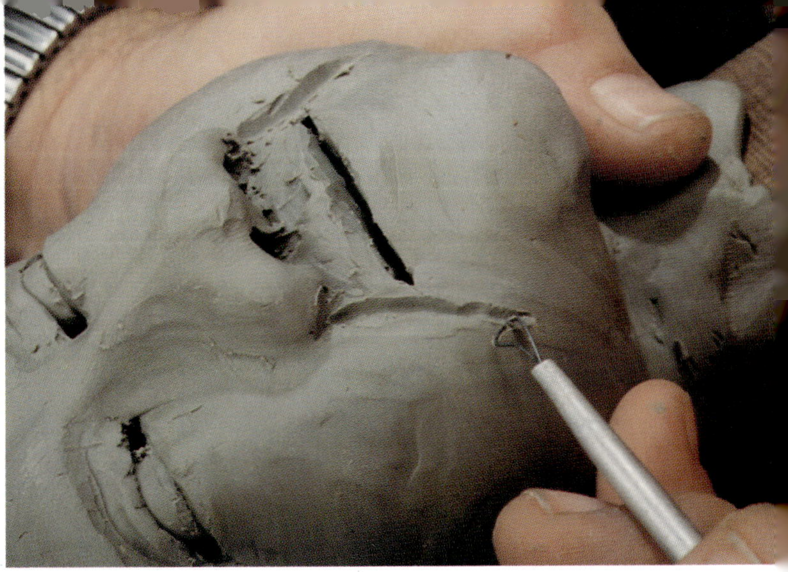

Cut in the smile lines.

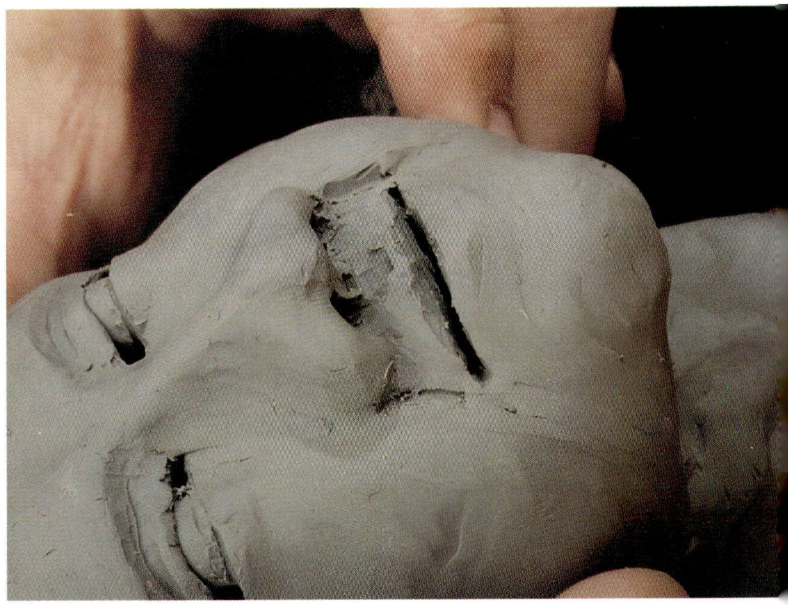

Blend in the sharp edges of the smile lines.

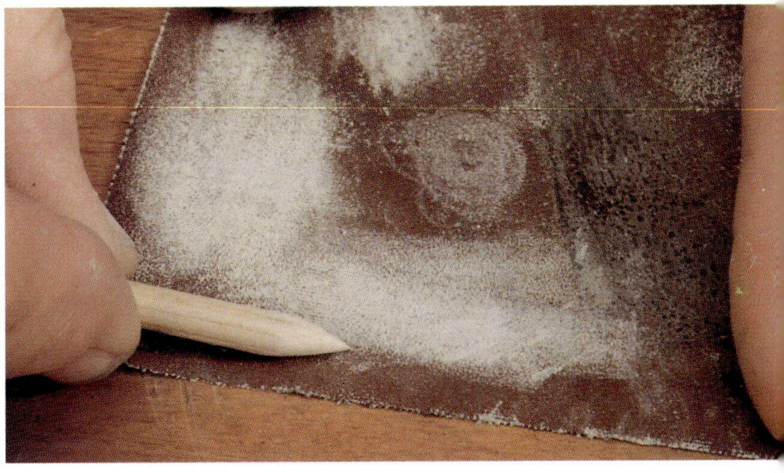

Fashion a tool to use to put in the pupils of the eyes. You can make one from a piece of round dowel, sharpening it with a knife and sanding it smooth.

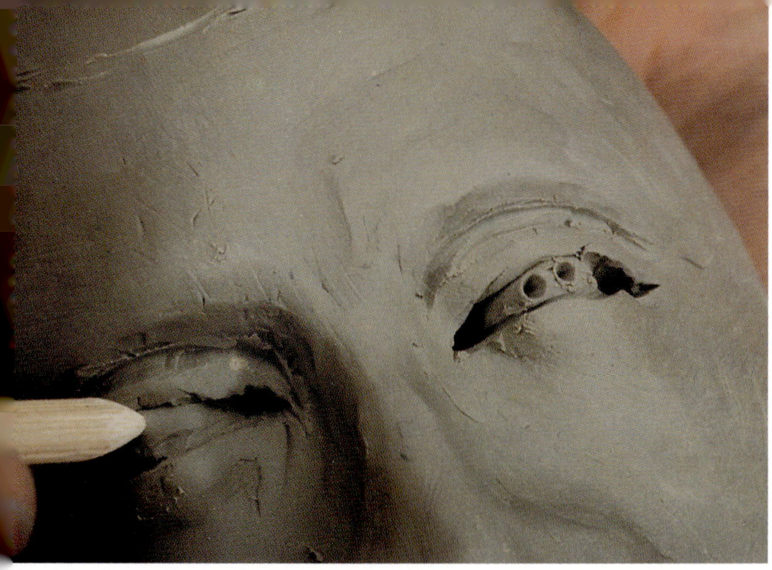

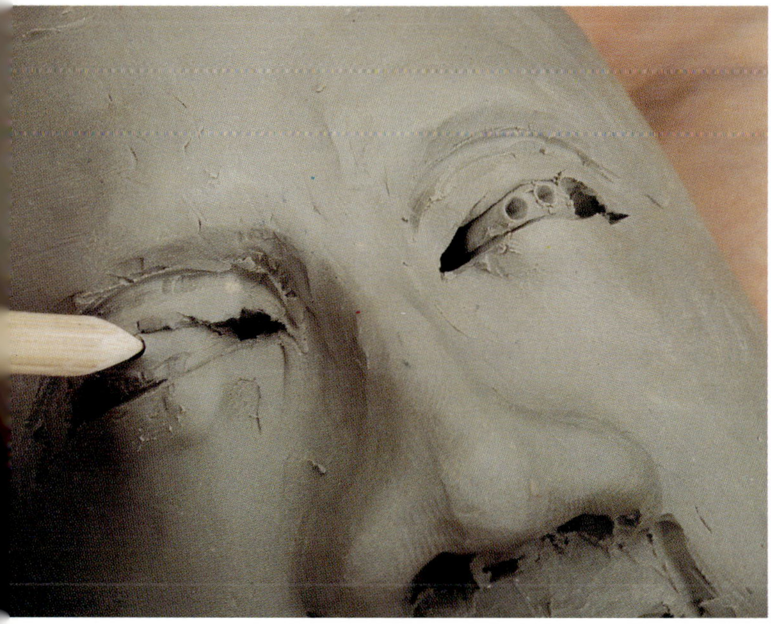

To begin forming the pupils, make two holes below the upper lid of each eye.

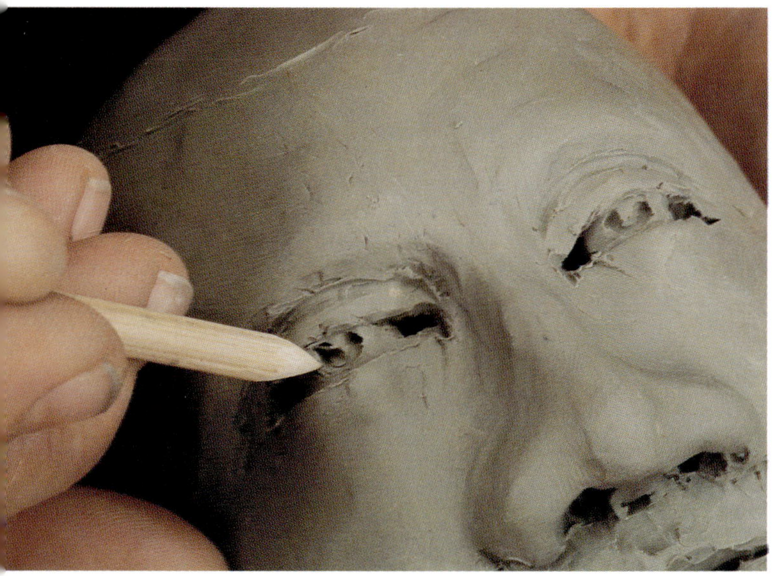

Connect the two dots with a U shape to complete the pupil.

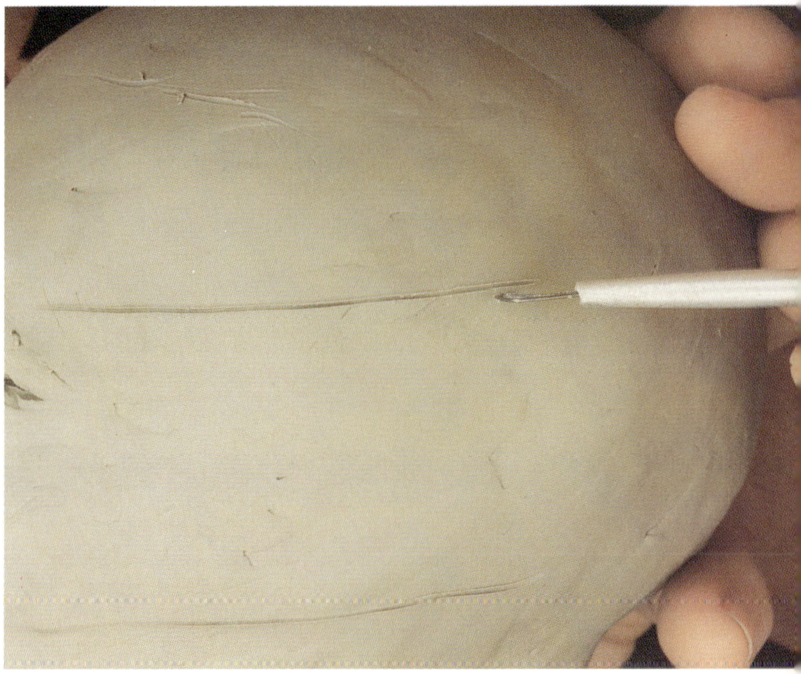

Start the layout for the ears by extending the lines from the bottom of the nose and the eyebrow to the sides of the head.

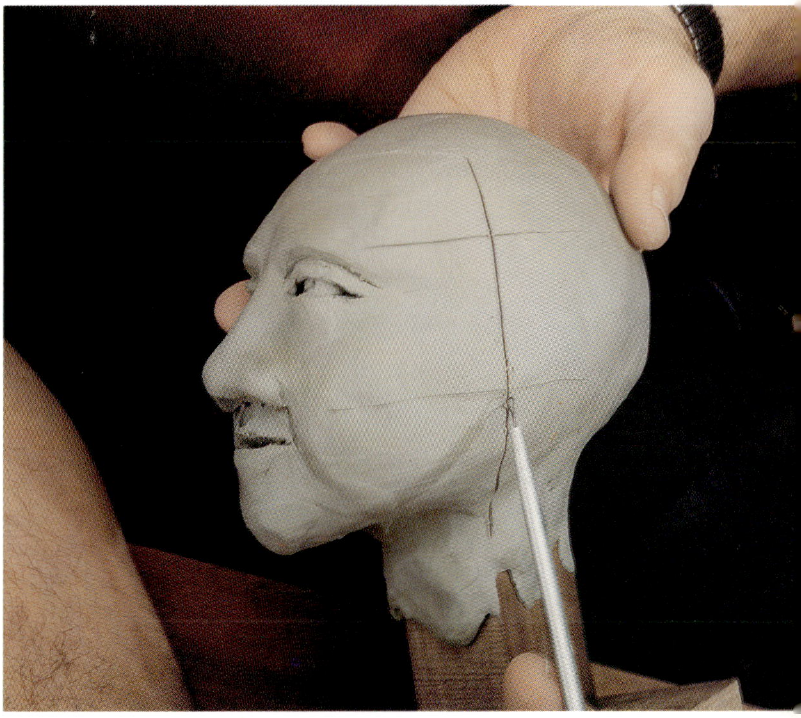

Locate the center of the head from front to back. Add the two line needed to locate the top and bottom of the ear.

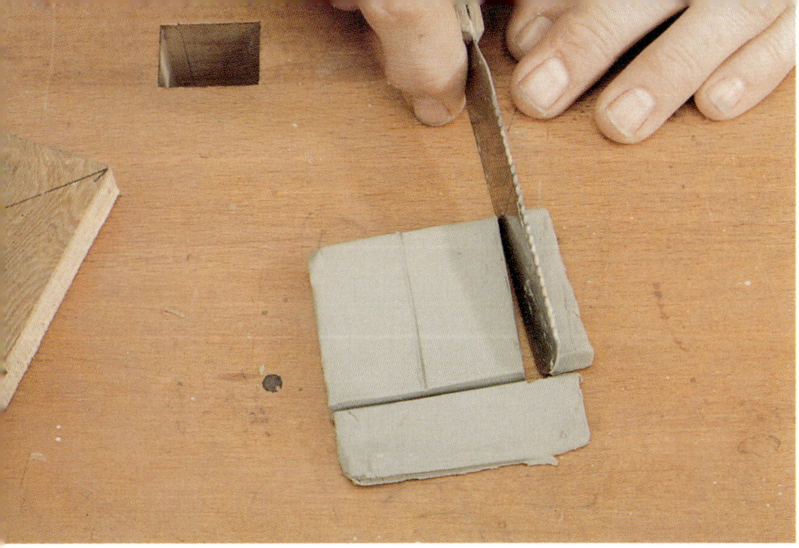

To construct the ears, take a slab of clay and roughly cut it down to size of two ears.

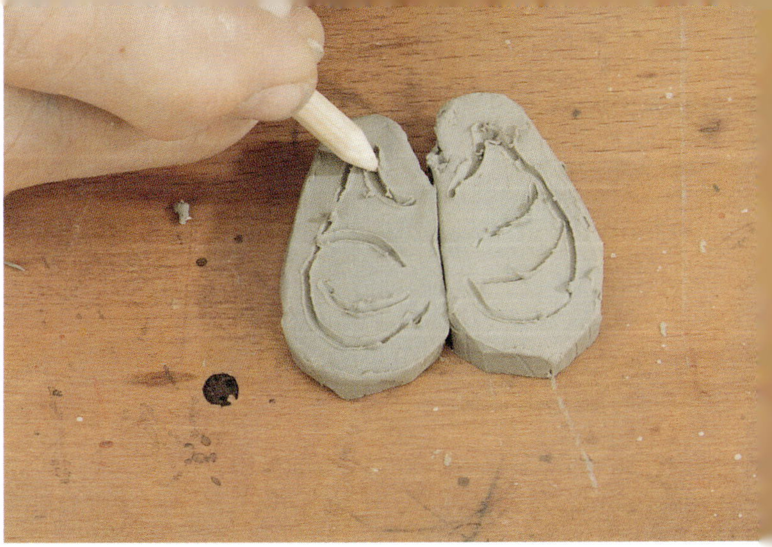

Separate the two pieces. You now have the shape for both ears. Go ahead and draw on the shapes of the inner ear.

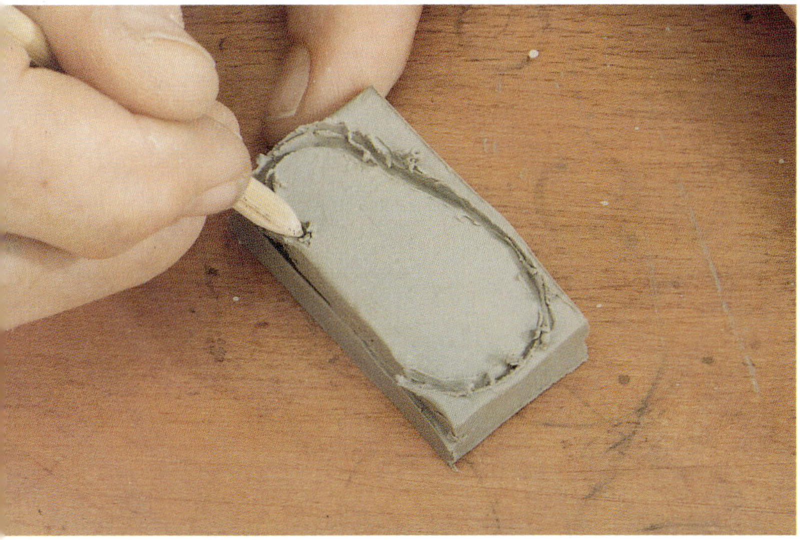

Stack one ear piece on top of the other and draw on the shape of the ear.

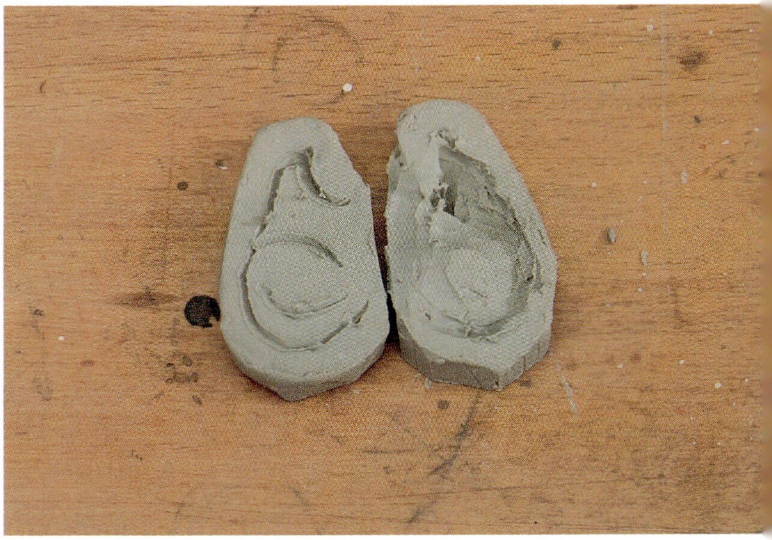

Rough in the shape of both ears.

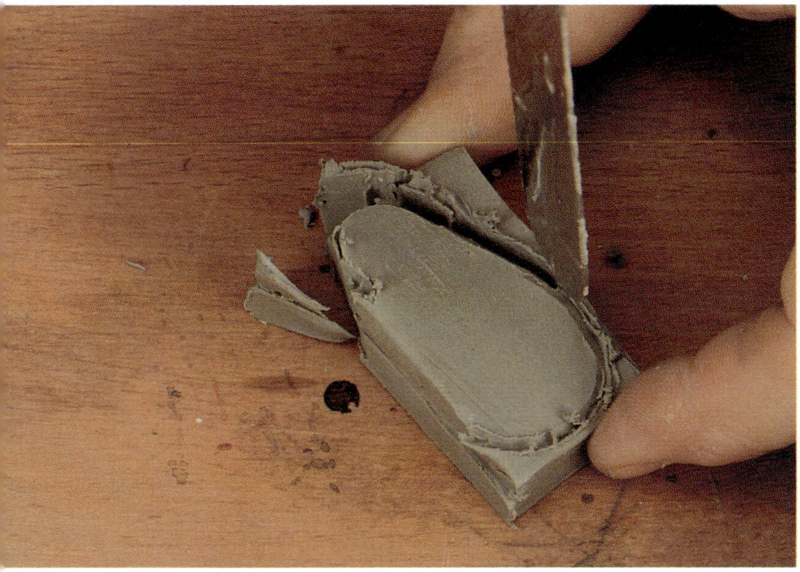

Roughly cut out the shape of the ears.

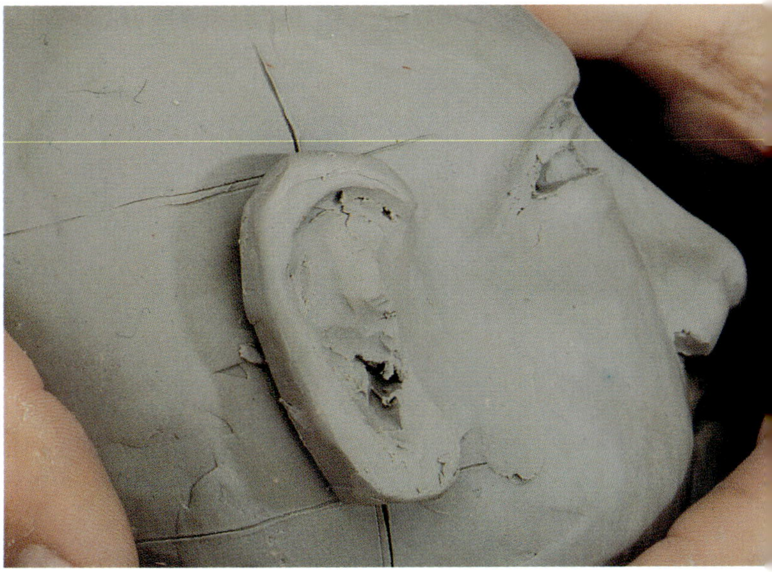

Attach the ear to the side of the head, following the guide lines.

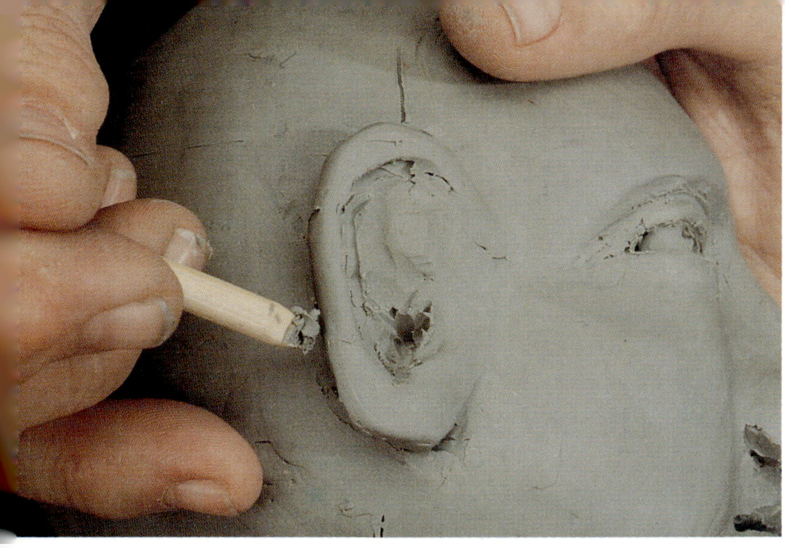

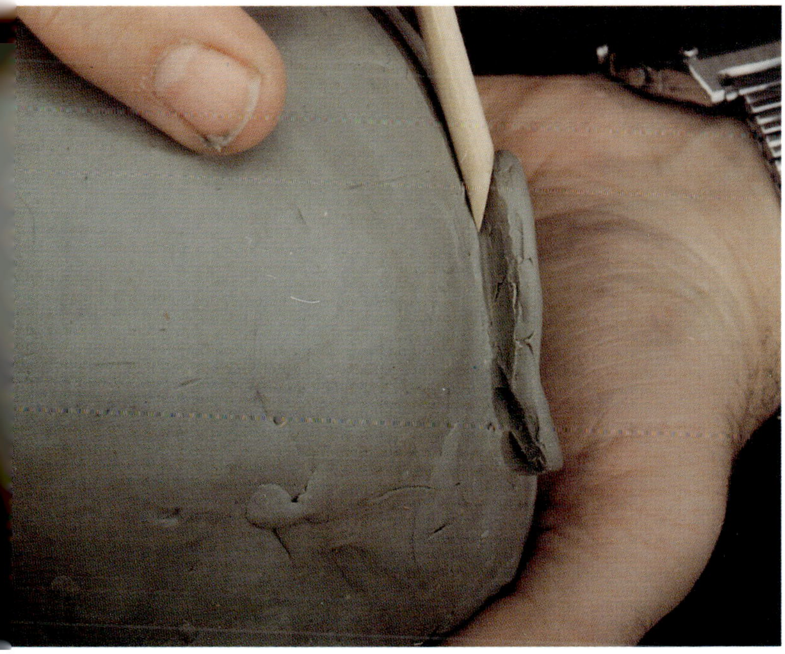

Blend the ear into the head. Don't forget to blend the back of the ear into the head as well.

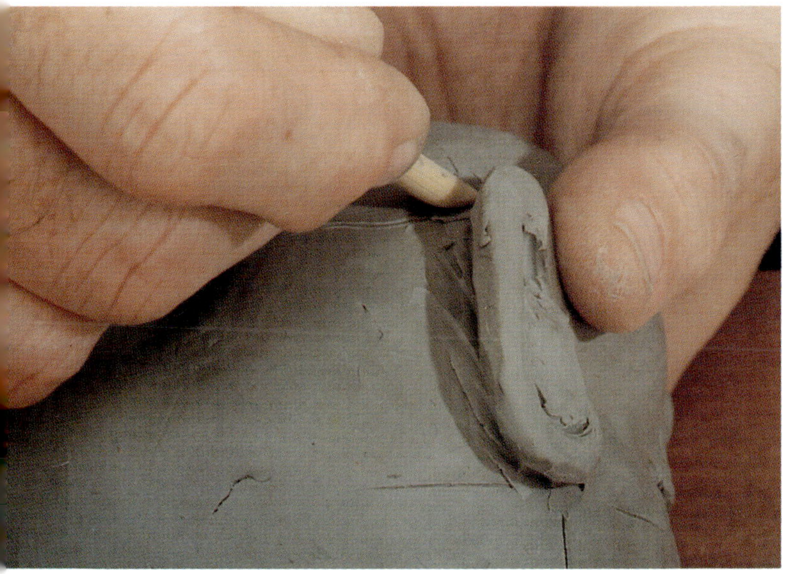

Repeat this process with the other ear.

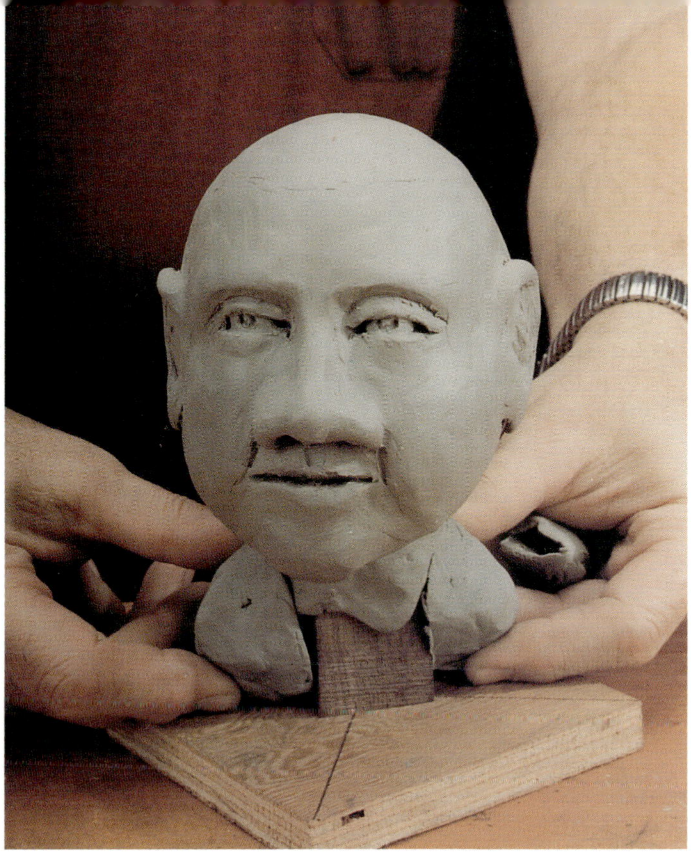

Add a lump to each side of the neck to start forming the shoulders.

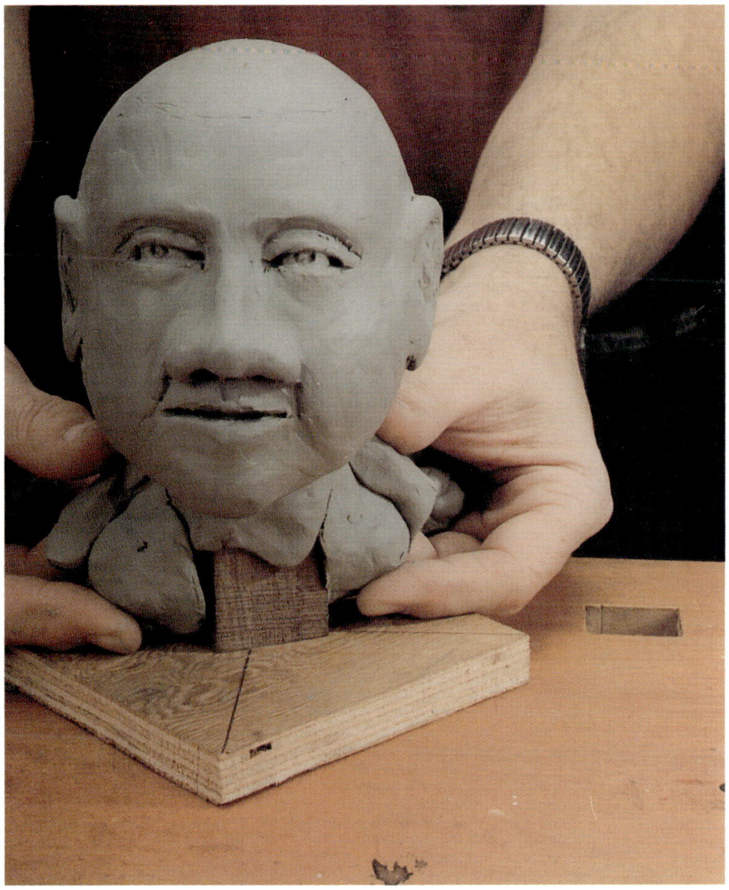

Next, add a coil of clay lining up with the sculpture's ear and running out onto the lump of the shoulder. This will begin representing the muscles that run down from the neck to the shoulder.

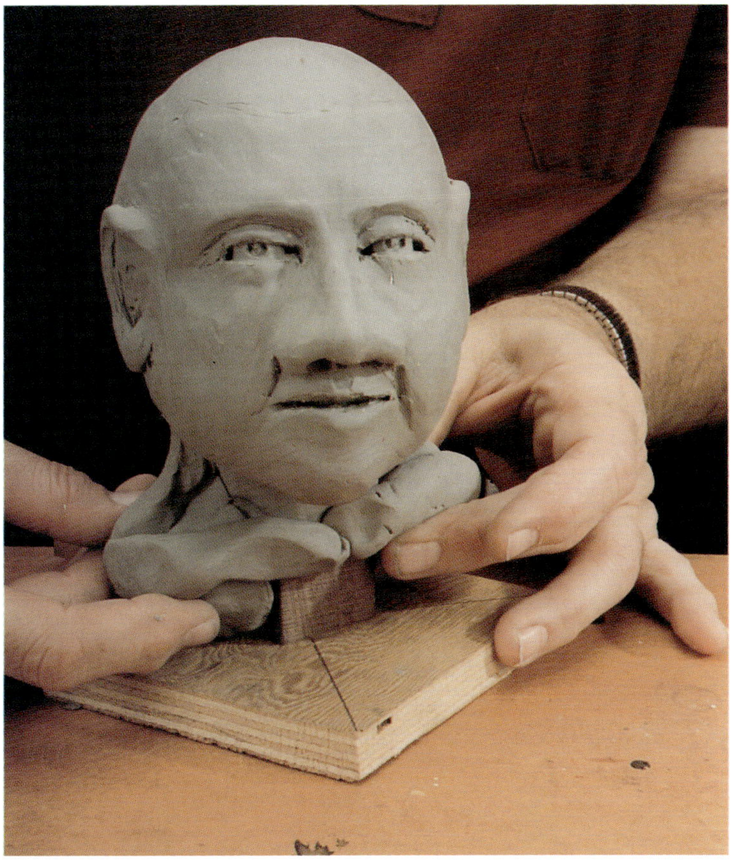

Run two more coils of clay across from the outer edges of the shoulder and ending at the neck to represent the collar bones.

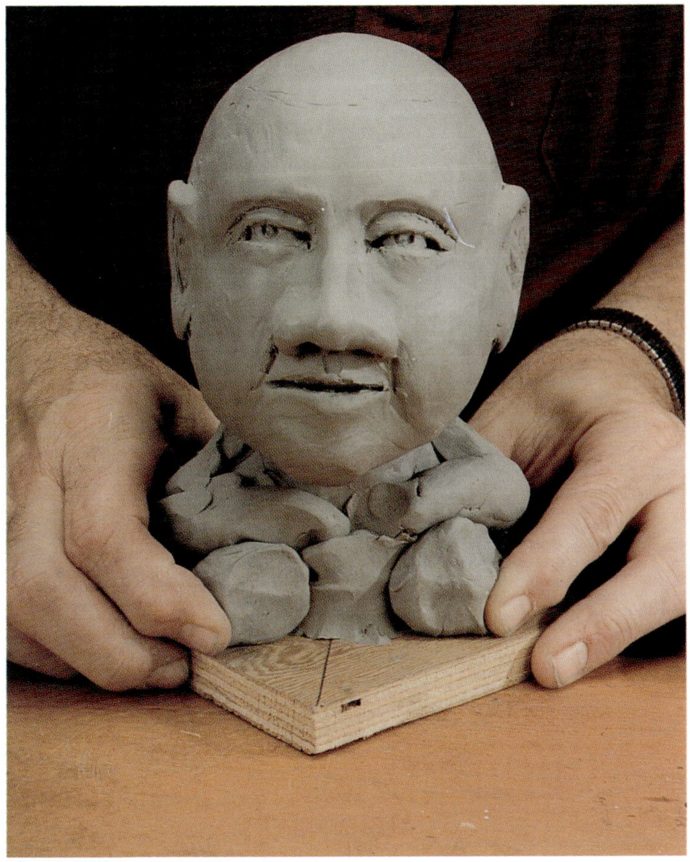

Put in a ball of clay on each side of the central chest muscles.

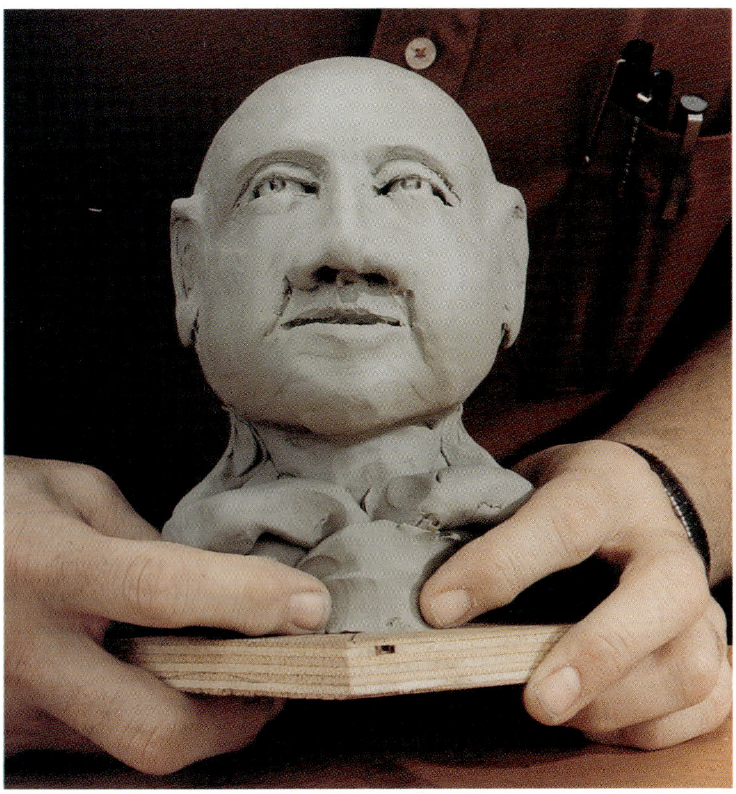

Put in a ball of clay below the collar bones to represent the muscles of the chest.

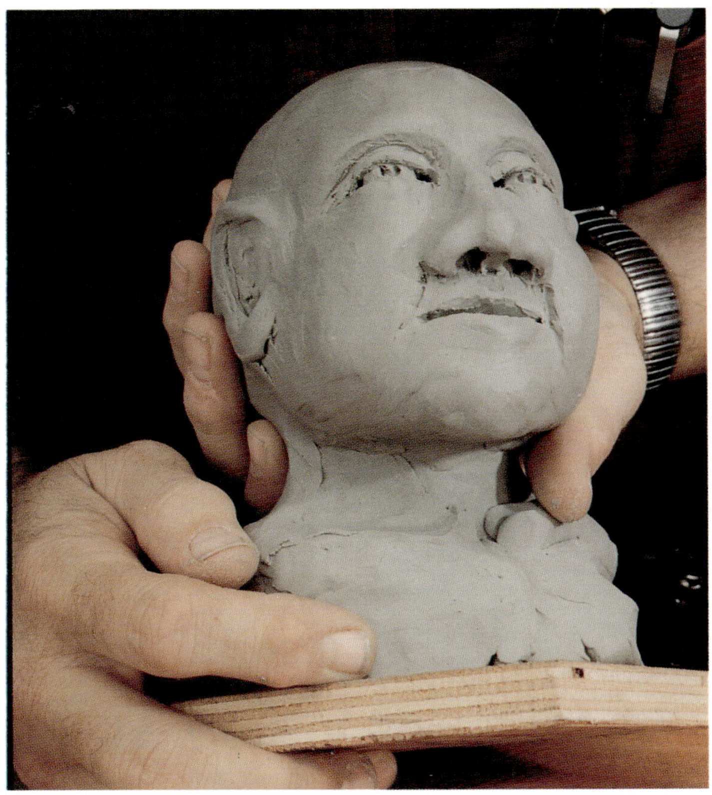

Start blending all of these masses together to shape the chest, shoulders, and neck.

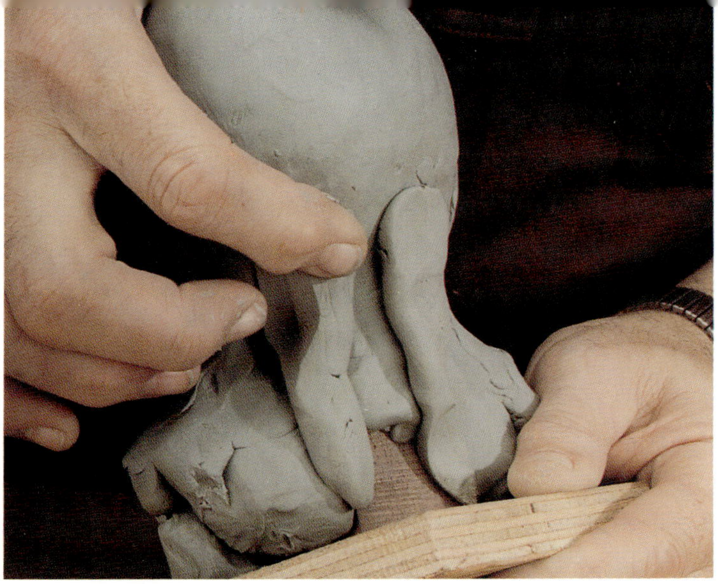

Add a couple coils down either side of the spine in the back.

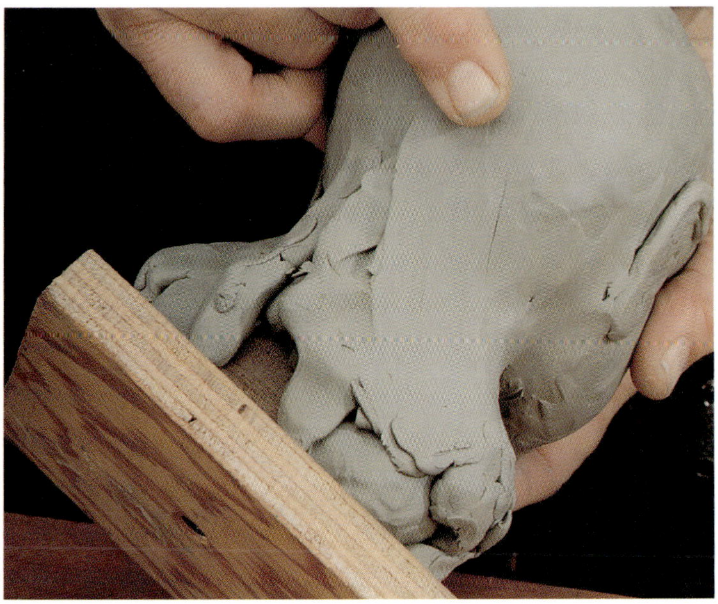

As you model this, show the muscles being pulled to one side as the head is slightly turned.

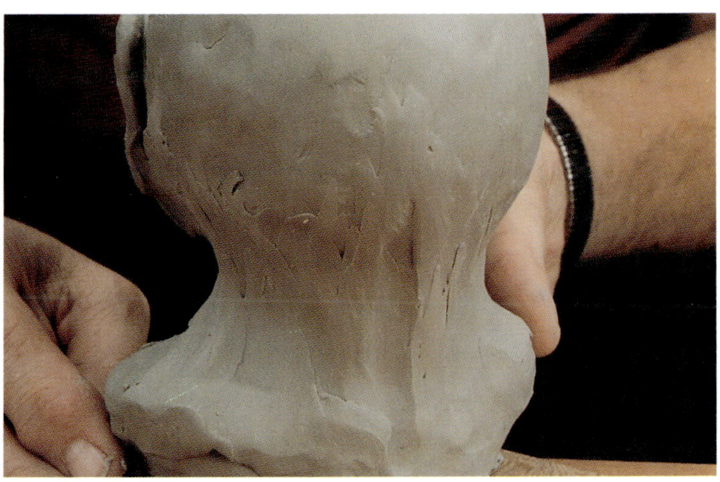

The back of the neck is formed. Allow the muscles and masses to show; the neck is not perfectly smooth.

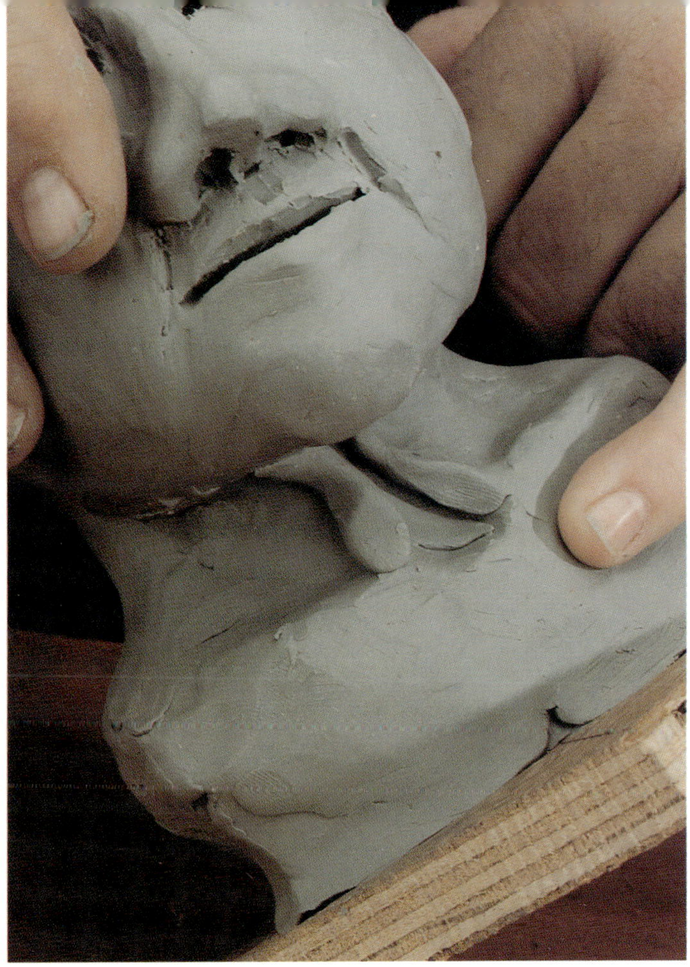

Apply two more small coils of clay on either side underneath the chin and down the throat to form the muscles of the Adam's apple. On a man, this is a prominent feature and on a woman, it is not.

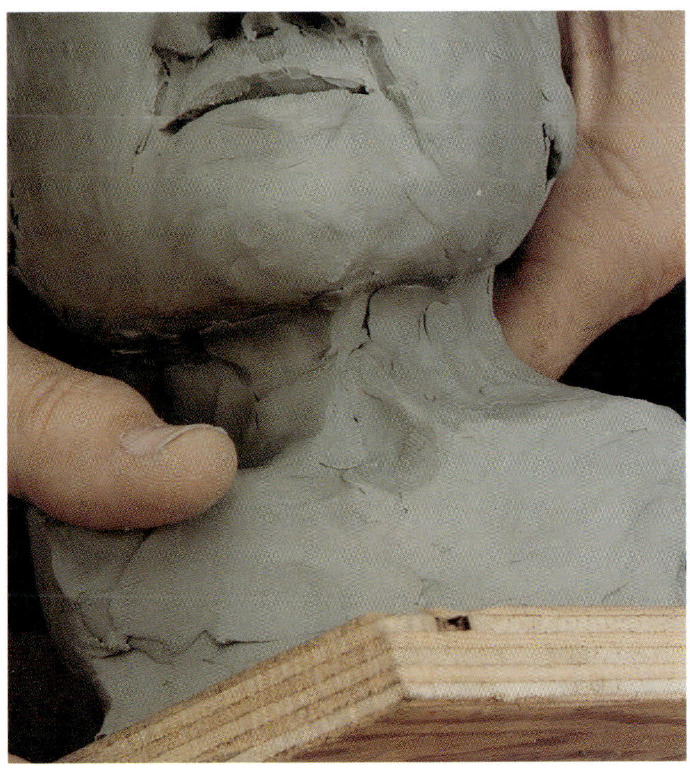

The completed Adam's apple has been sculpted.

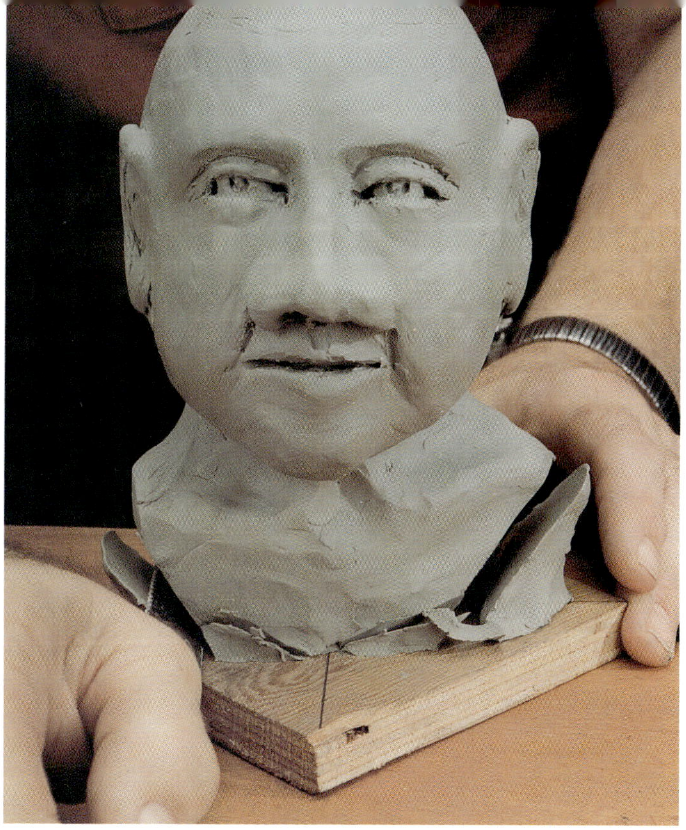

Shape up the base to give it a more finished look.

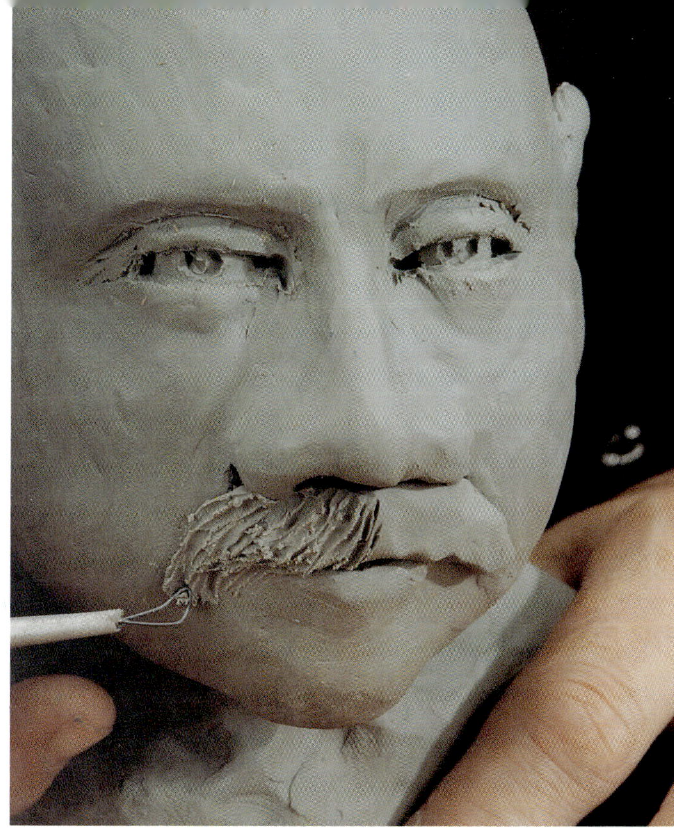

Cut in the mustache hair.

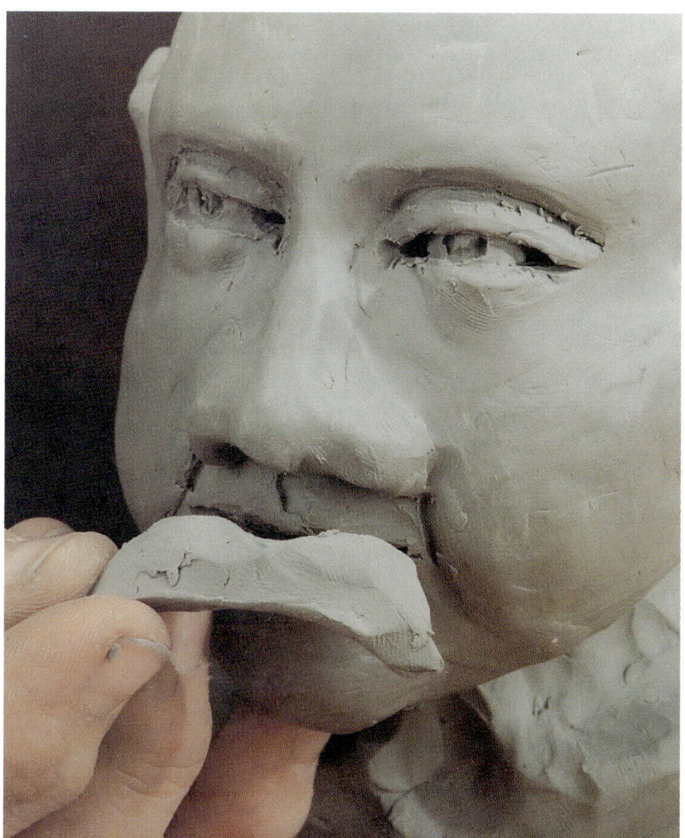

Now is the time to make the choice of how much more finishing you are going to do. These choices include how much hair to sculpt, of what length should the hair be, and whether or not to include a mustache or beard. To lay on a mustache, you roughly shape it down and gently put it in place.

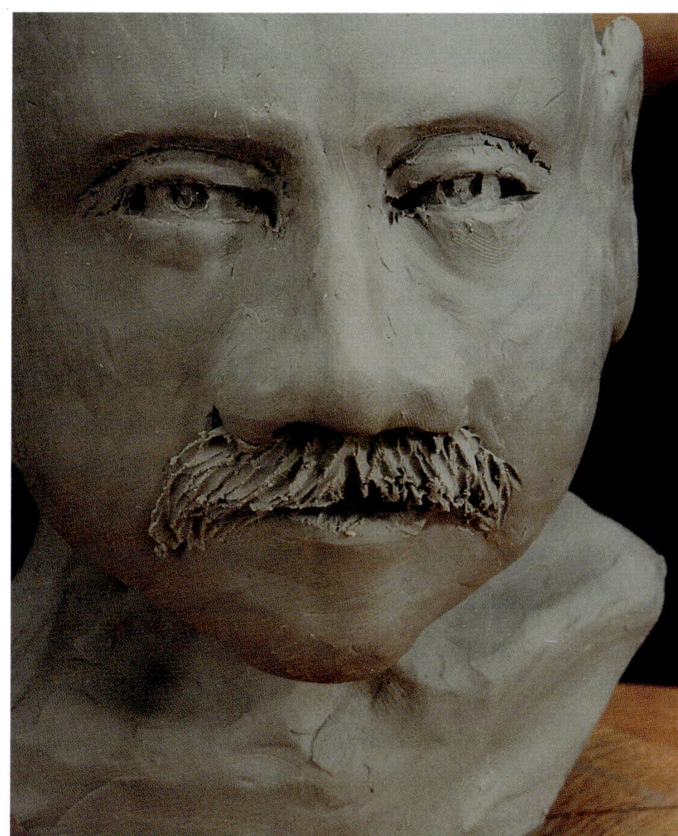

The mustache is finished. You can stop here or go on.

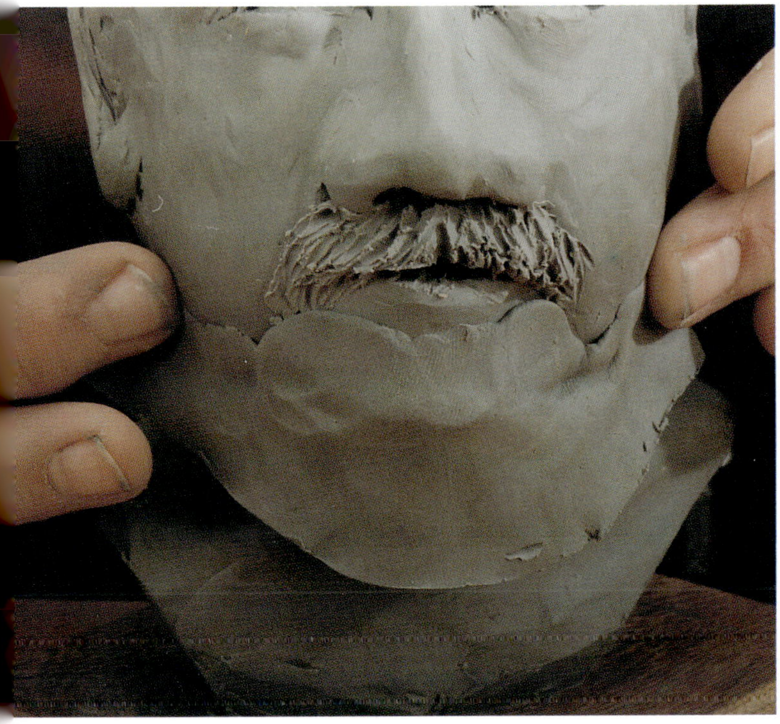

Flatten a sheet of clay, making it thin at the top edge to blend in easily with the face. Rough this flattened shape into a beard. Place it gently on the face and attach the top end to the face.

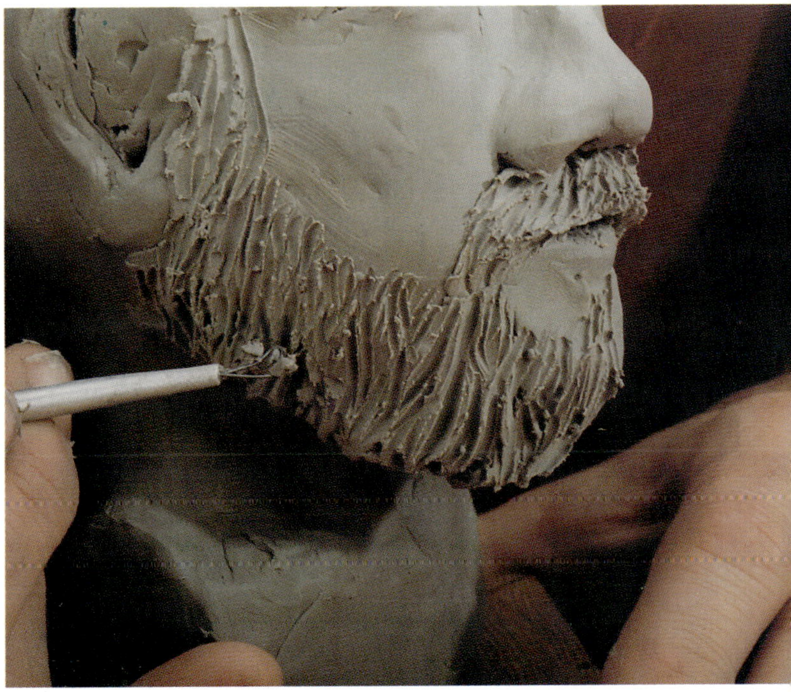

When cutting in the beard, remember that you are only cutting in masses of hairs during this process, not individual hairs.

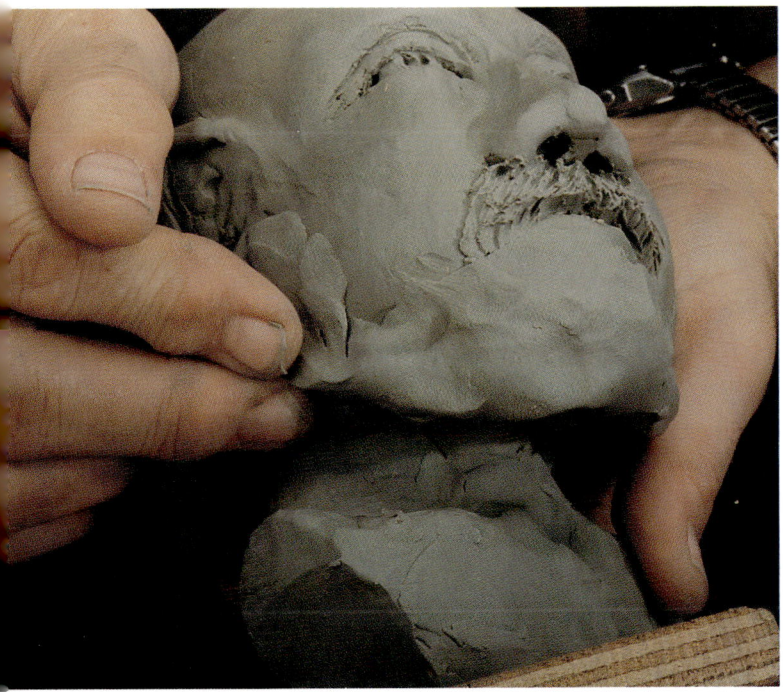

Fold the bottom edge underneath to shape it to the contours of the face.

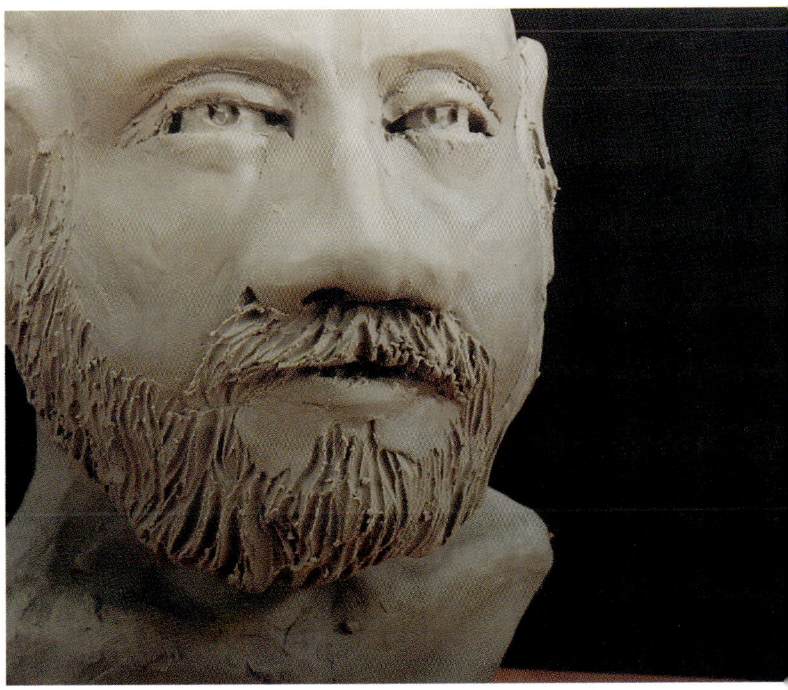

The beard is sculpted in.

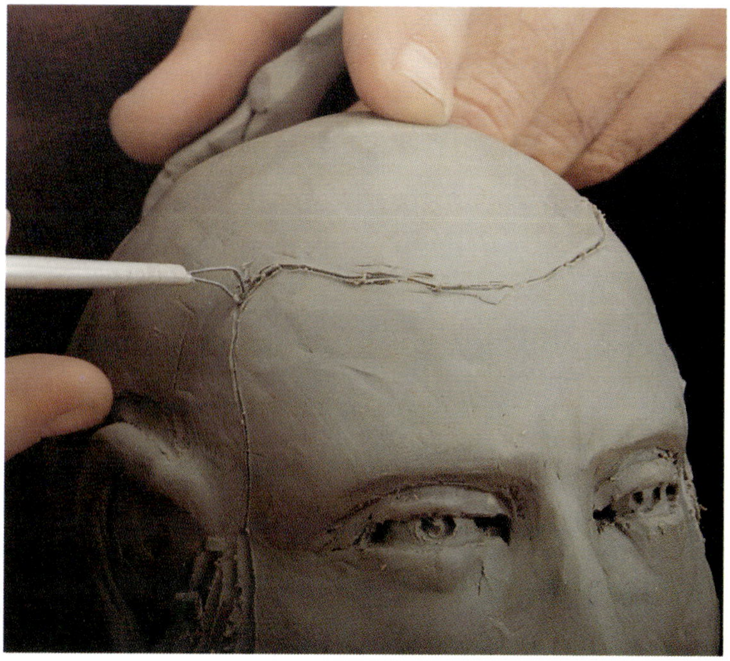

Decide what sort of hair line this gentleman will have. Normally a man with a full head of hair has that hair falling half way between the top of his head and his eyebrows.

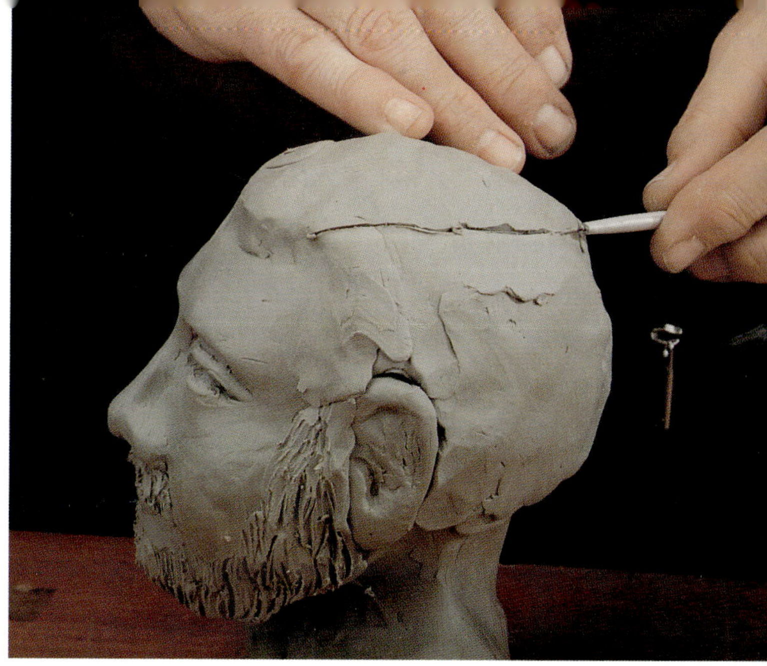

Since this is a well kept gentleman, we'll put a part in his hair.

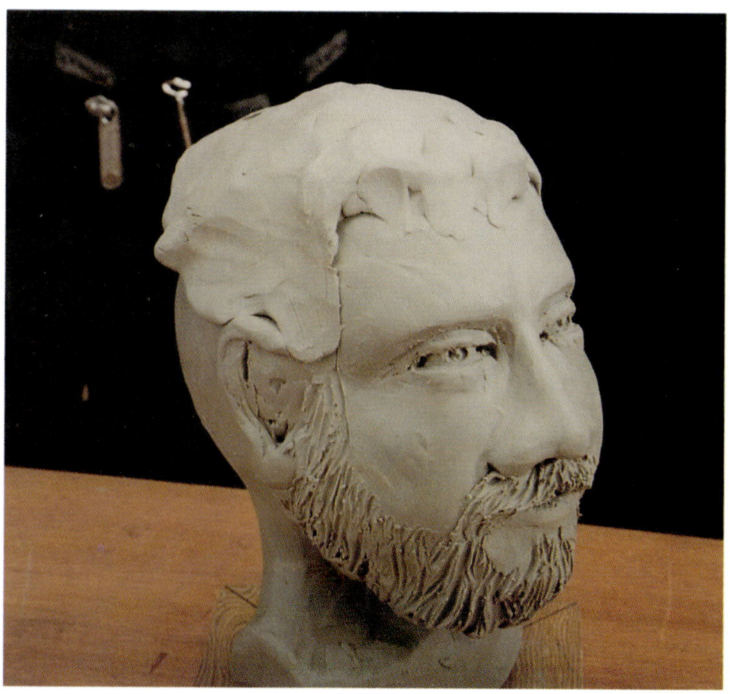

Lay on a sheet of clay that can be sculpted to form his hair. Blend in the edges.

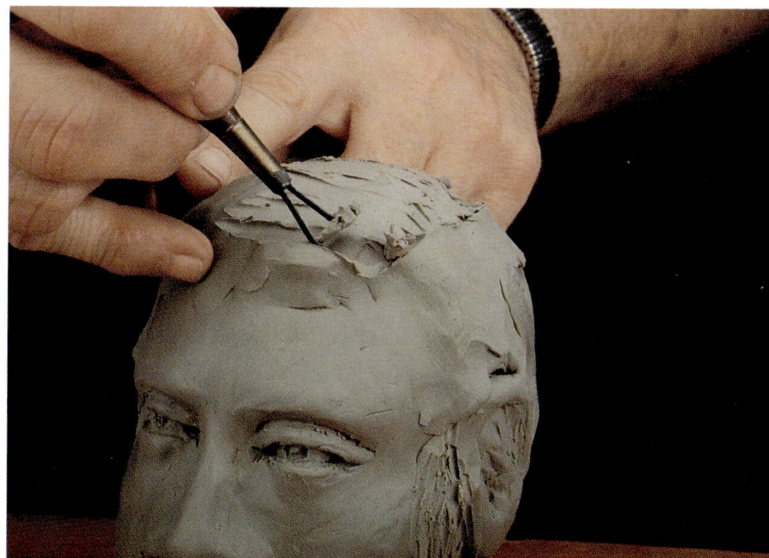

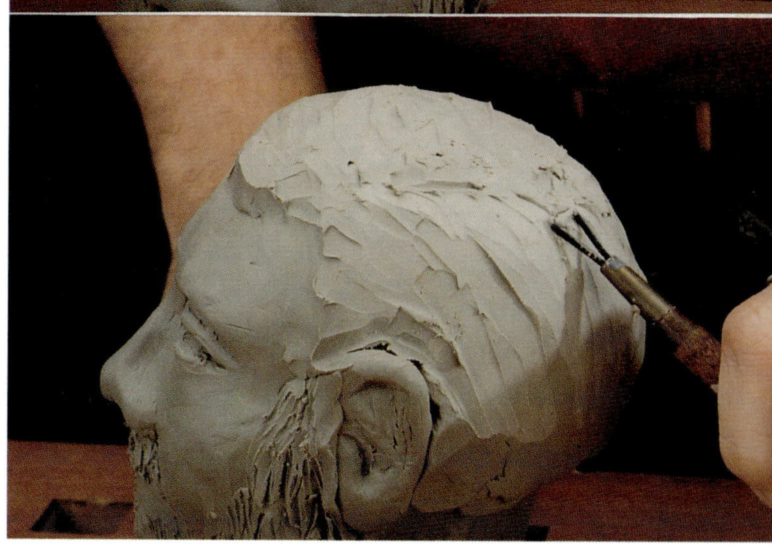

Pull the hair away from the part in both directions.

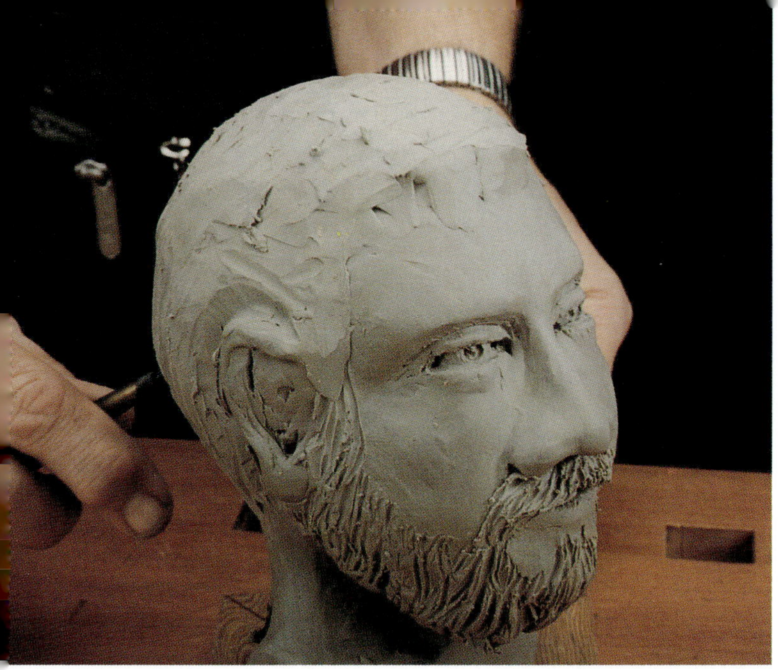

Sculpt in the large masses of hair to create the general shape of the hair.

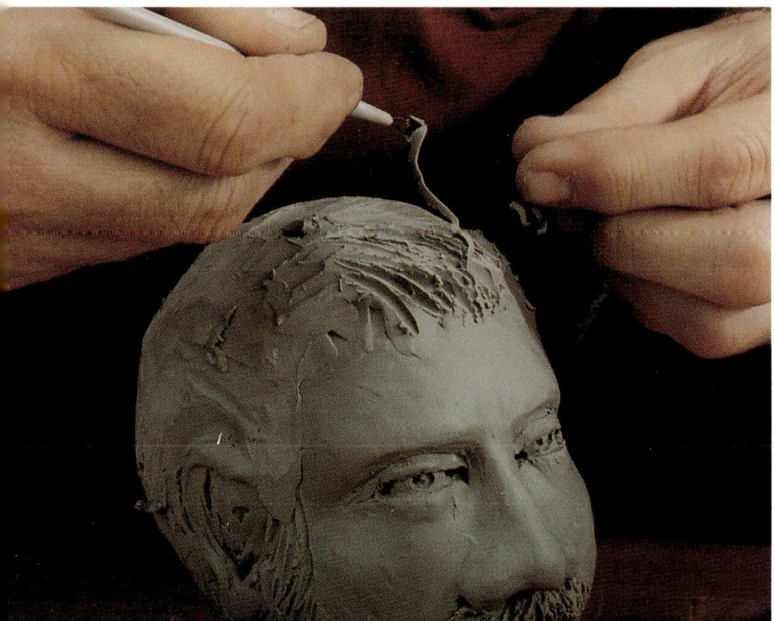

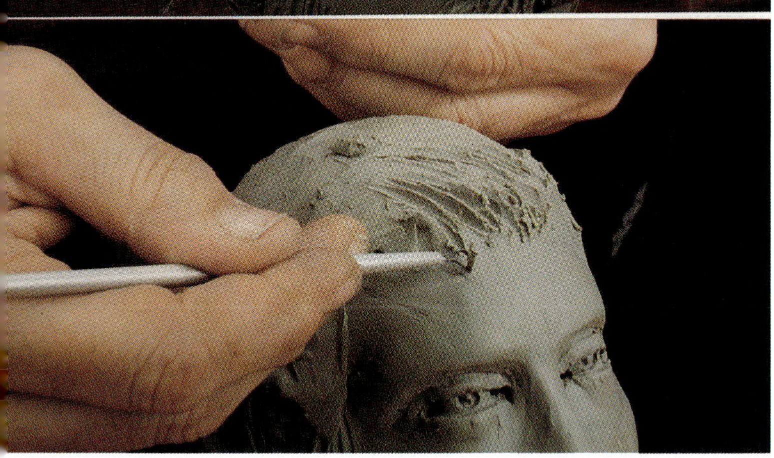

Take a small tool and put in a few hairs in the front, indicating where the hair grows from the scalp.

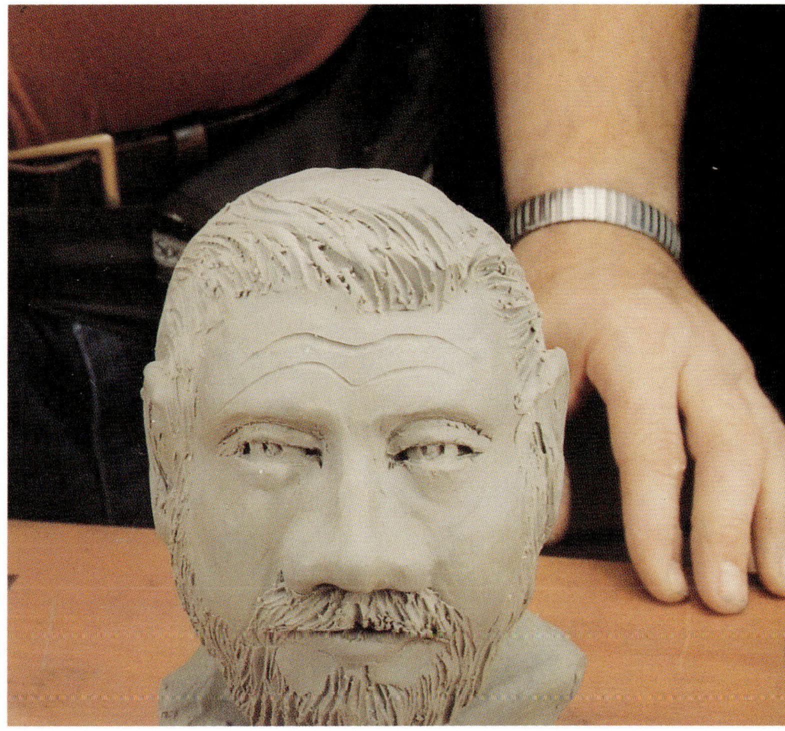

Feel free to age him as much as you like, adding wrinkles as you go.

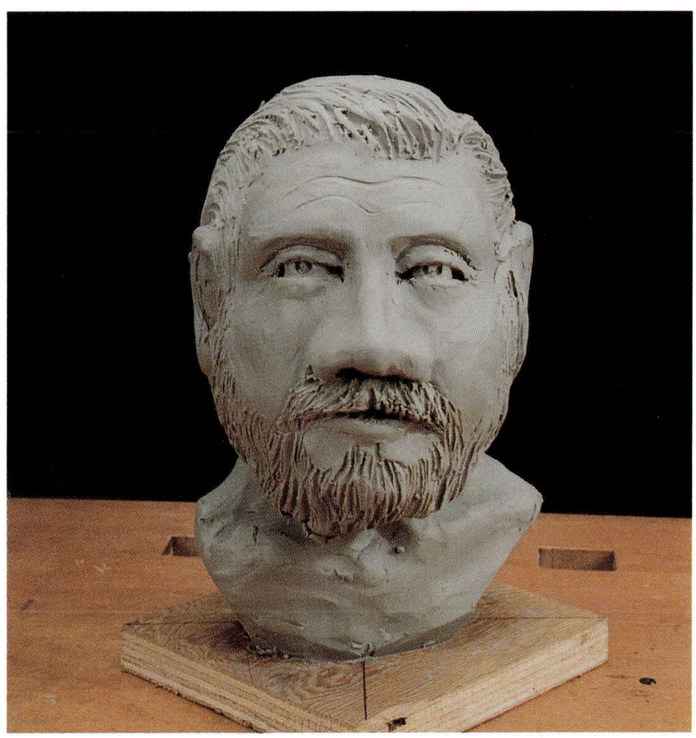

As you have noticed, there are no eyebrows indicated. It is perfectly all right to leave this face that way or you can add them to change the appearance of the person.

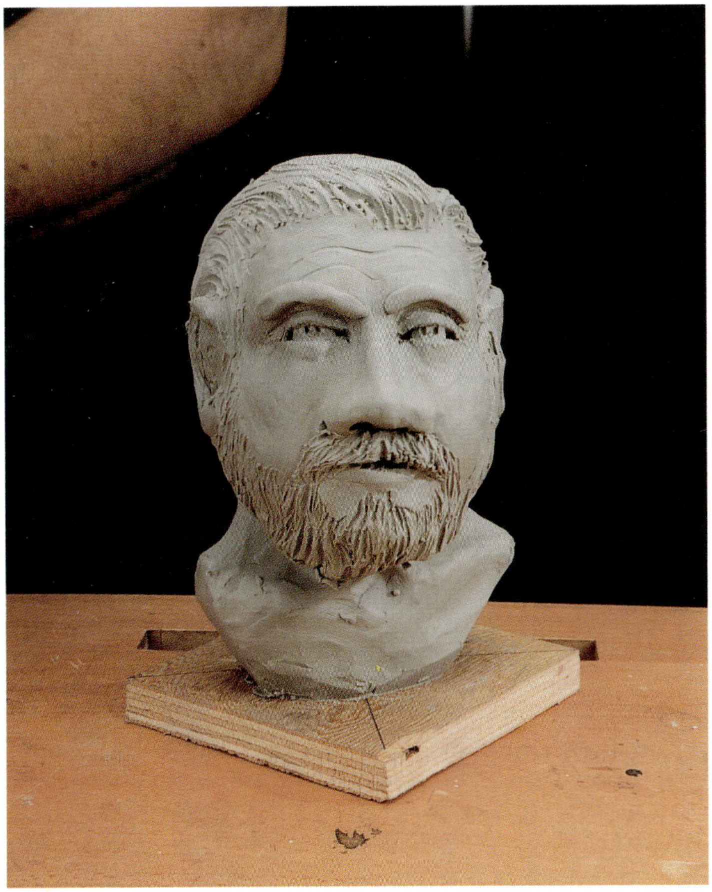

To add eyebrows, make two coils and flatten them in place.

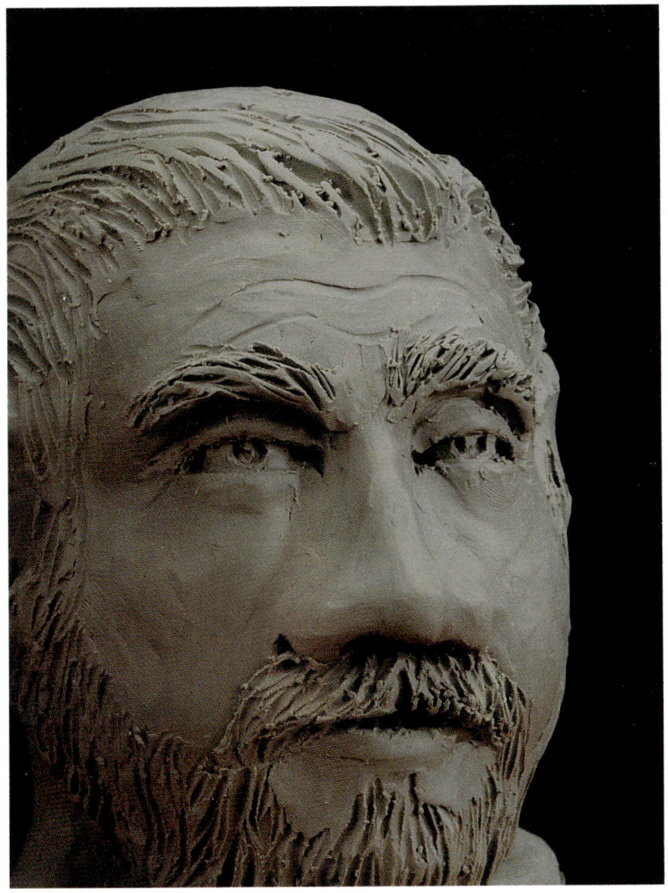

The eyebrows are in place.

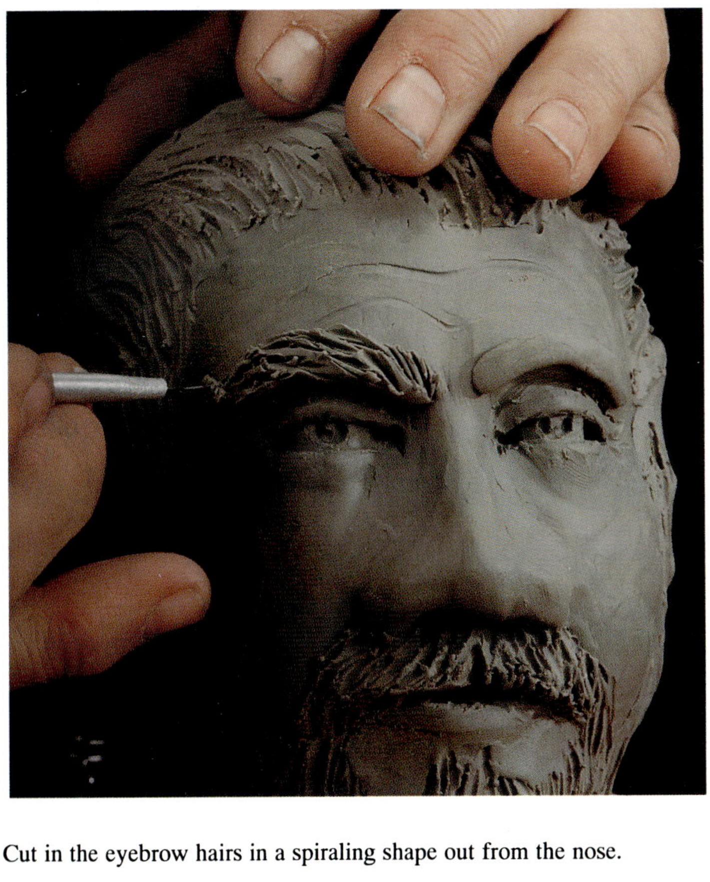

Cut in the eyebrow hairs in a spiraling shape out from the nose.

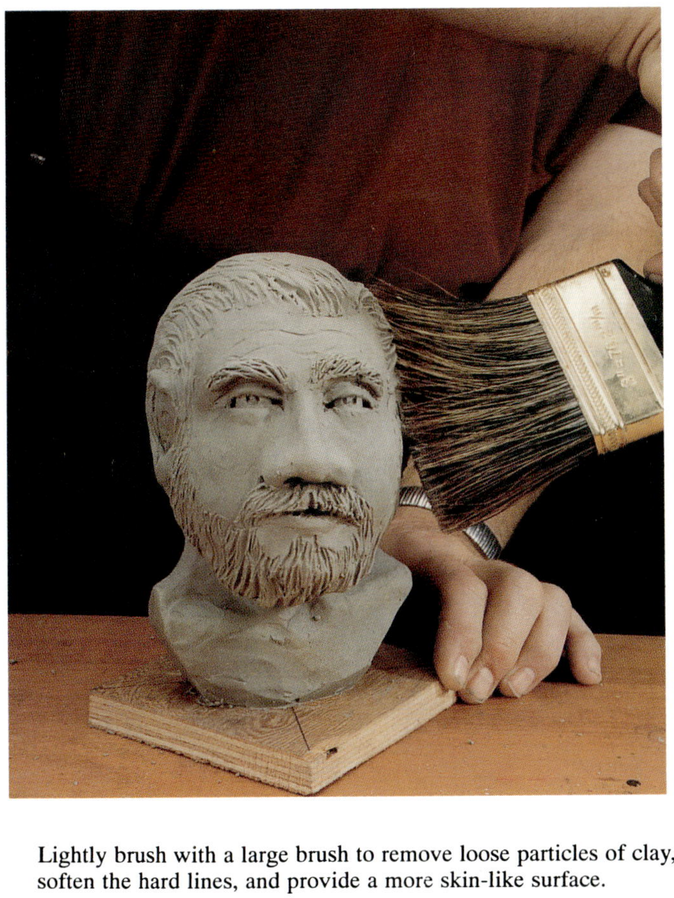

Lightly brush with a large brush to remove loose particles of clay, soften the hard lines, and provide a more skin-like surface.

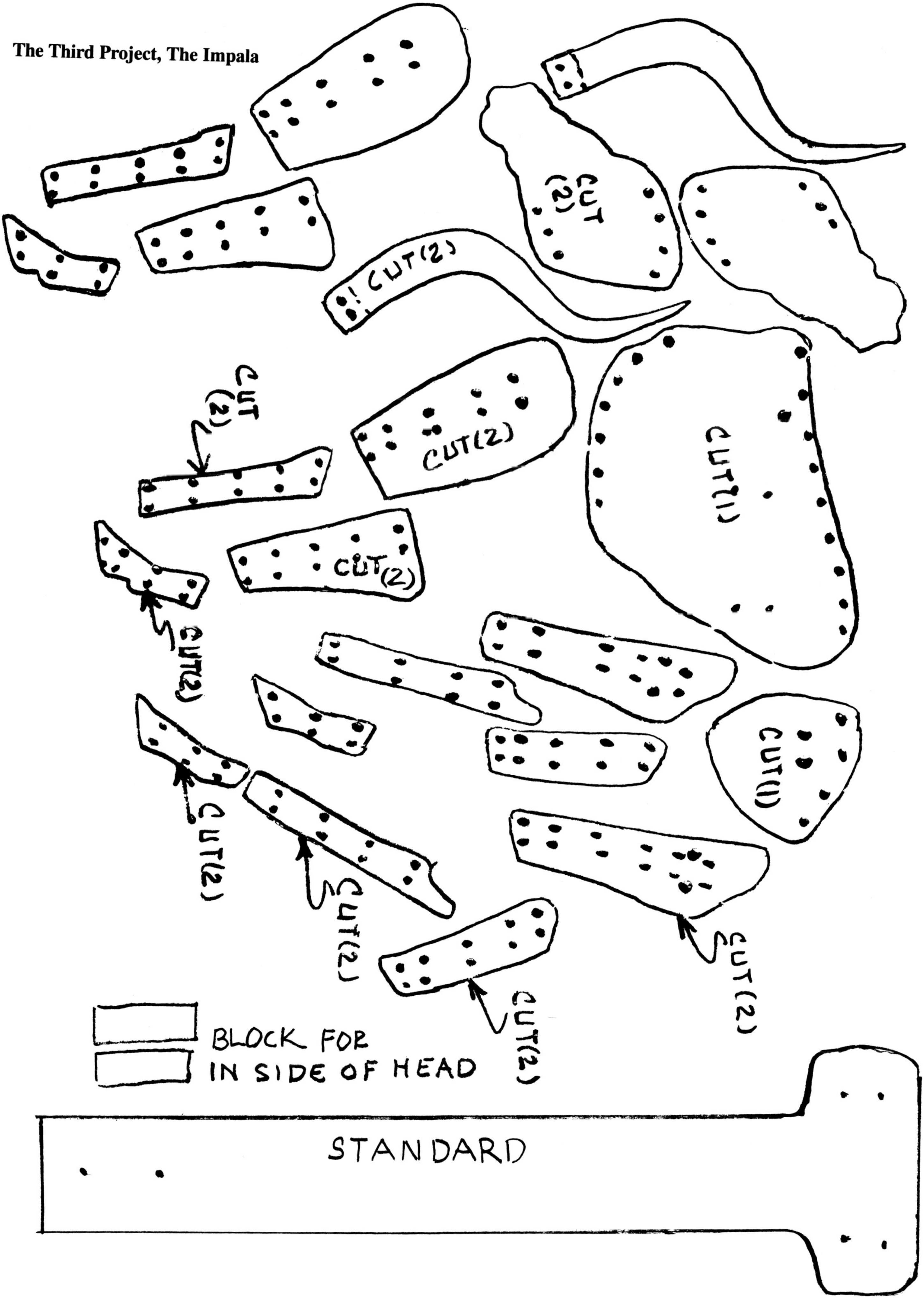
CUT (2)
CUT(2)
CUT(2)
CUT (2)
CUT(1)
CUT(2)
CUT(2)
CUT(2)
CUT(1)
CUT(2)
CUT(2)
CUT(2)
CUT(2)
BLOCK FOR
IN SIDE OF HEAD
STANDARD

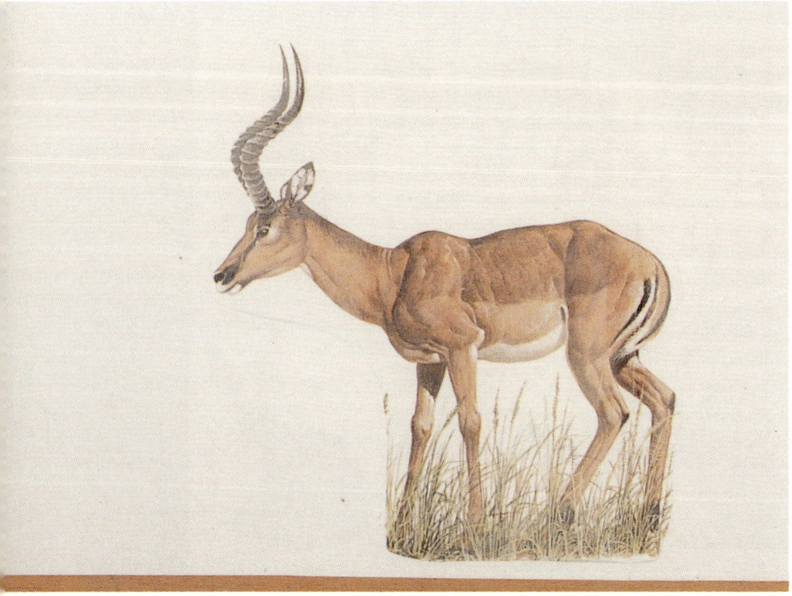

This is the reference image we will use to create our impala.

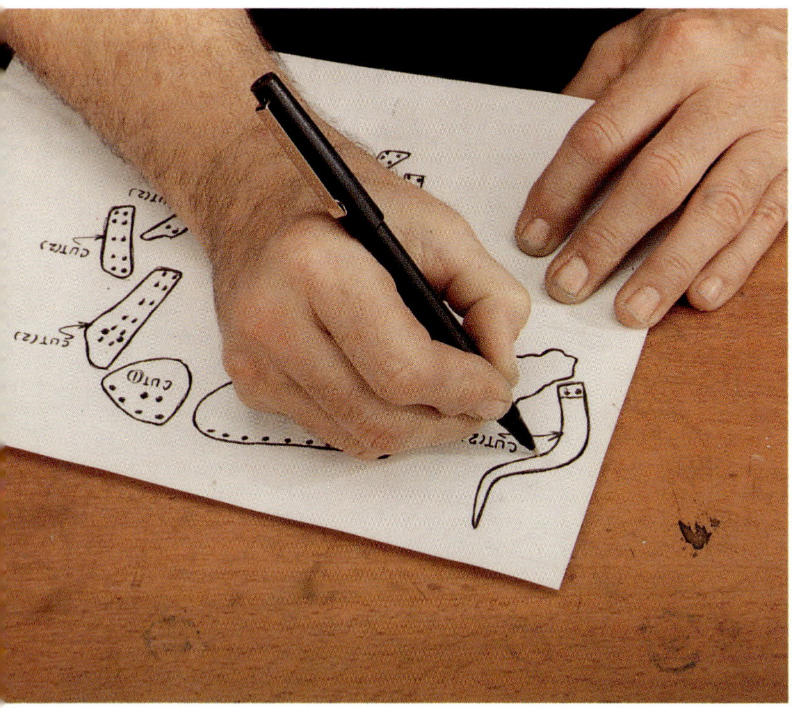

Transfer the impala pattern to the 1/8" thick plywood. We are now making a mannequin of four footed animals — in this case, the mannequin for an impala.

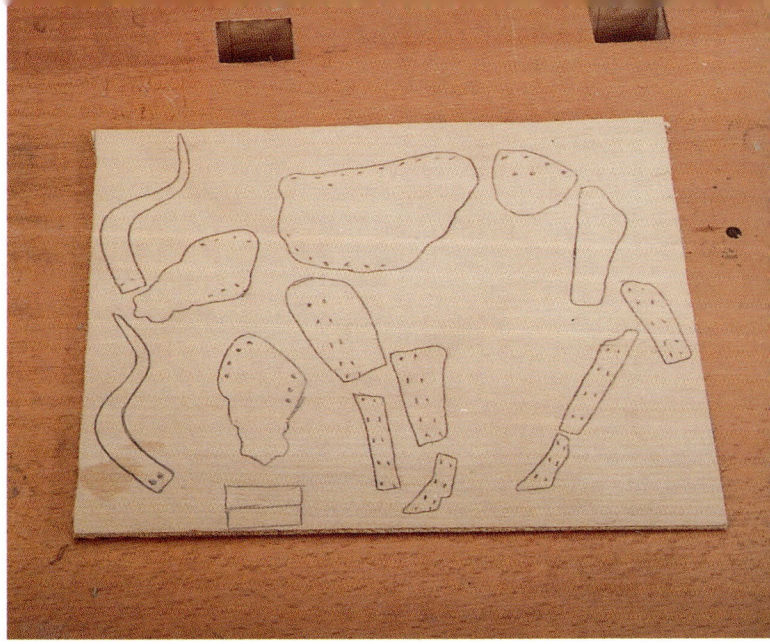

The patterns are transferred.

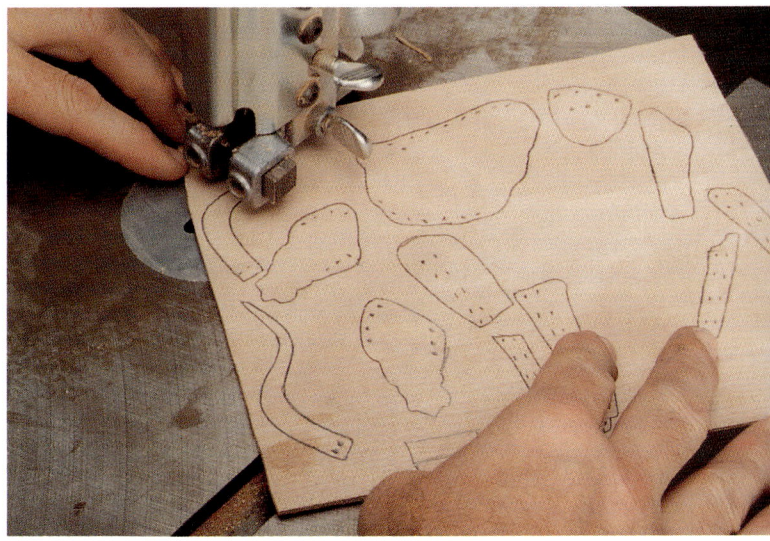

Cut out the patterns with the band saw.

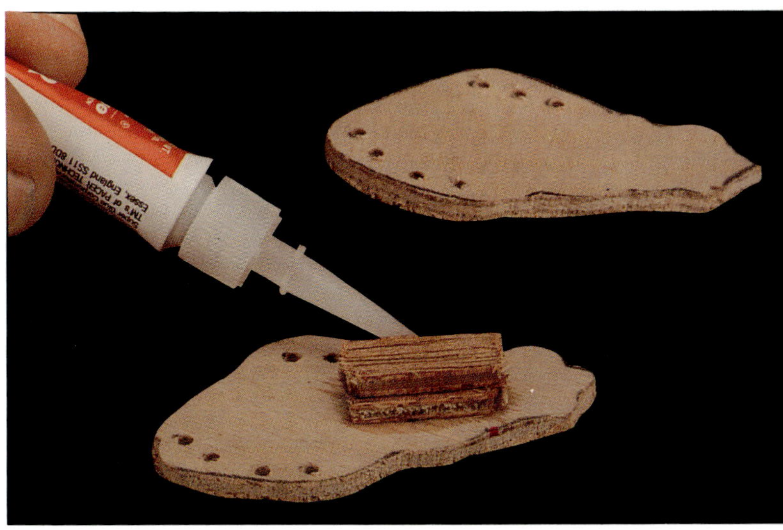

After cutting out the patterns and drilling all of the holes indicated in the pattern, you are going to assemble the head by gluing two small blocks inside first.

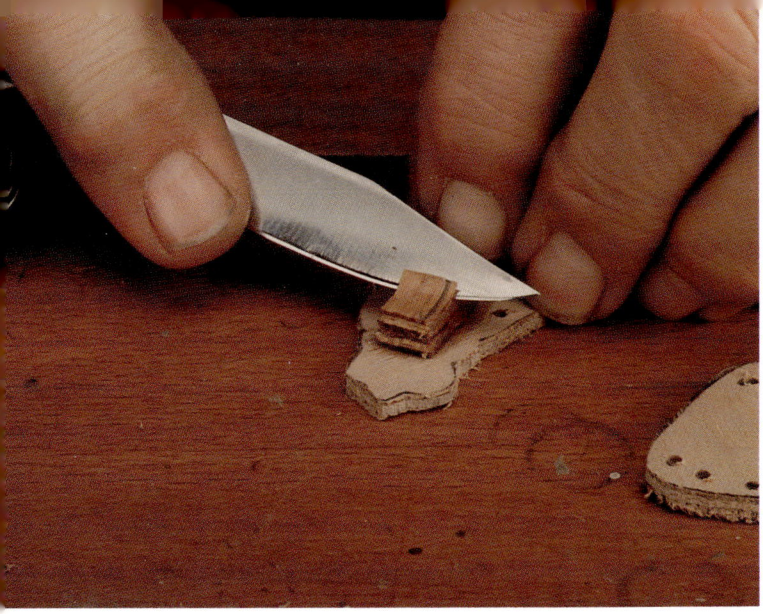

Starting about half way back, shape down the block where the nose will come to a point.

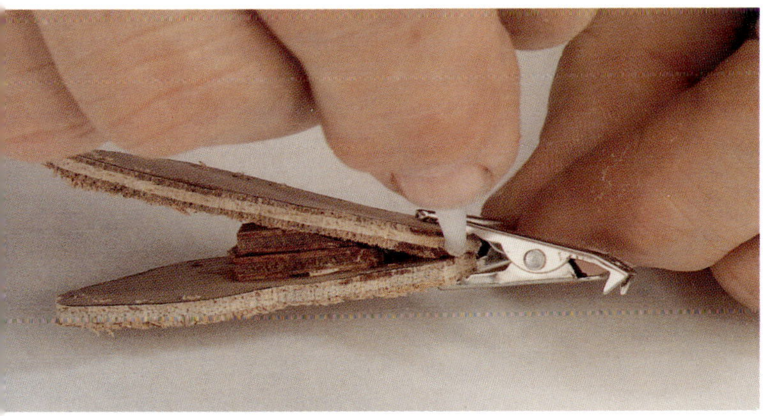

Hold the two nose pieces together with small clamps. Glue the head together with Super Glue.

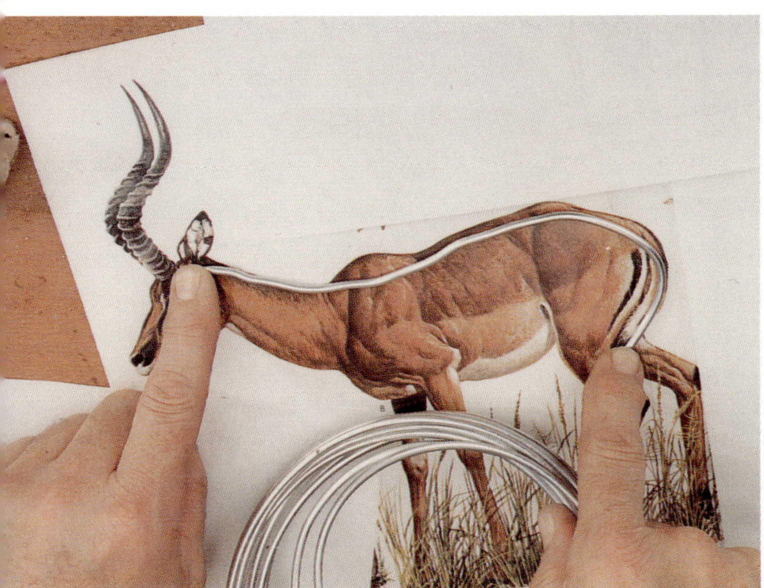

Set the head aside to dry. Shape the wire for the spinal column. Run it right on around and down to the tail.

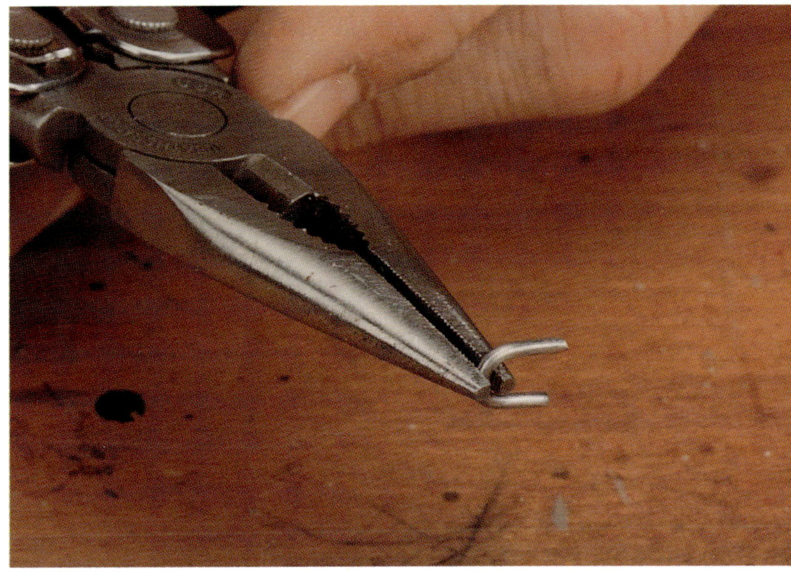

It is time to use 1/16" wire to fasten the horns in place. Shape the wire with needle nose pliers into basically a small U shaped piece.

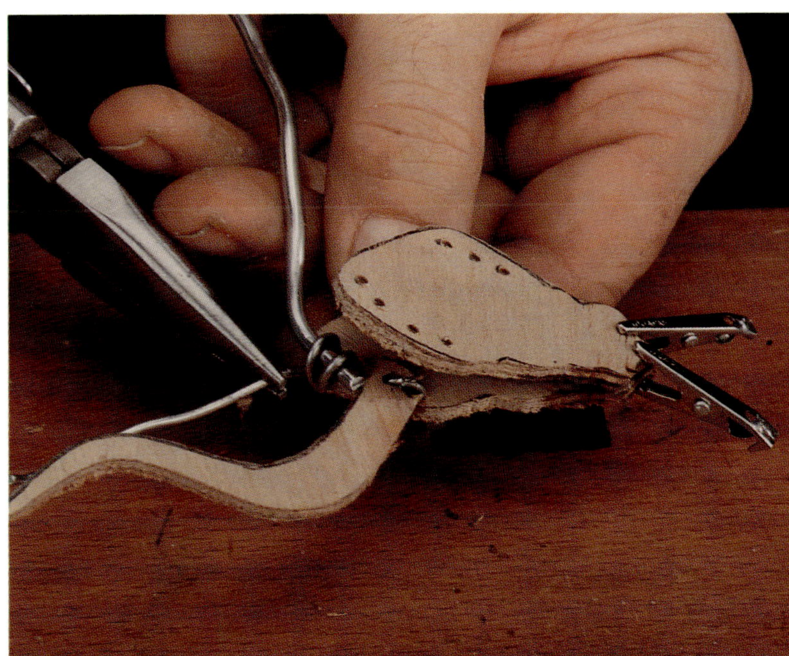

Fasten the horns and the spine in place with the 1/16" wire. Continue to attach the rest of the body to the spine.

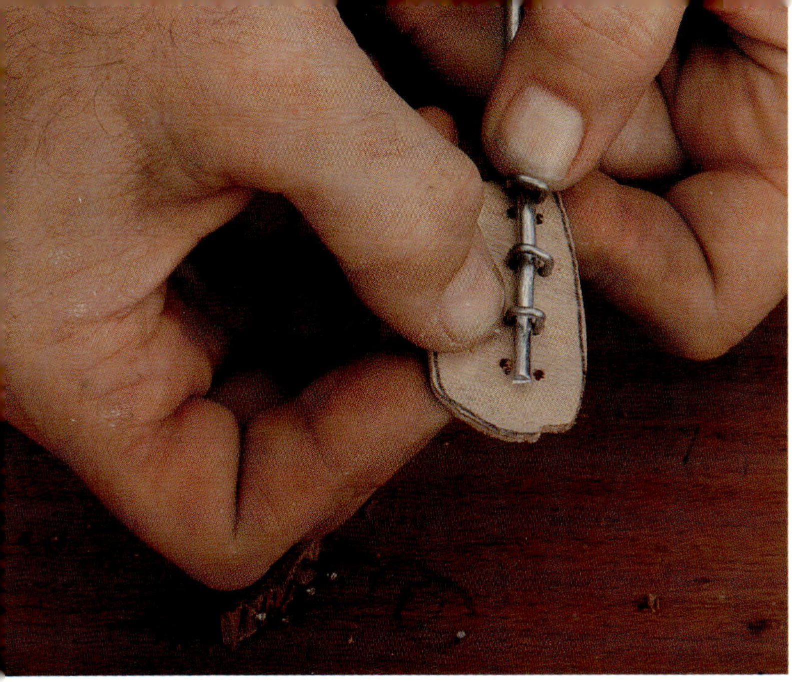

For the legs, starting in the second set of holes, insert at least three 1/16" wire fasteners through the plywood in order to attach the 1/8" wire in place and crimp them over on the back side. The upper portion of the leg is held in place.

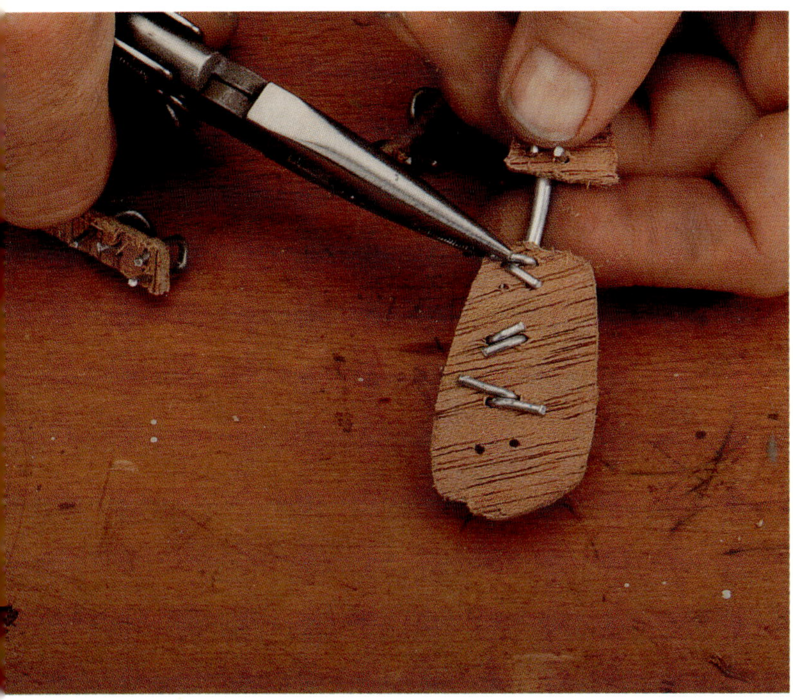

Crimp the 1/16" wires in place in back.

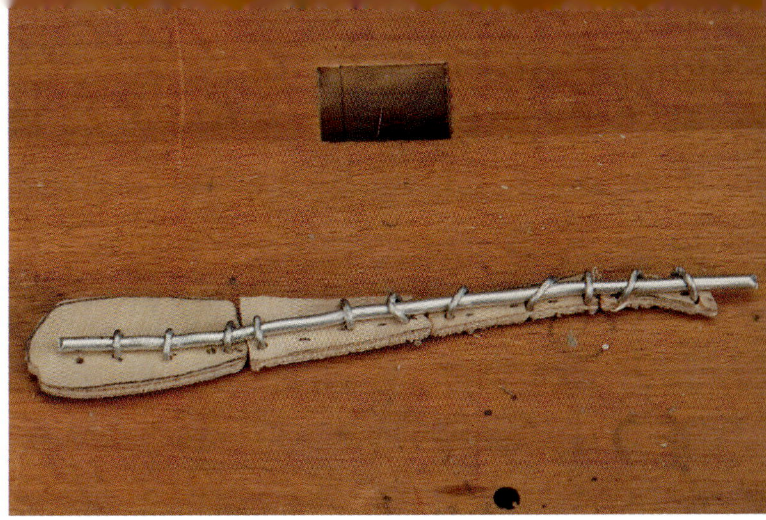

The front leg is fully assembled. Assemble the rest of the legs in the same fashion.

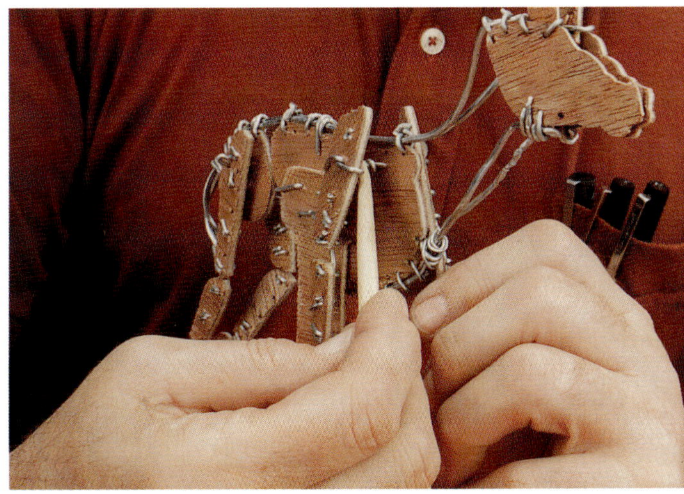

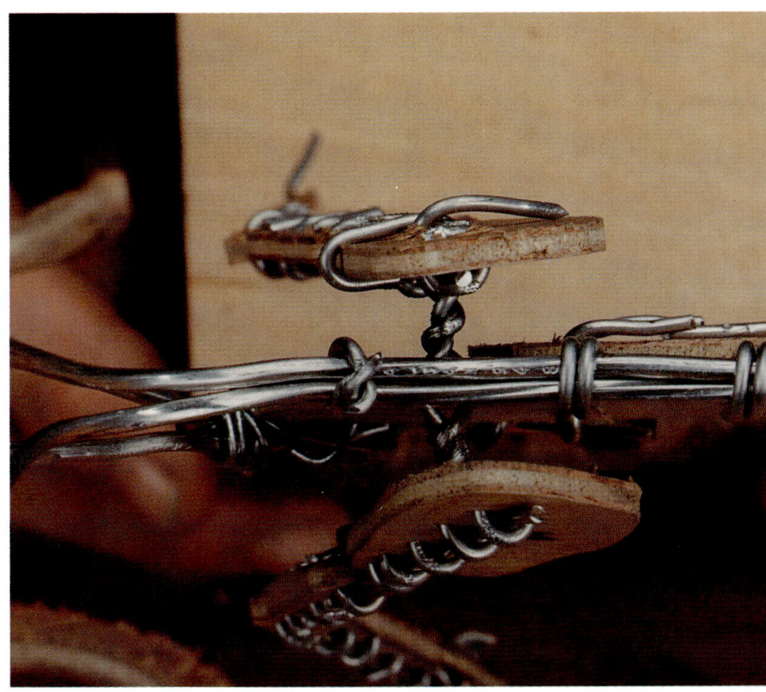

Run a 1/16" wire through the first set of holes that were left open on the legs. Twist the wire three times, then run it through the corresponding set of holes on the central armature. Twist the wire three times, then it through the leg on the opposite side and clench it over.

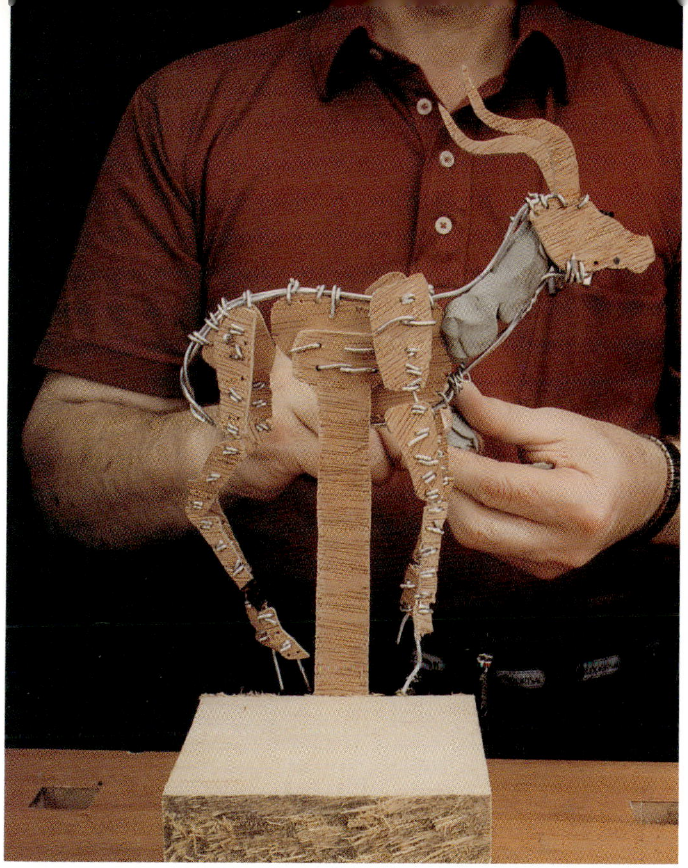

Attach the standard to the armature to a block of wood. Using #2 medium Plastilina, begin to create the sculpture. Start by filling in the voids in the armature with clay.

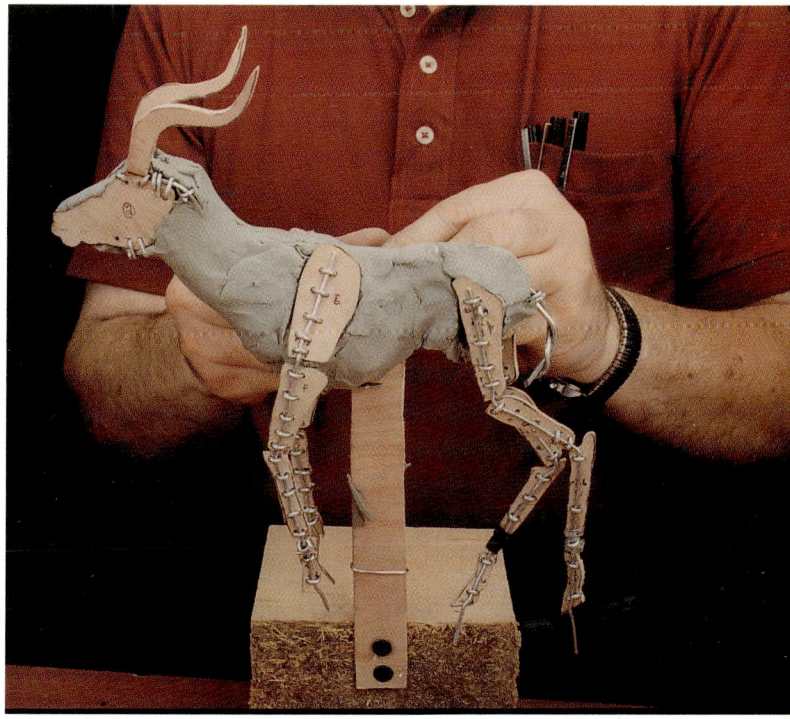

Start filling the void underneath the legs so that the legs can be positioned later on.

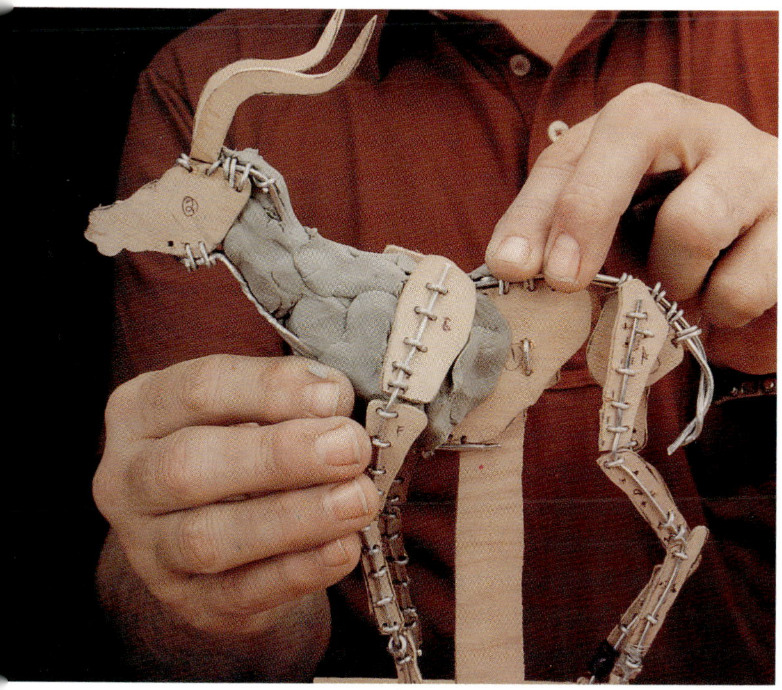

Between the shoulders, the thickness of the body with the clay in place one head length long from the base of the horns to the tip of the nose.

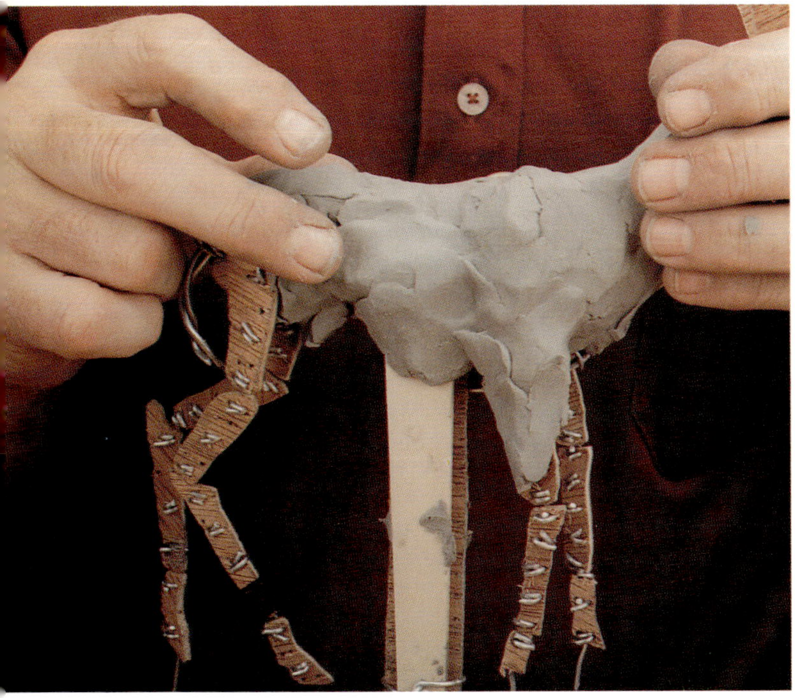

Continue filling the body with clay. Lay the clay in as if it were muscle.

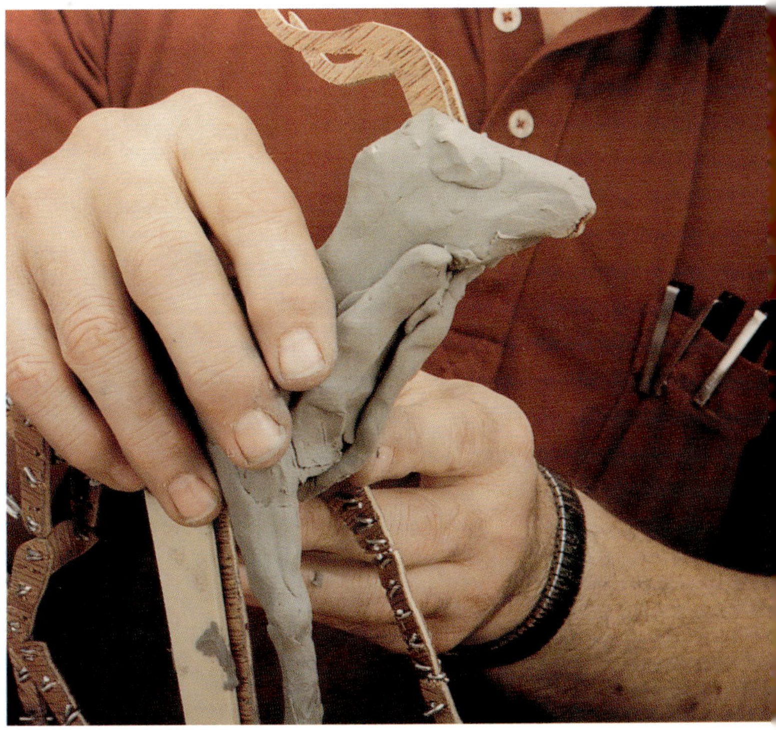

Start filling in the neck with a long roll of clay.

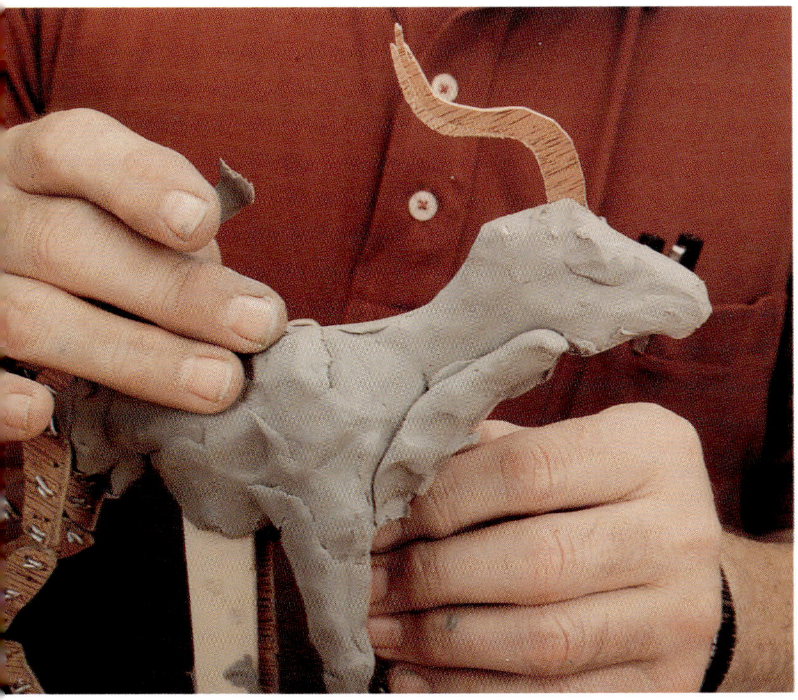

Begin laying in the clay down the legs.

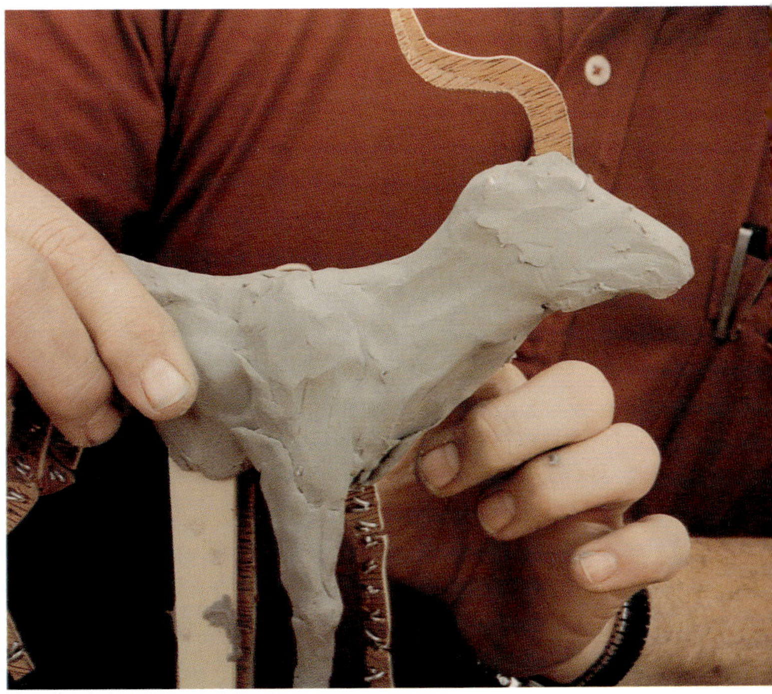

Put another roll right down the front edge of the throat and start blending those rolls together.

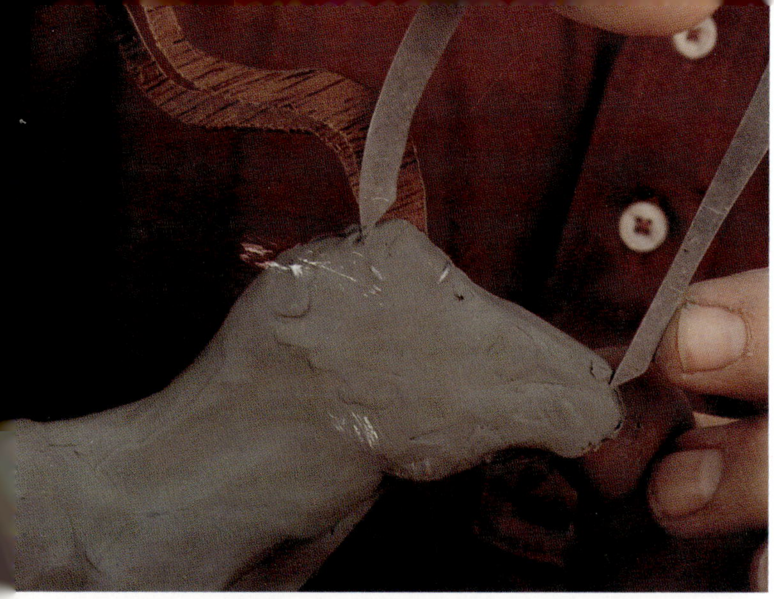

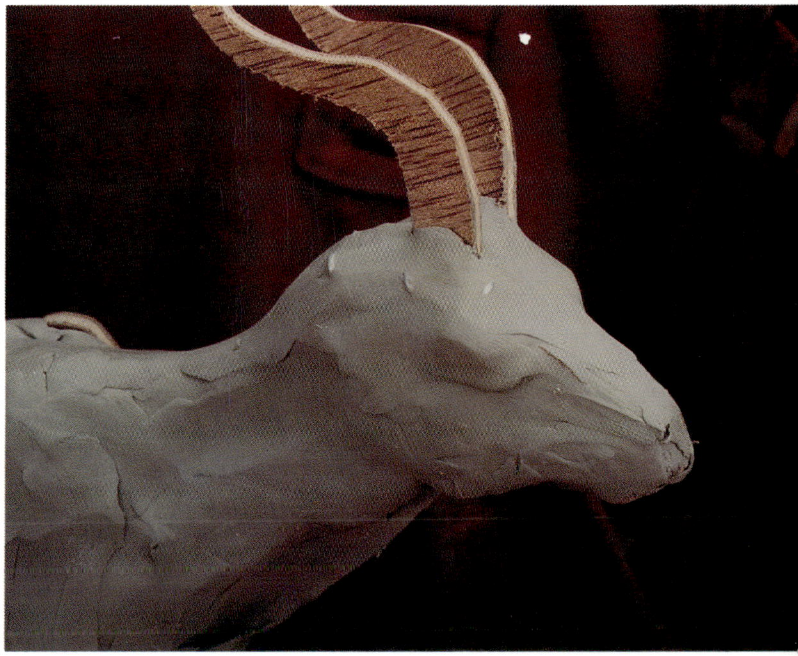

Smooth them down and blend them into the head.

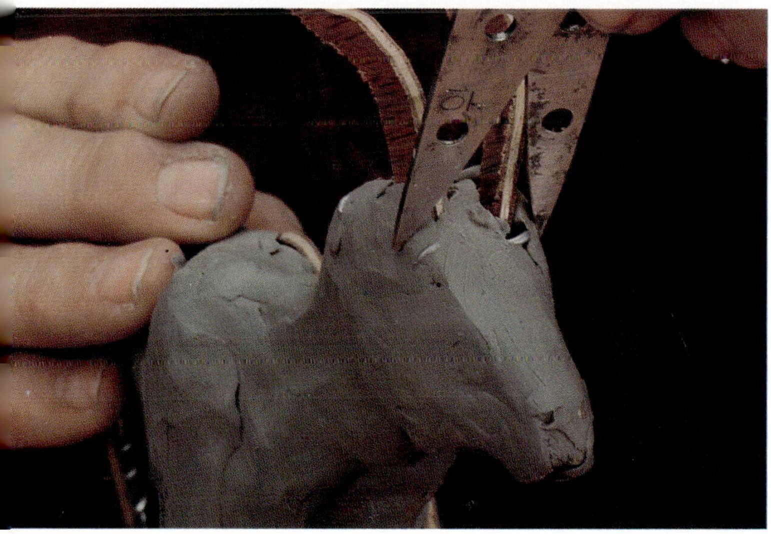

Half of the full length of the head will give you the width of the head at the base of the horns.

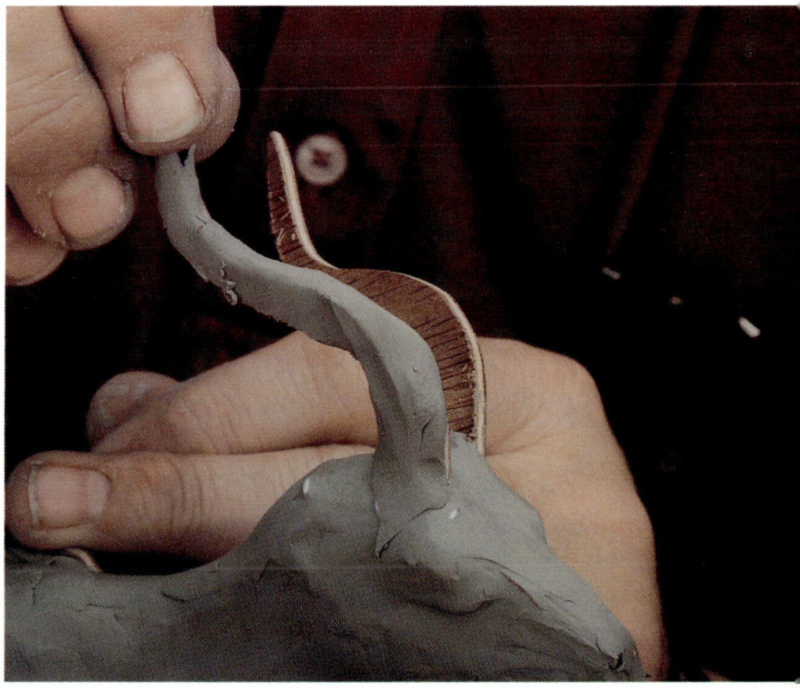

Make little ropes of clay to cover the horns. Cover both sides of each horn.

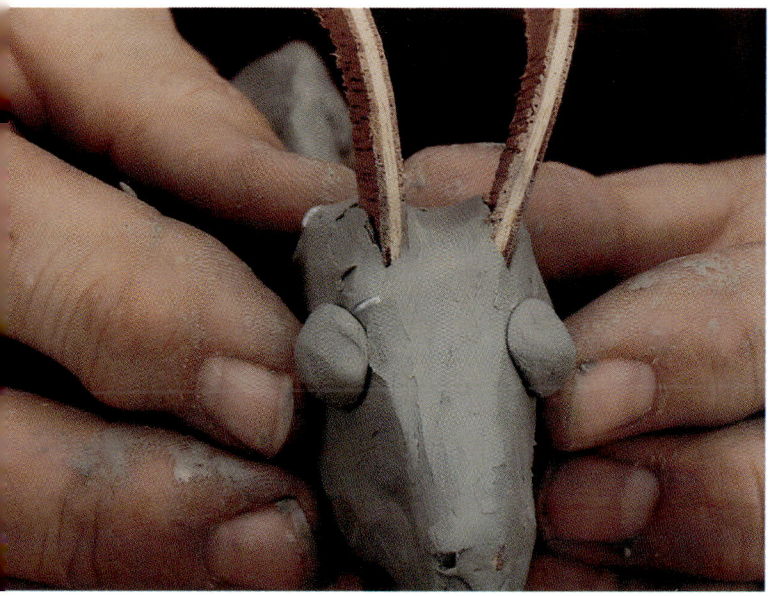

Put in two round pieces of clay below the horns for eyes.

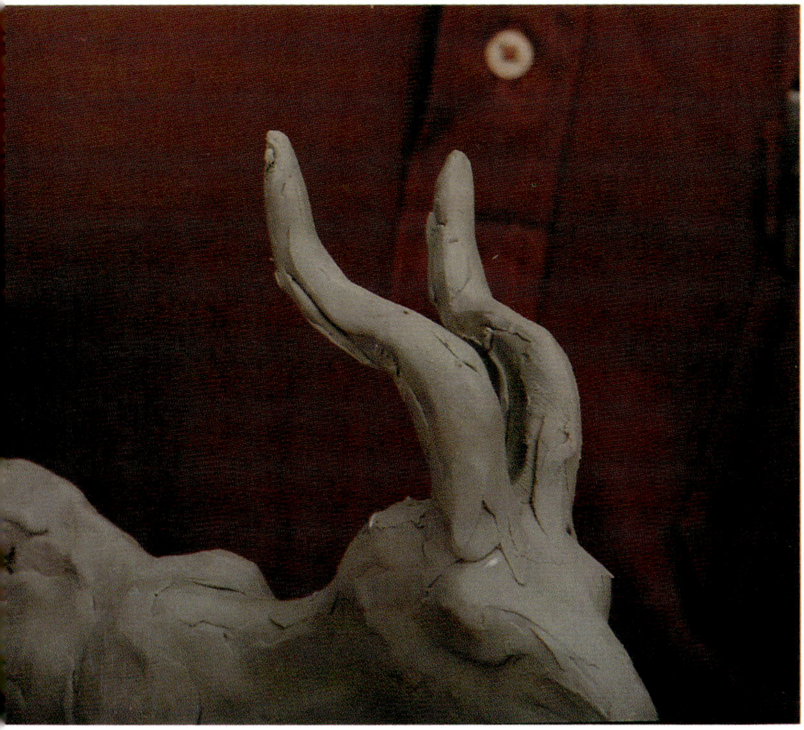

The horns are covered.

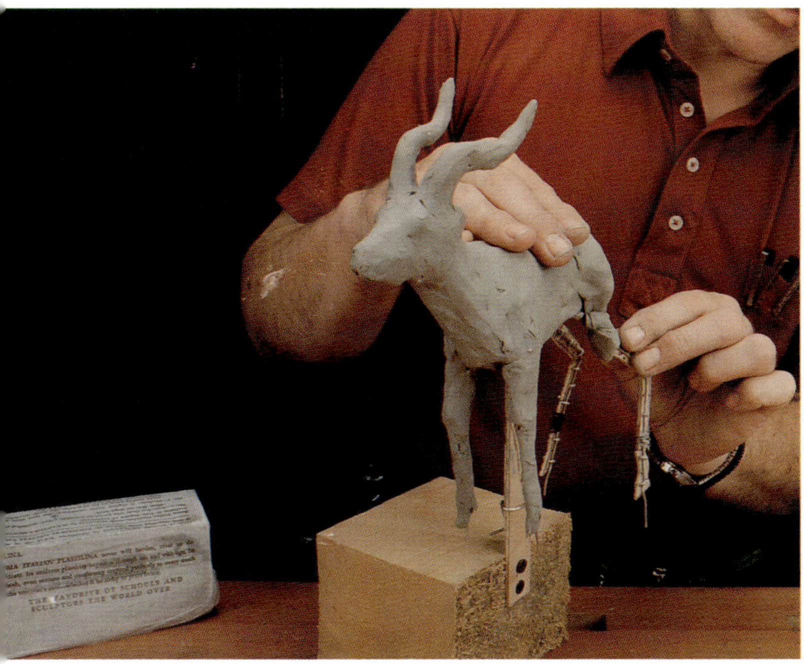

Continuing to build the clay up on the armature.

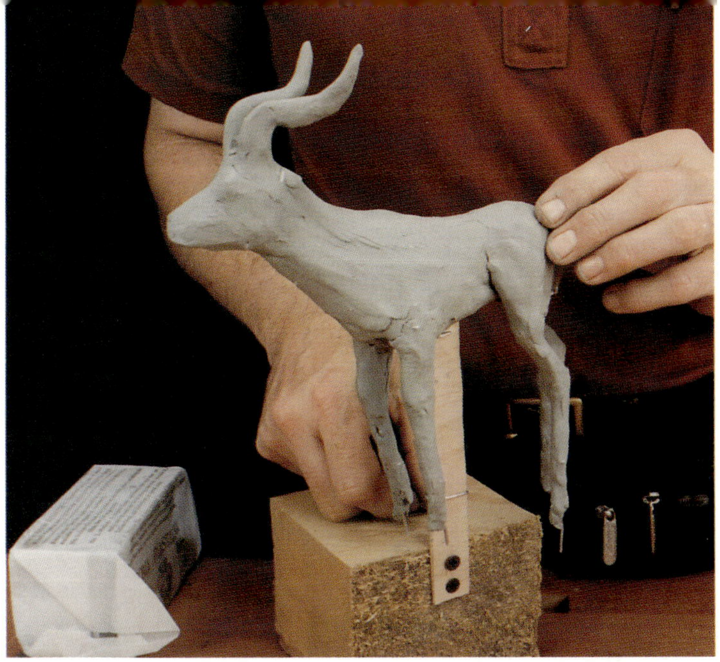

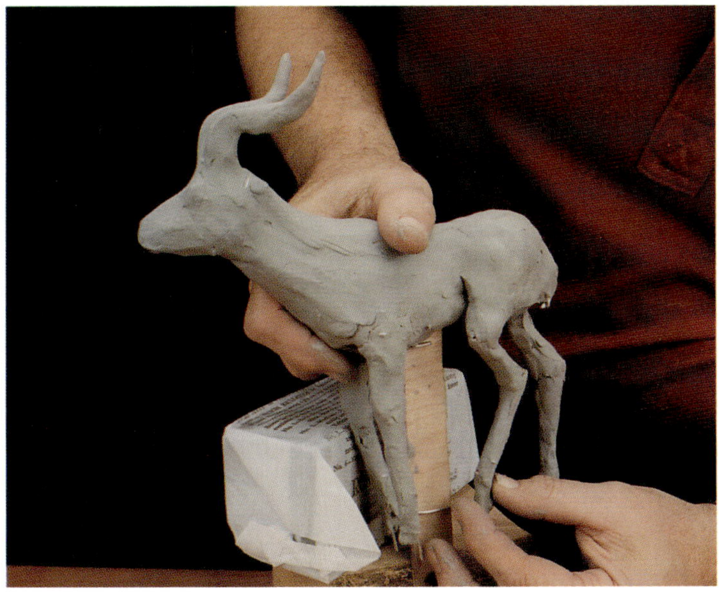

Now is the time to decide how the legs are to be positioned. Gently move the back leg slightly forward and put a bend in it.

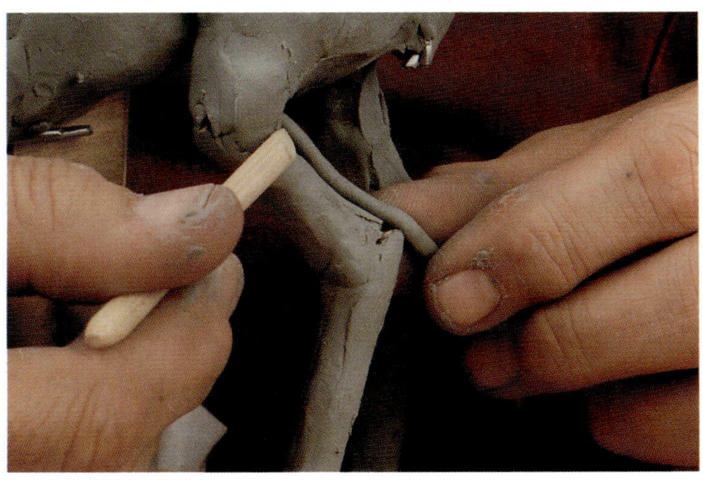

Start adding detail to the positioned back leg. Lay a small ribbon of clay along the back of the leg to approximate the tendon.

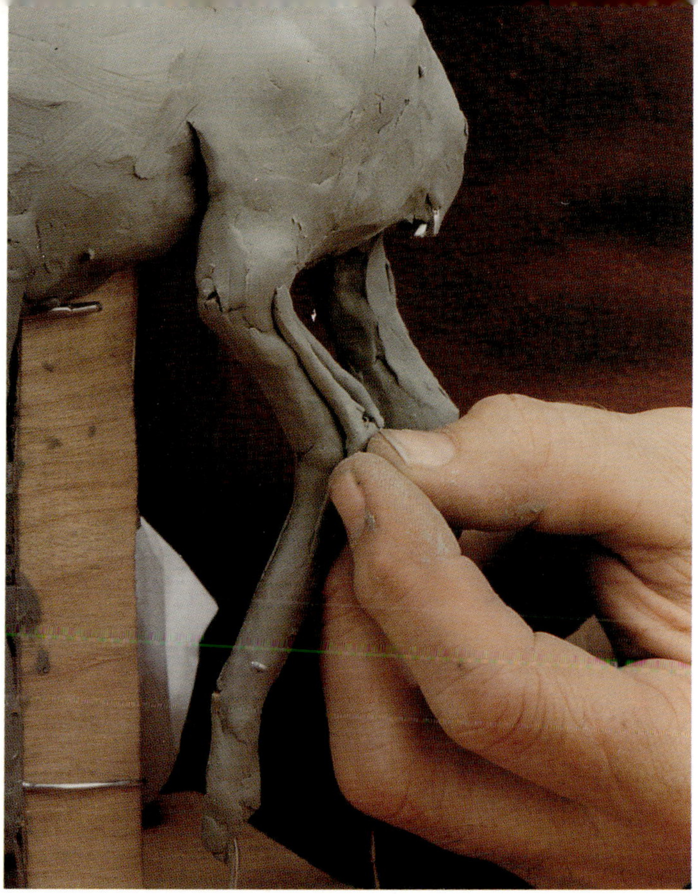

Lay the second muscle in down the leg.

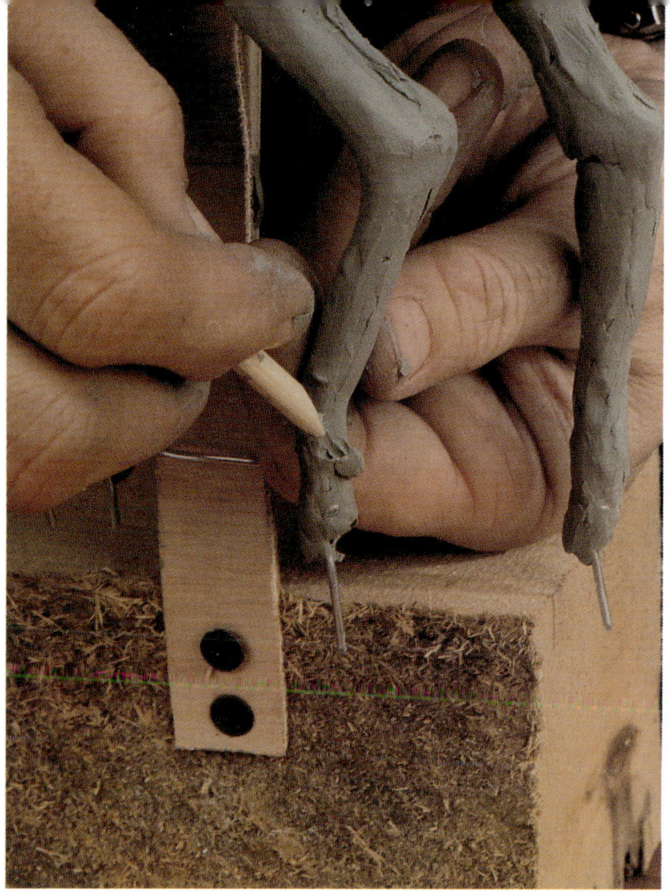

The dew claws are put in with two very small pellets of clay. Blend them into the leg.

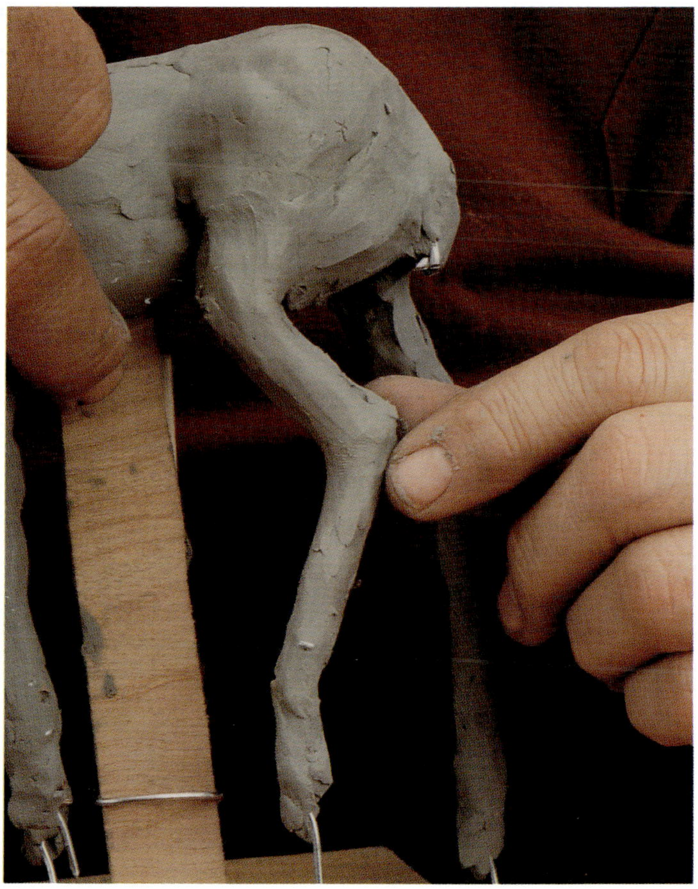

Blend the muscles into the leg and shape the joint. The leg below this joint is very thin and bony. Don't let it get built up too much.

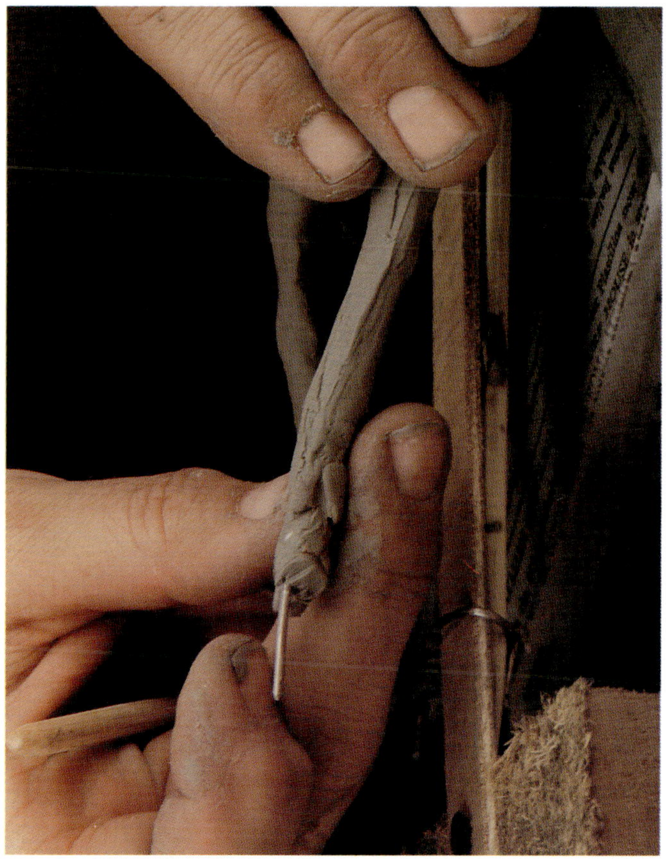

The blended dew claw.

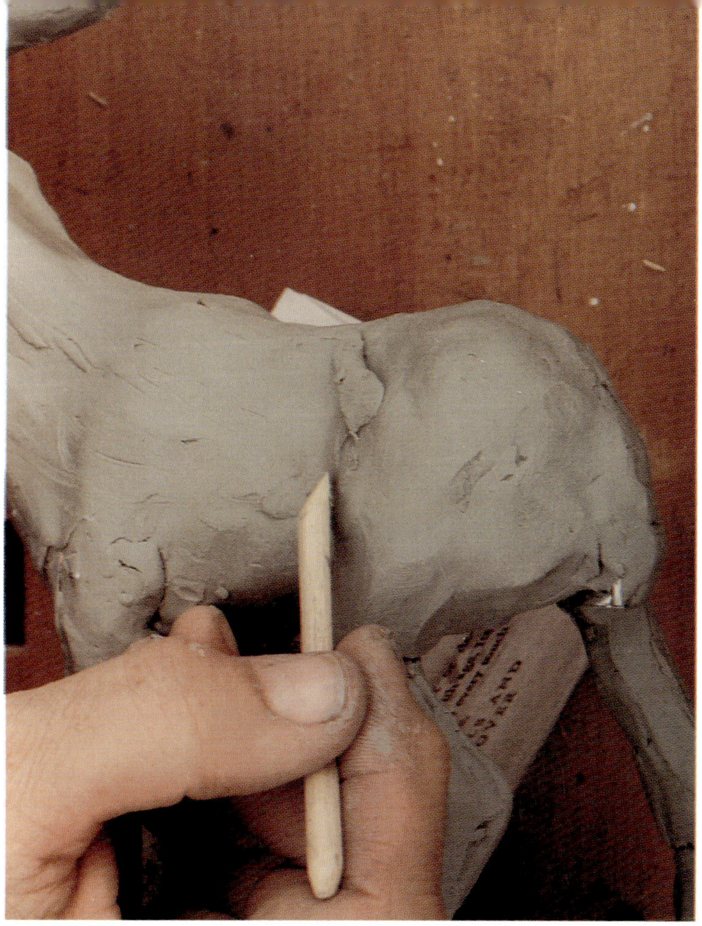

Laying in a muscle mass along the hips with a series of small rolls.
The hips measure 3/4 of the length of the head at the widest point.

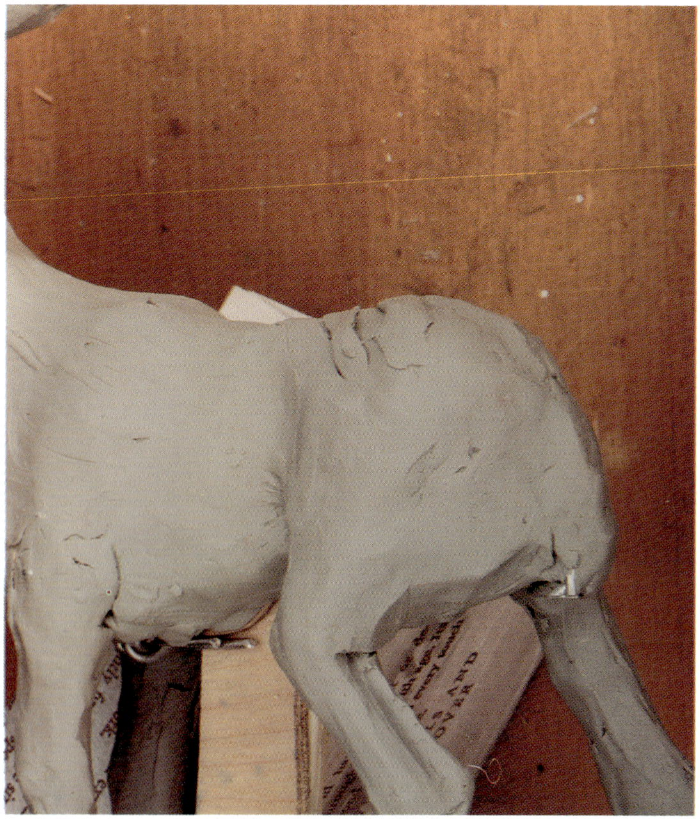

Laying in additional muscles and blending them into place.

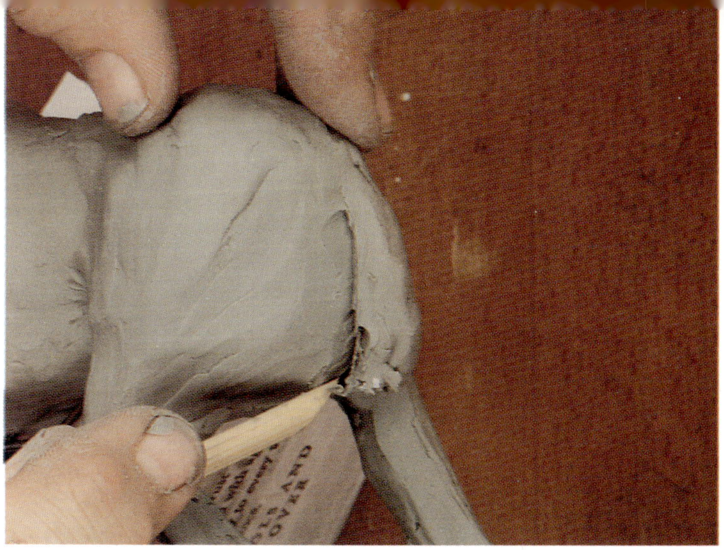

Detail the separation between the tail and the flank.

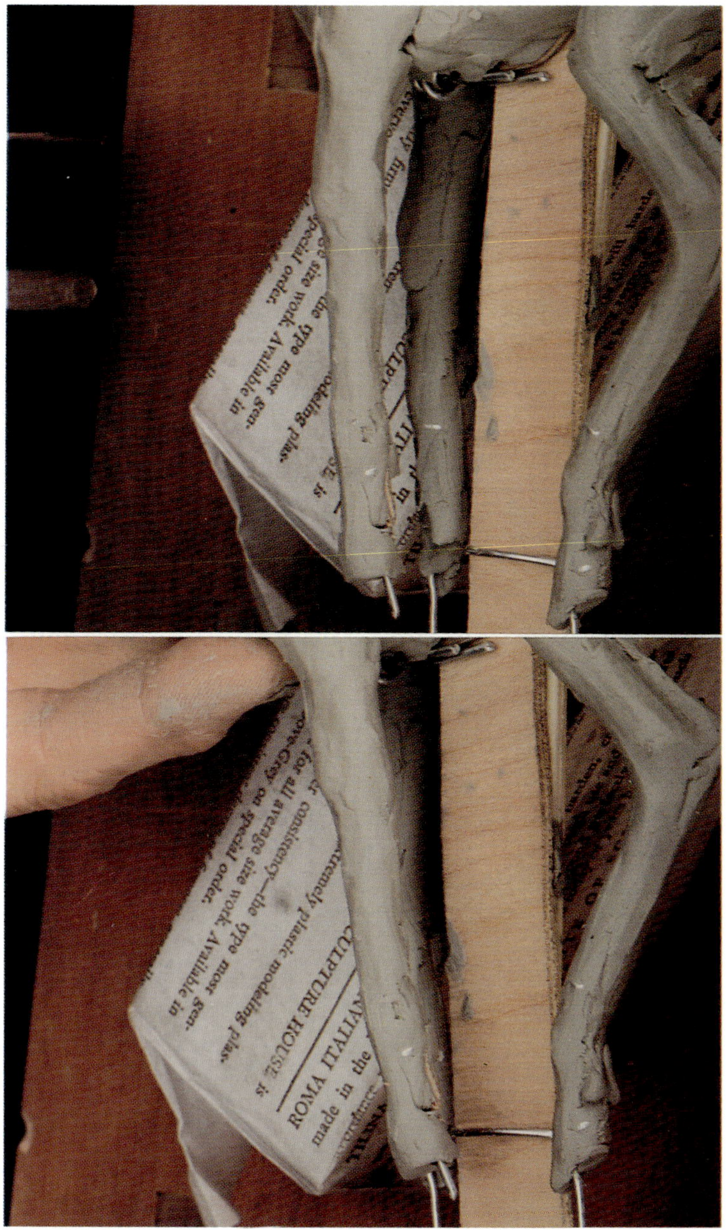

Reposition the front leg and refill any separation that happens in the clay.

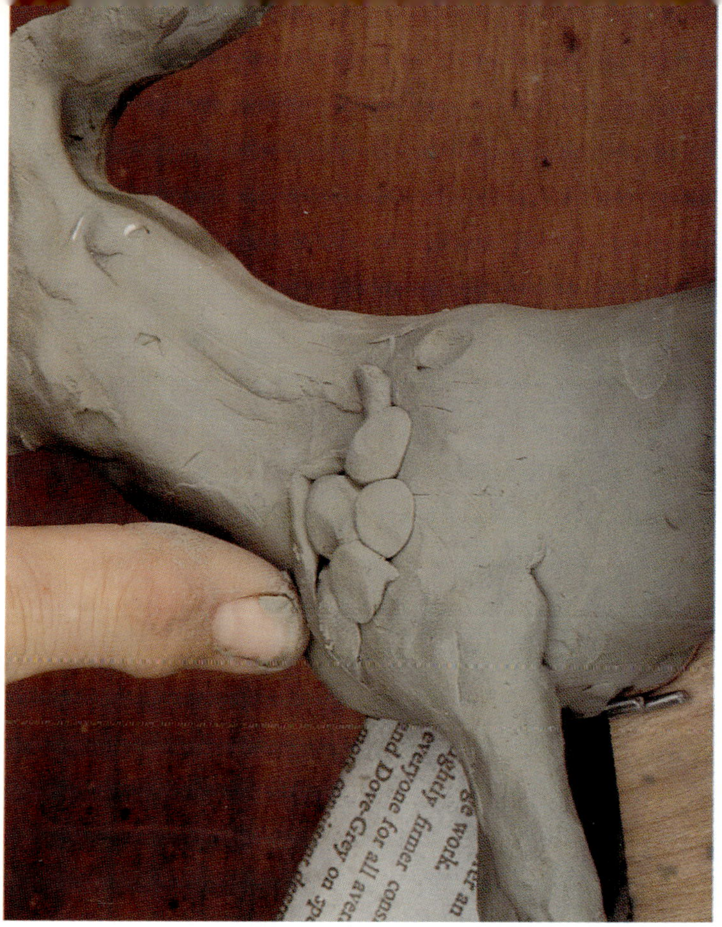

Add muscle mass that forms the front shoulder. Add some small pellets of clay to represent the muscles.

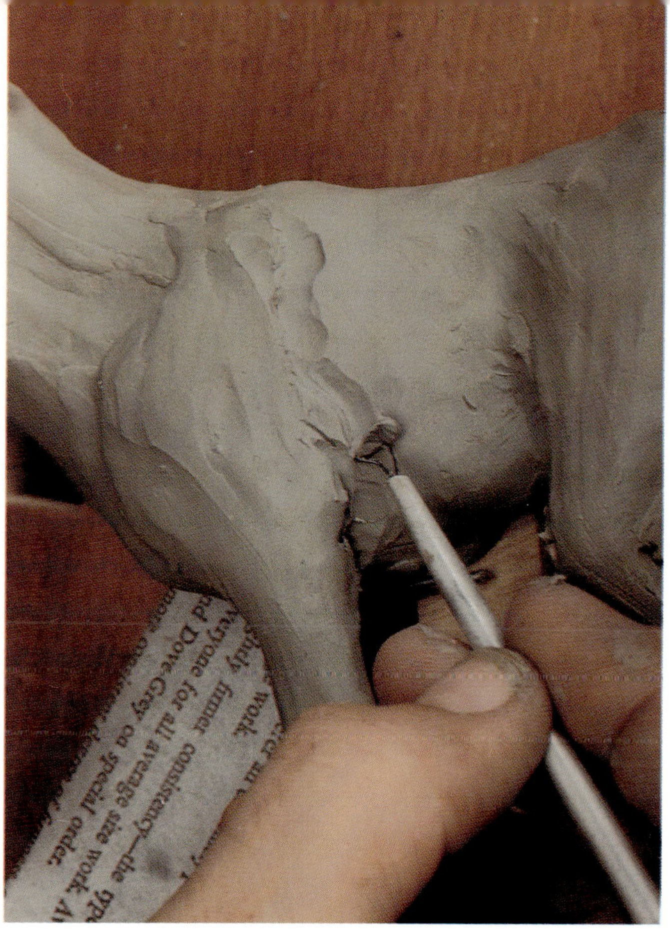

Sculpt in the way the leg lays along the body.

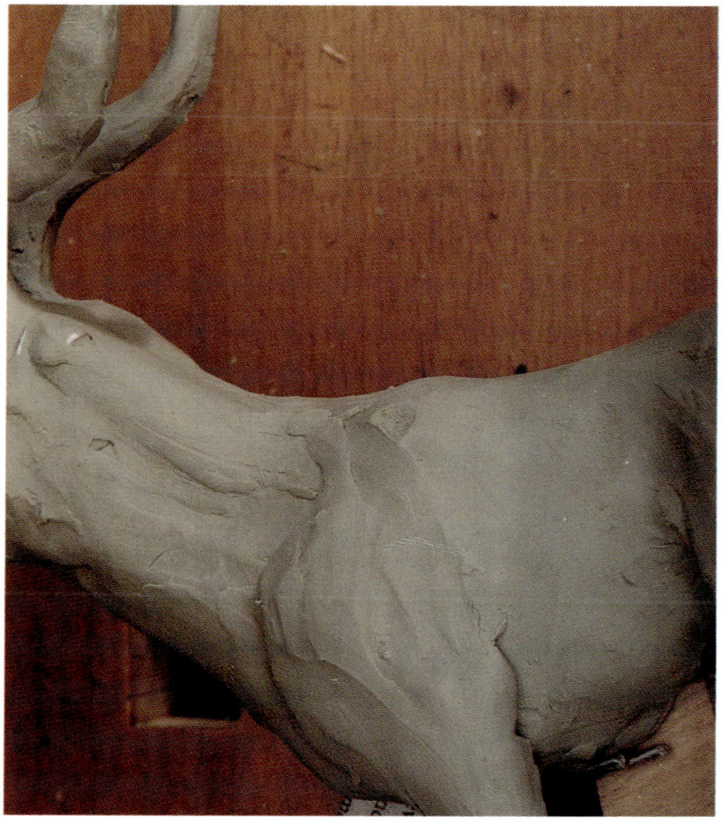

Smooth out the muscles masses.

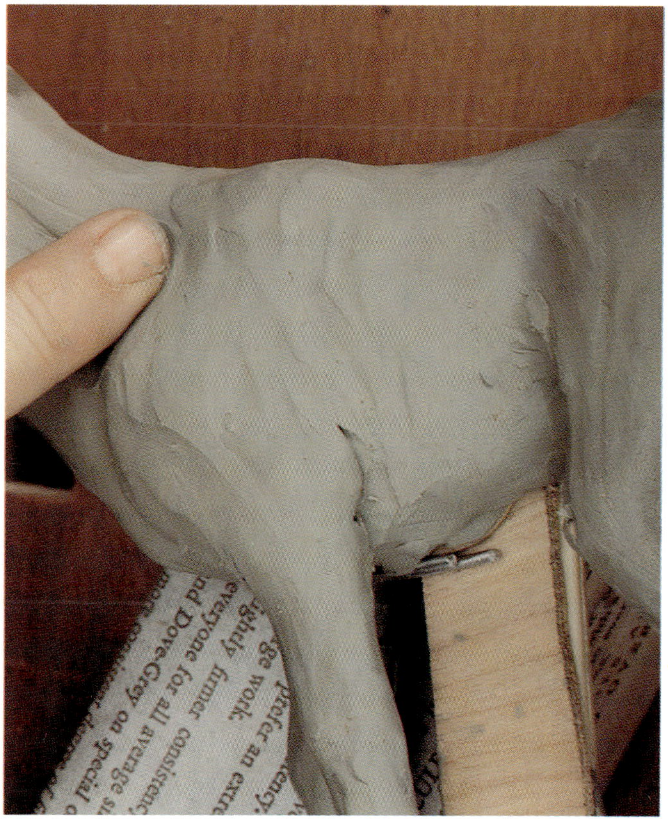

Smooth down these sculpted lines so that the muscles and leg ripple along the body rather than stand out starkly against it.

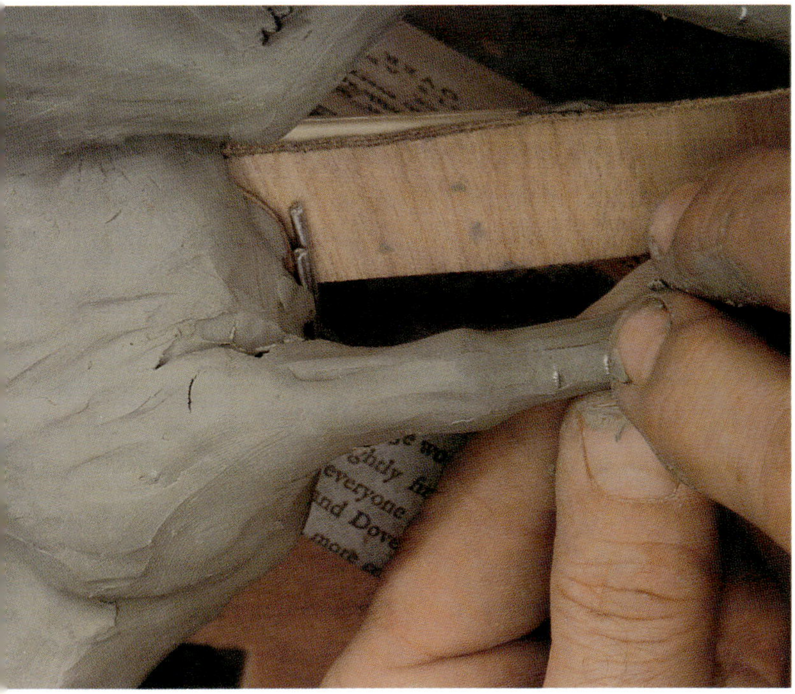

As we work down the leg, make sure that below the joint the leg remains quite bony and thin. The joint itself it prominent.

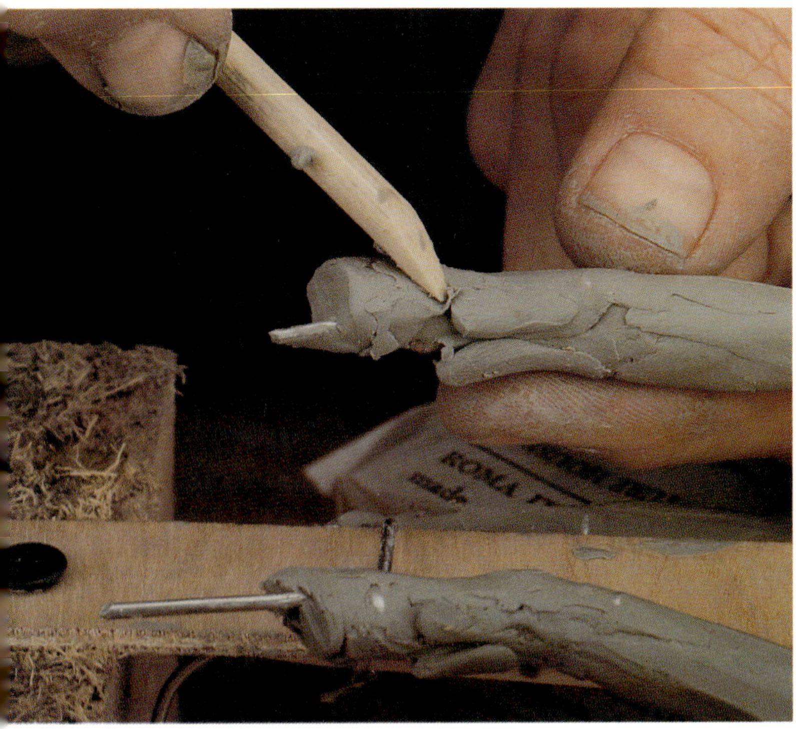

Attach and smooth in the dew claw.

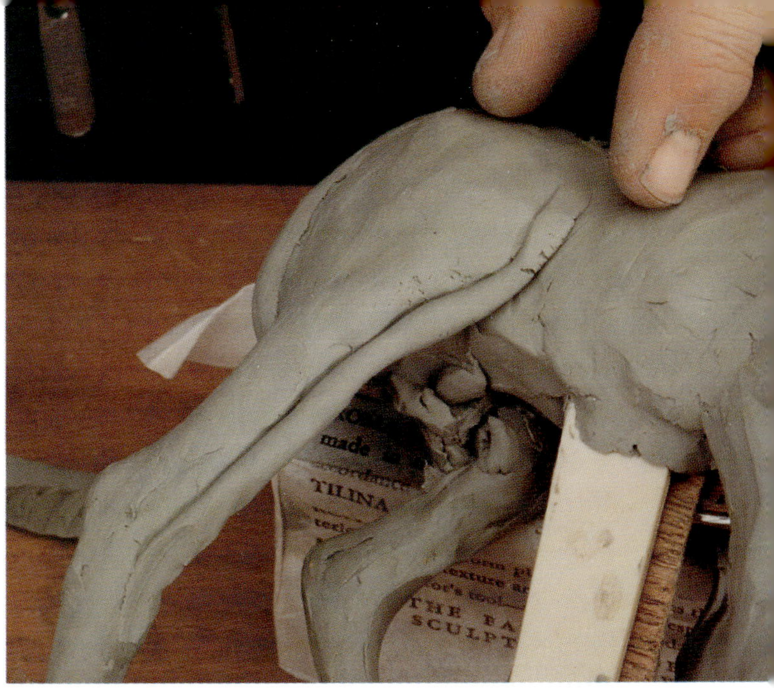

Lay in a long roll of muscle to fill in the front of the extended right rear leg.

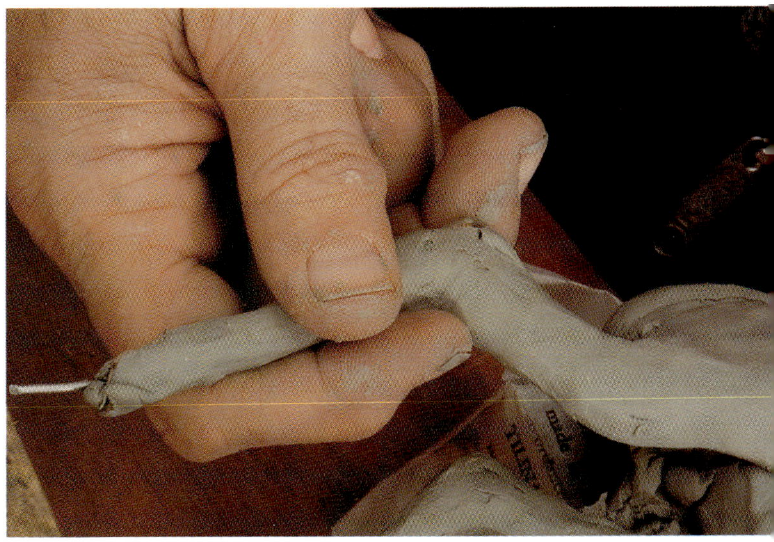

Reposition that leg and smooth in the muscle mass.

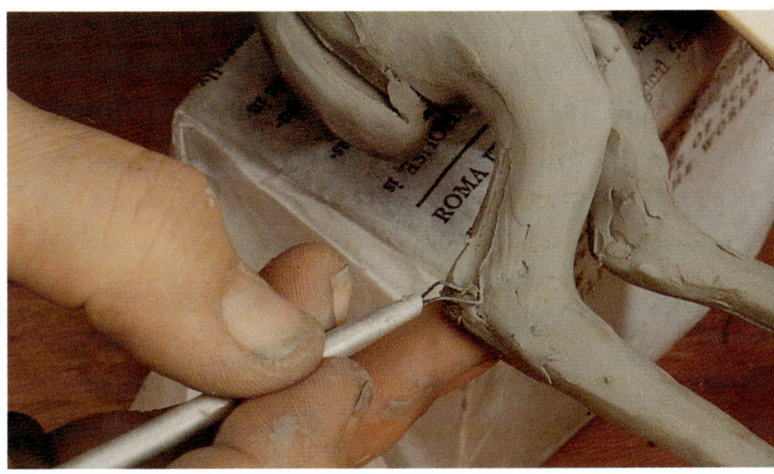

Cut in the tendon.

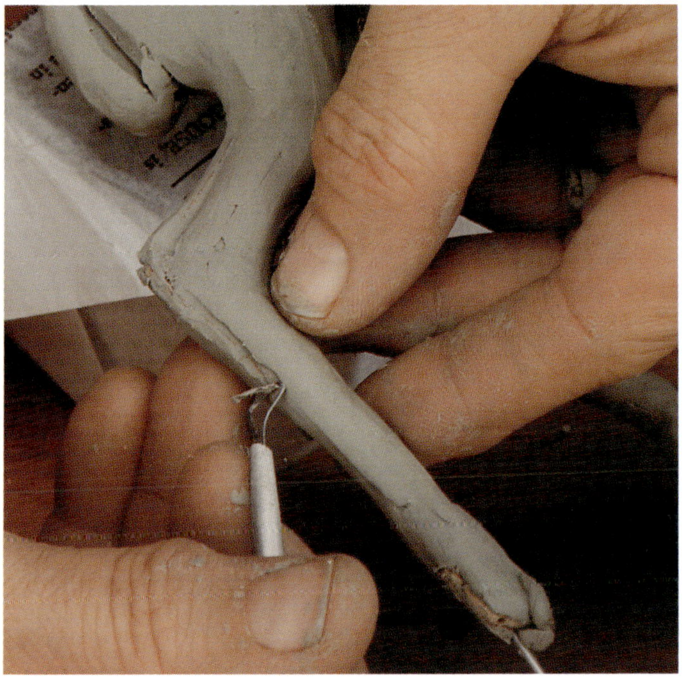

Sculpt in the tendon going on down the leg.

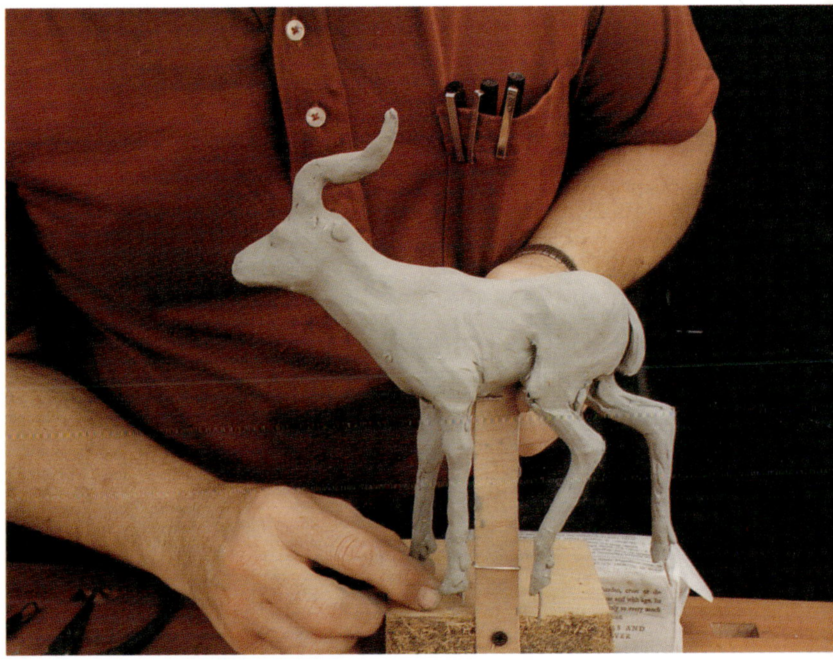

The body is now fairly well finished.

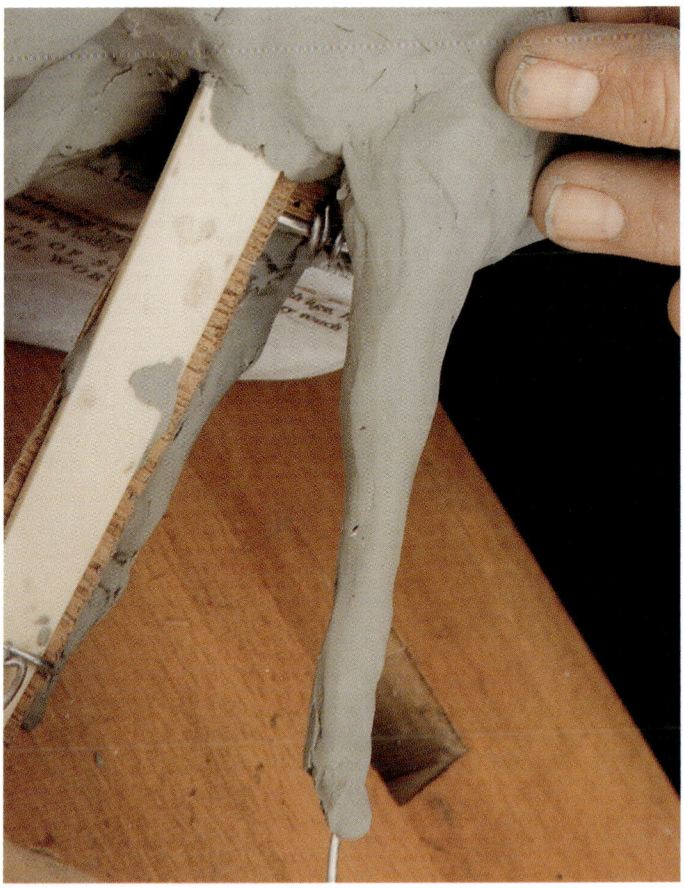

Reposition the right front leg and repeat the procedures to finish it. The hooves will be finished later, after the landscape has been built up beneath the legs.

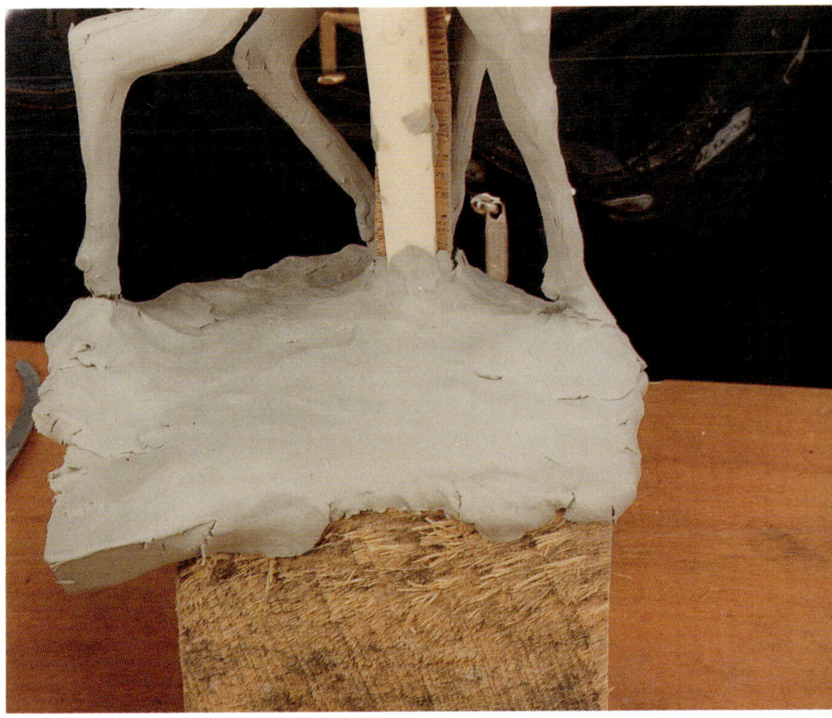

This is a good time to put in a little ground work to help support the sculpture before applying detail to the face.

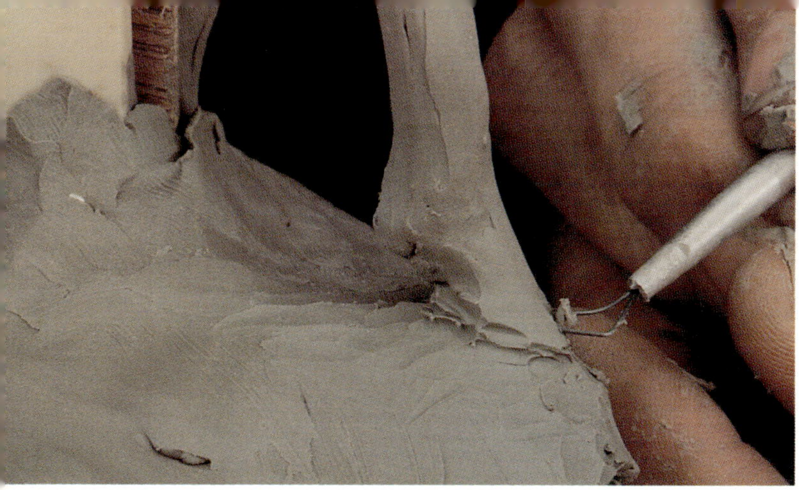

Begin to detail the hoof.

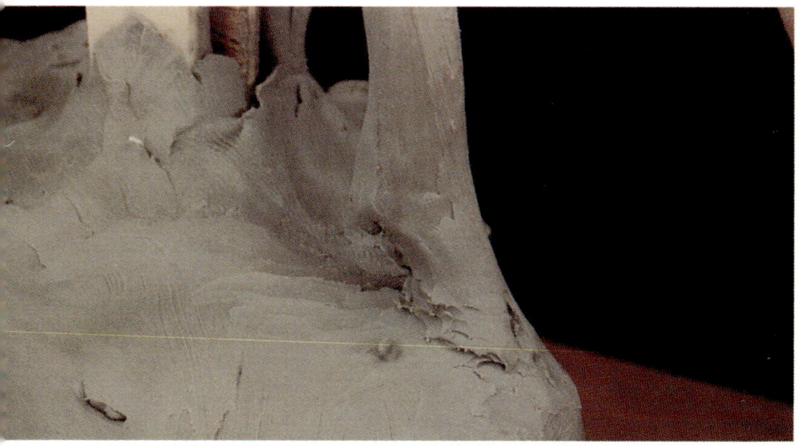

Split the hoof.

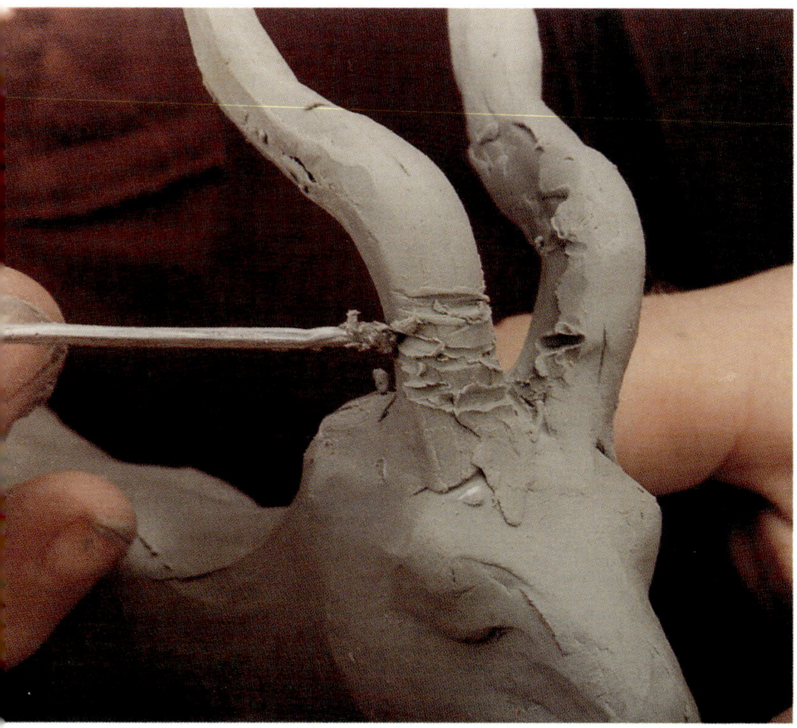

Lightly sculpt in rings around the horns.

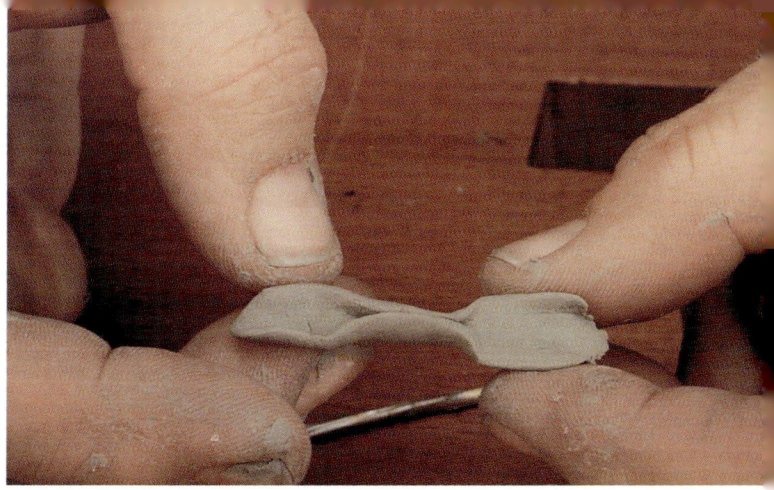

Take a small flat piece of clay, pinch it in the middle, and cut it in two at the pinched middle so that you have two halves.

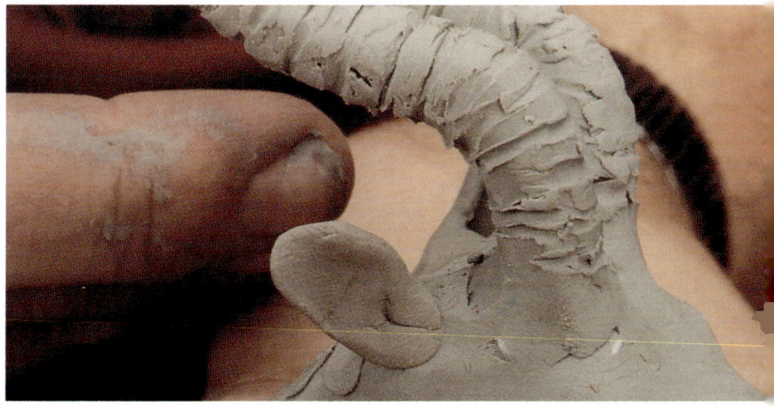

Place one half on each side of the head behind the horns and shape into ears.

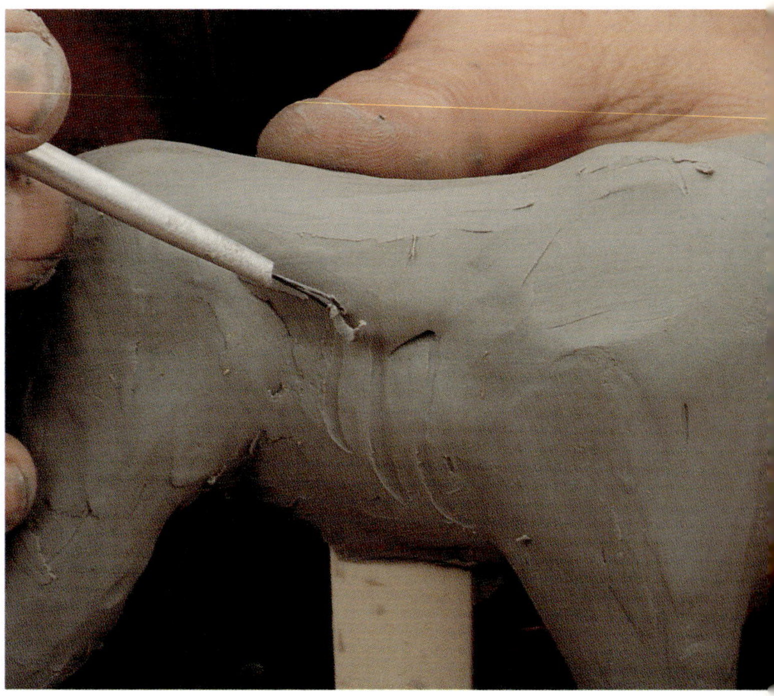

Lightly score in three ribs on each side and smooth them out with your finger so that the lines are not so definite.

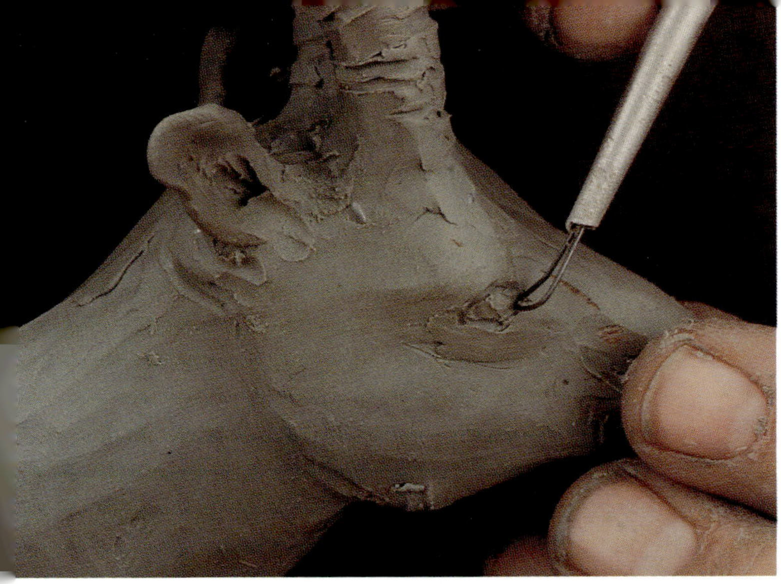

Cut in the eye.

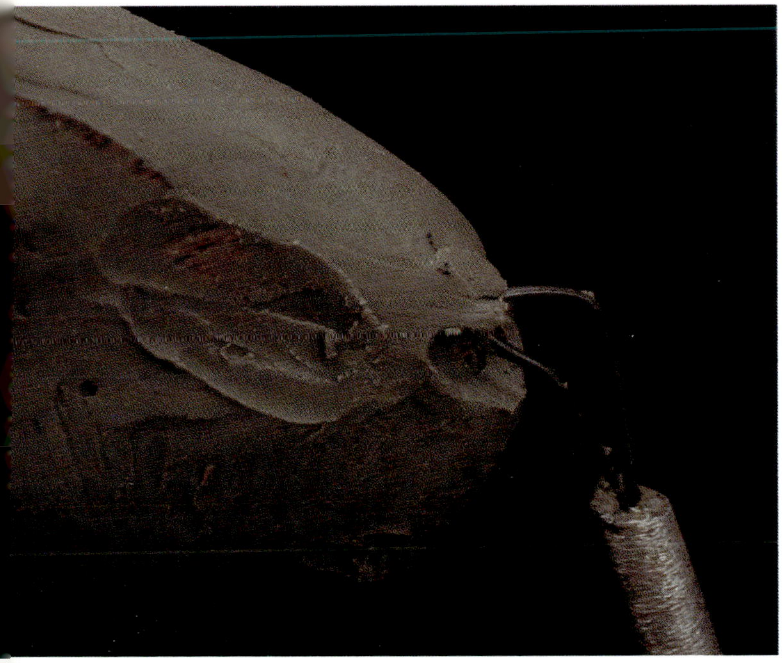

Cut in the nose, making it a teardrop with the smaller part in the back and the larger part wrapping around the front of the face.

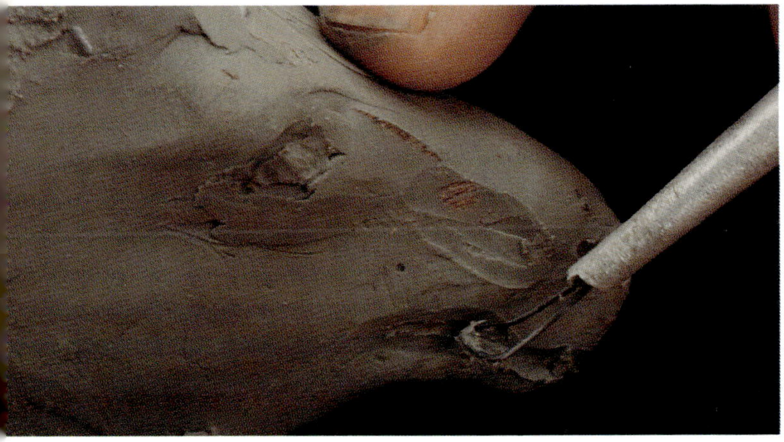

Use small cuts to indicate the muscles in the face and the mouth.

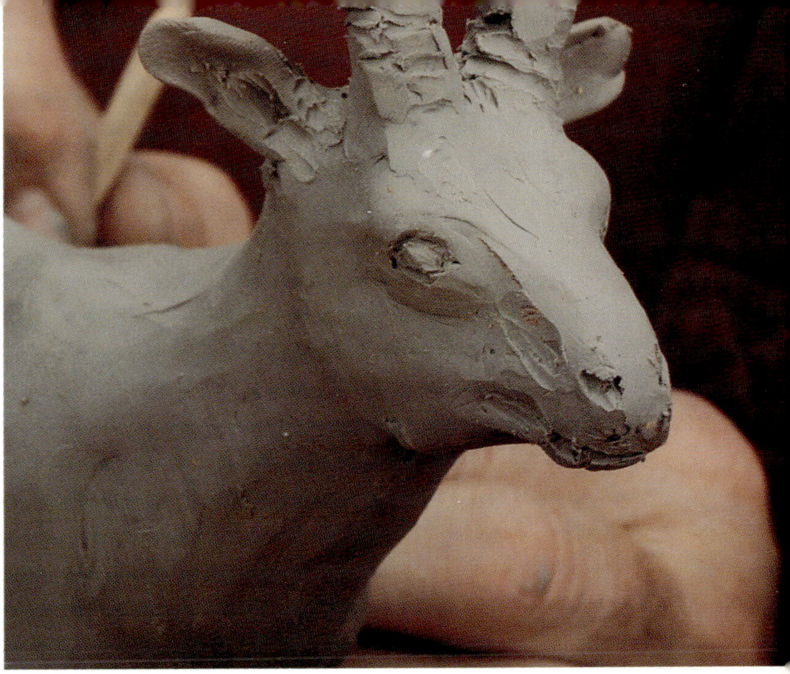

The face and the impala are basically complete. You can go back now and put in as much extra detail as you care to.

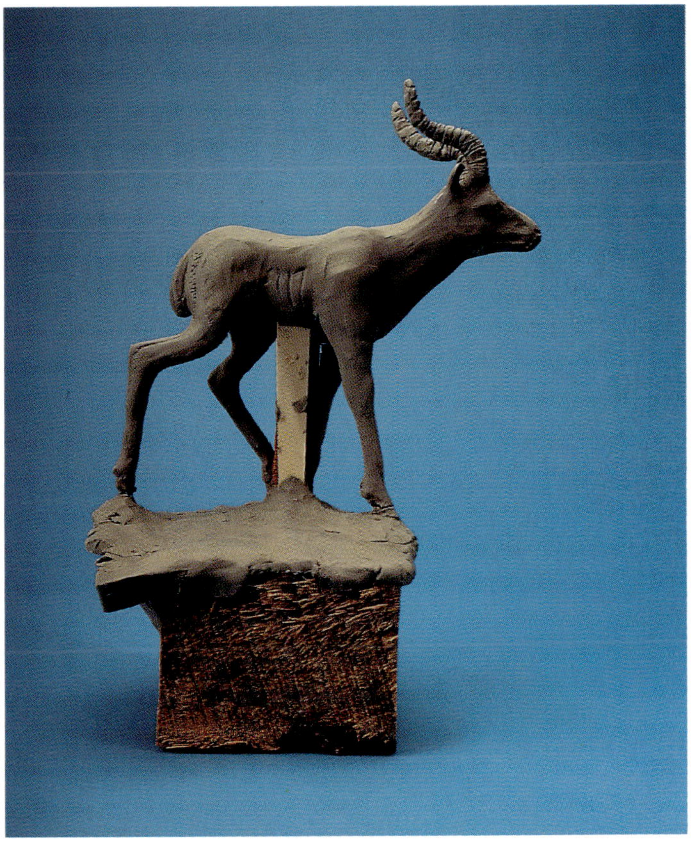

The completed impala.

Gallery

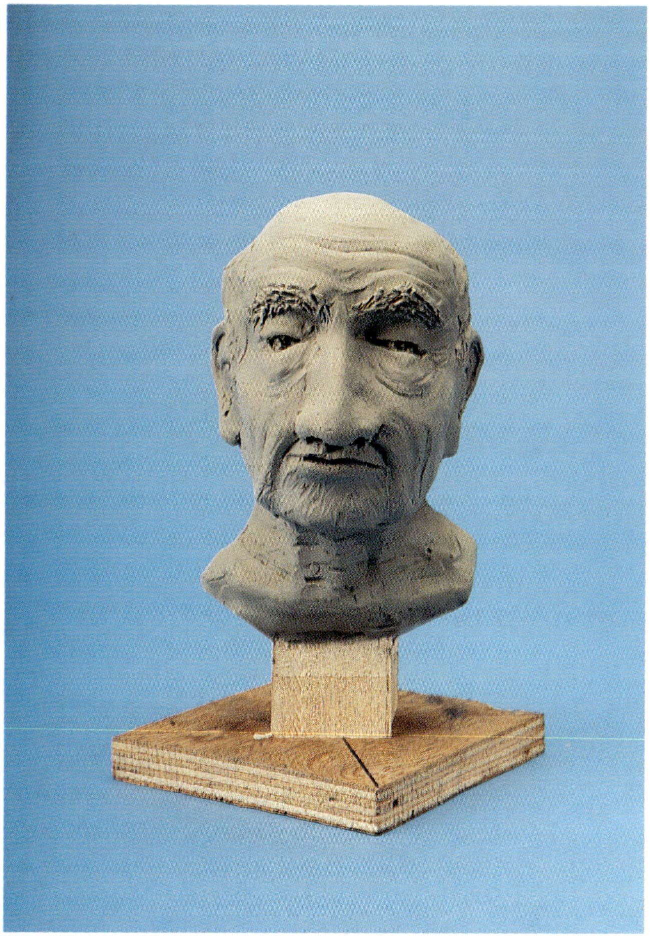

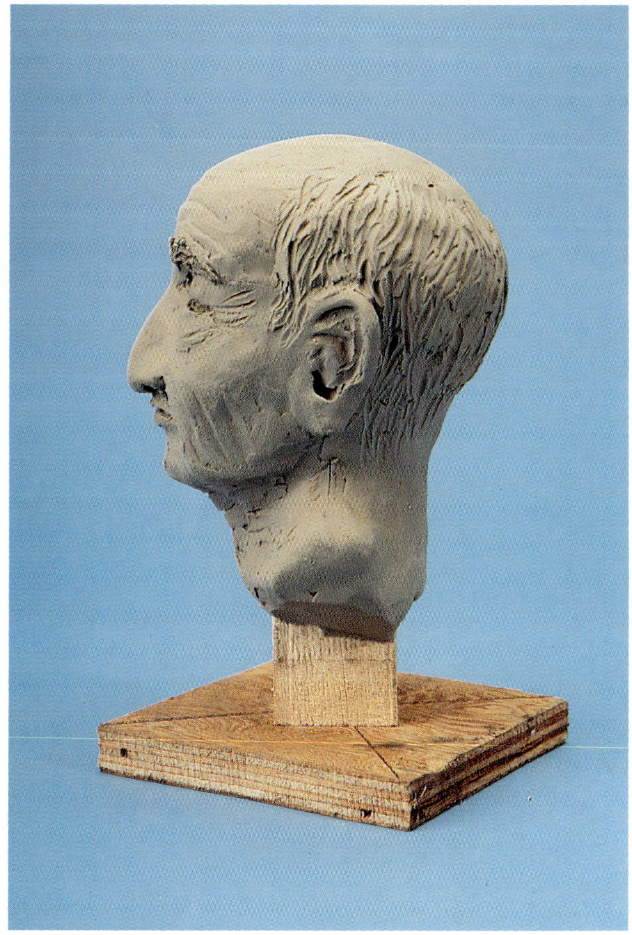

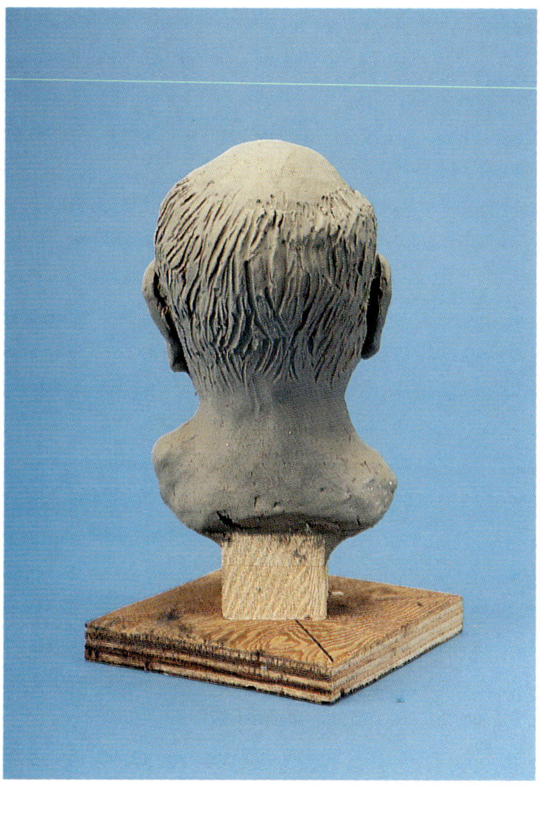

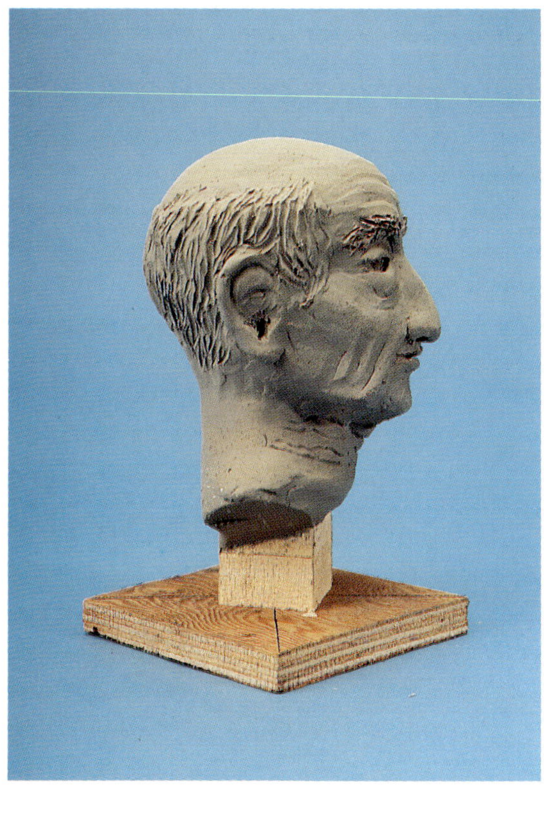

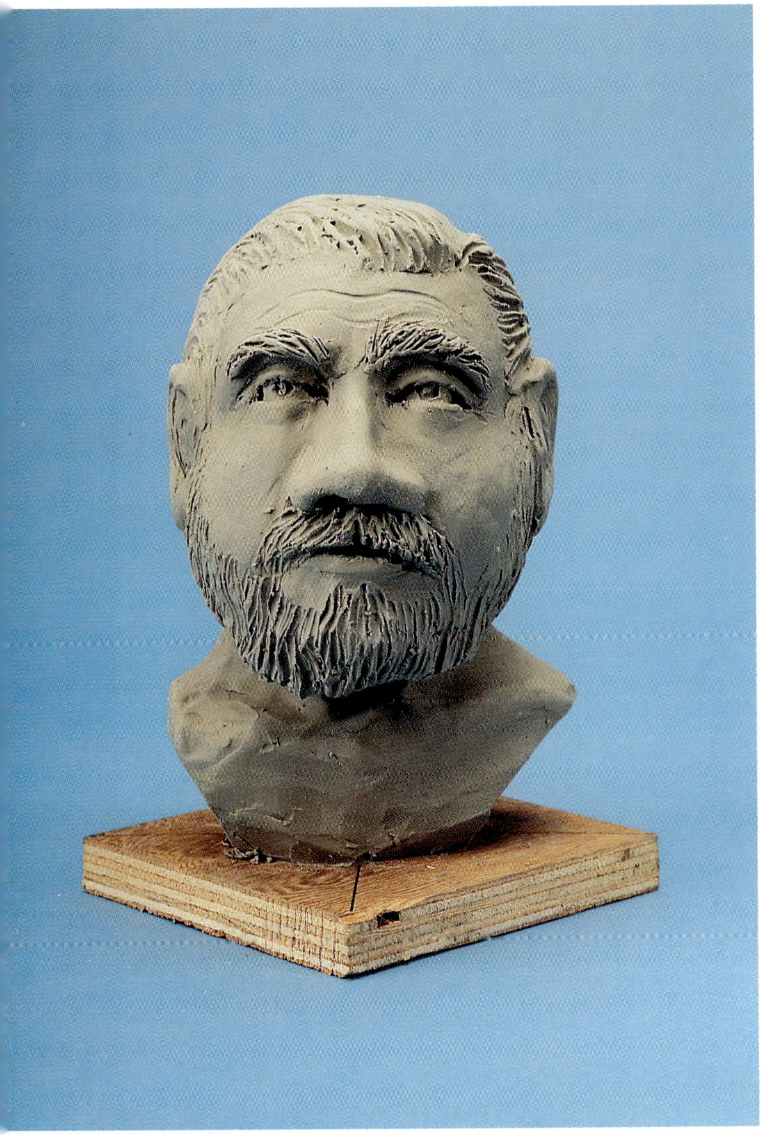

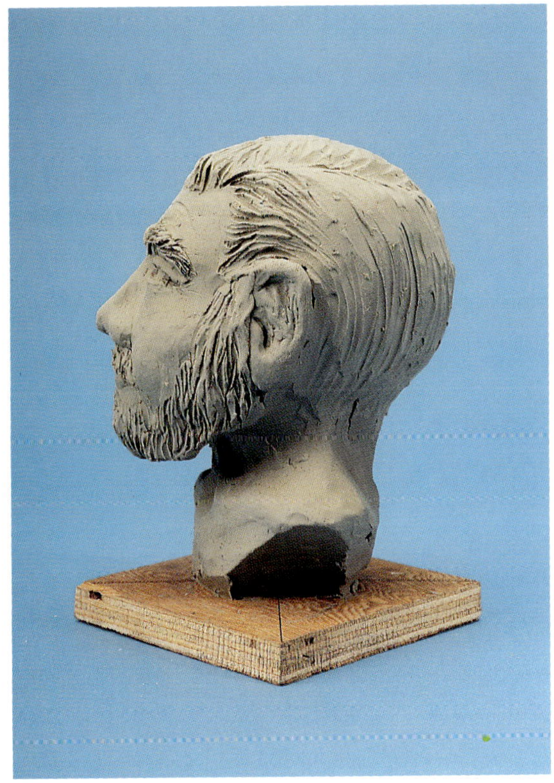

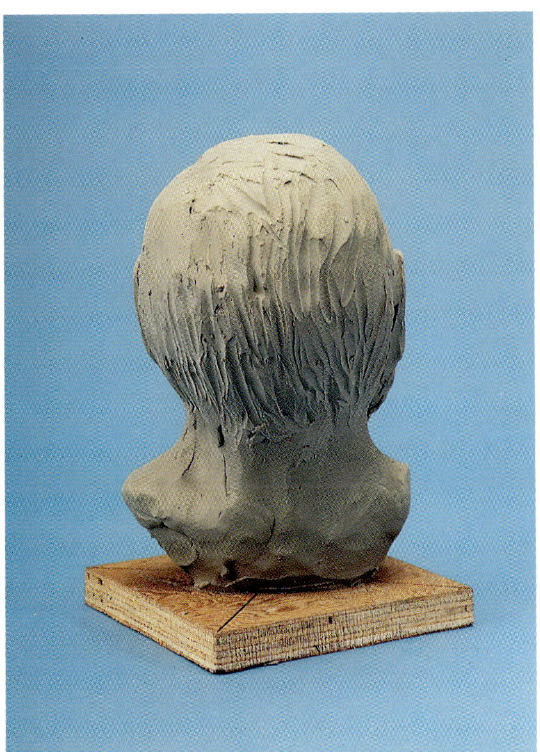

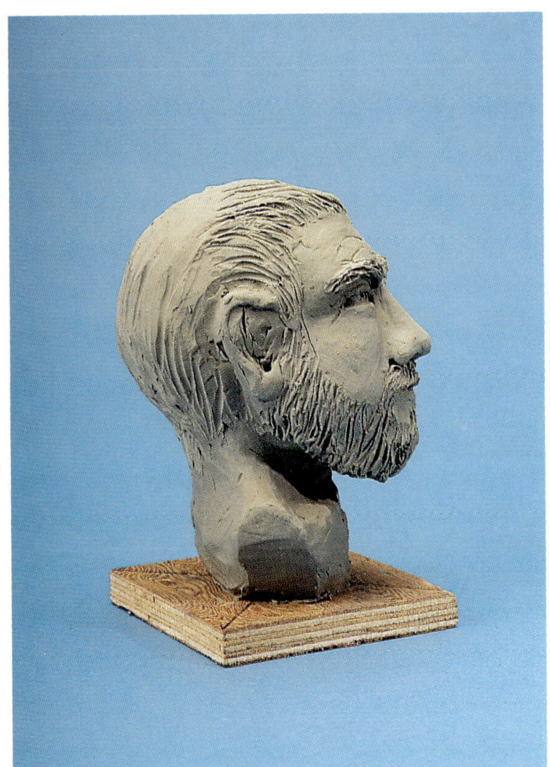

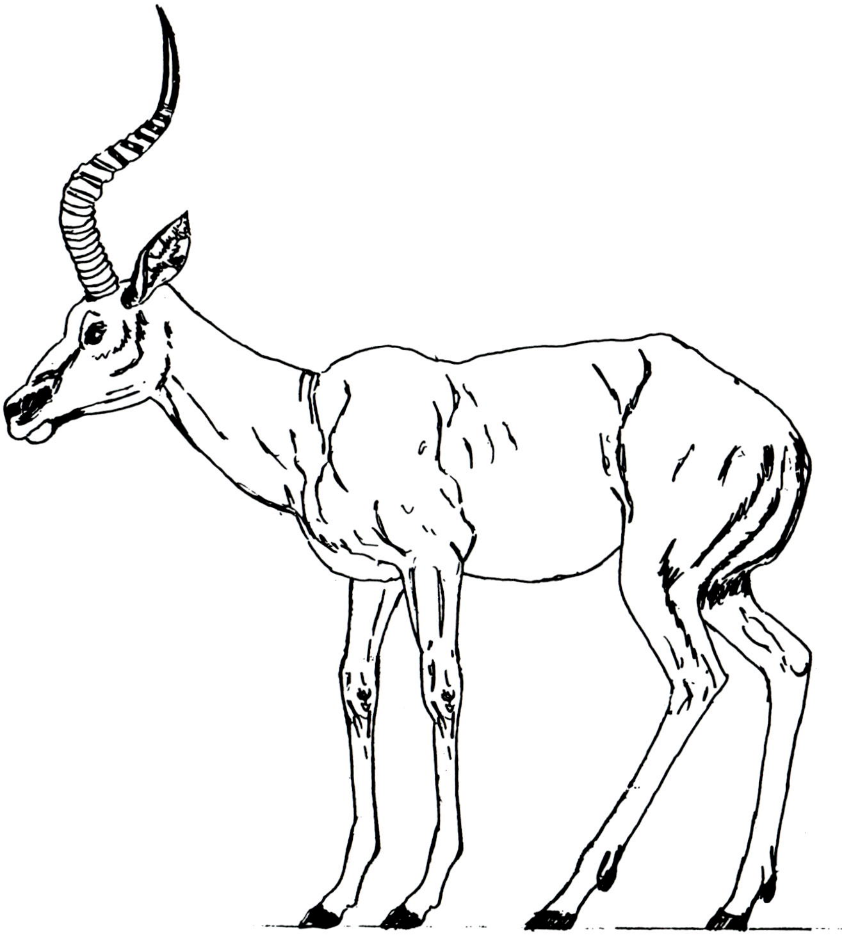

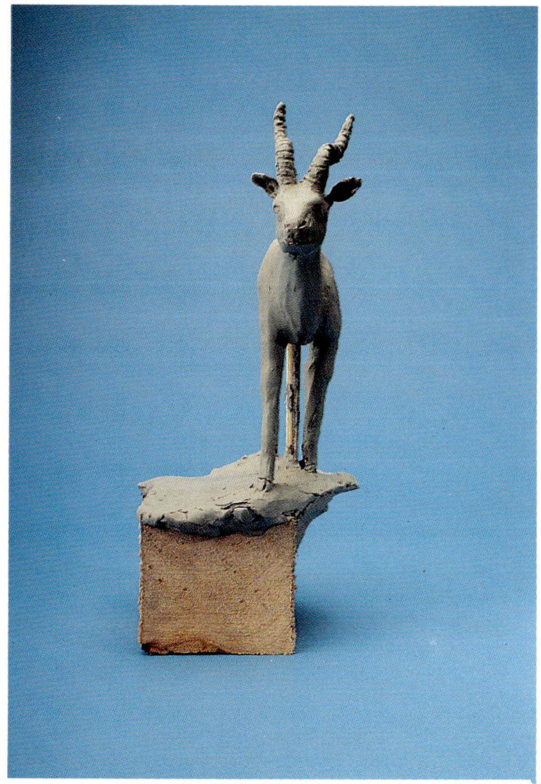

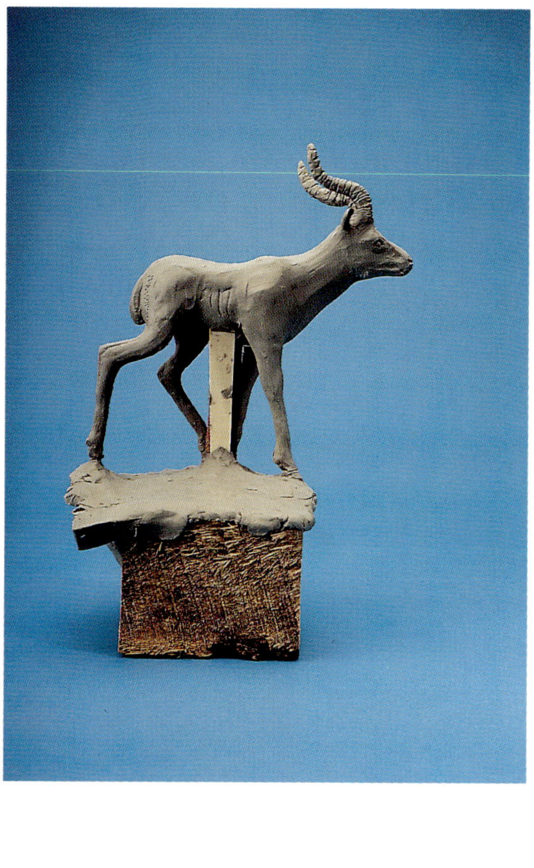

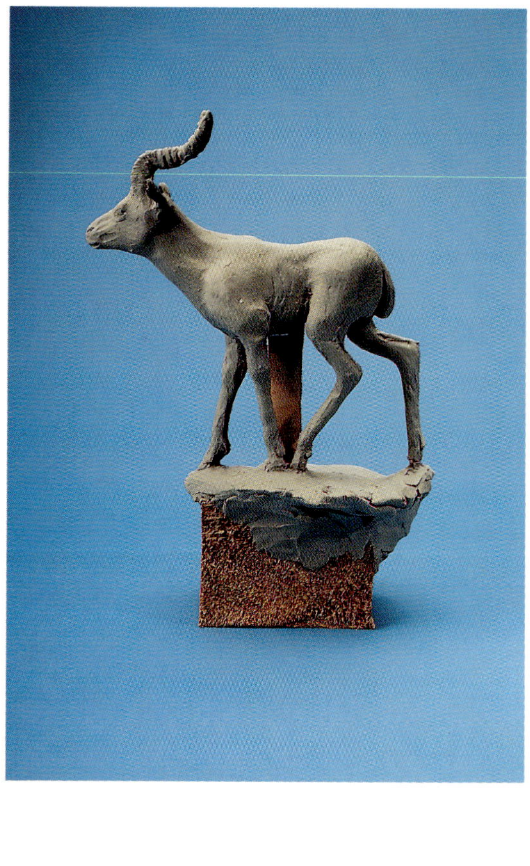

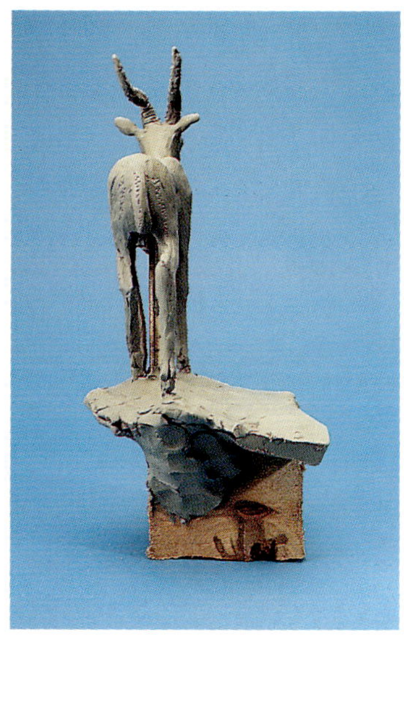

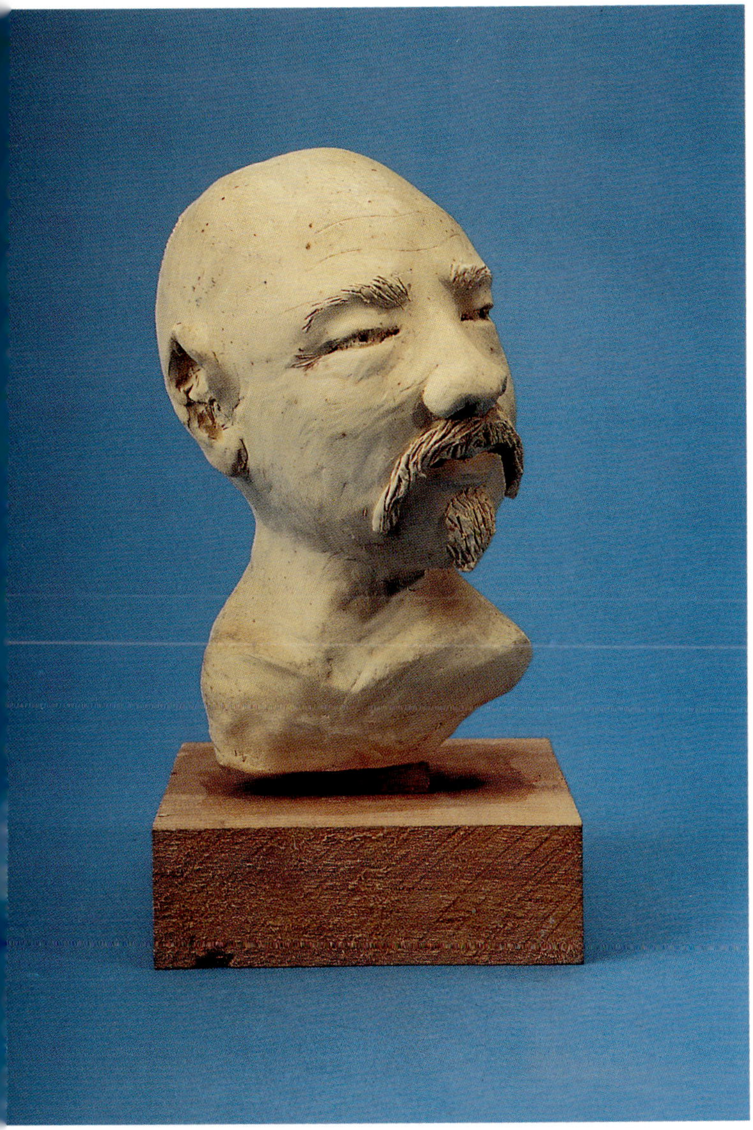

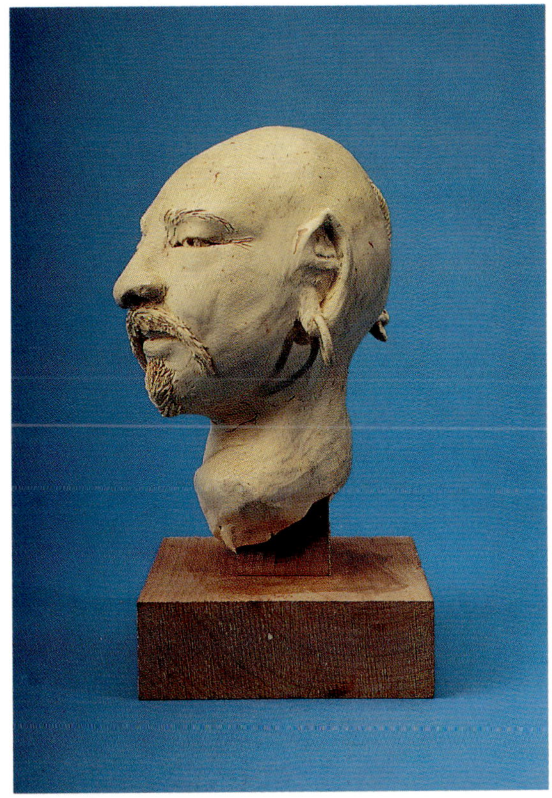

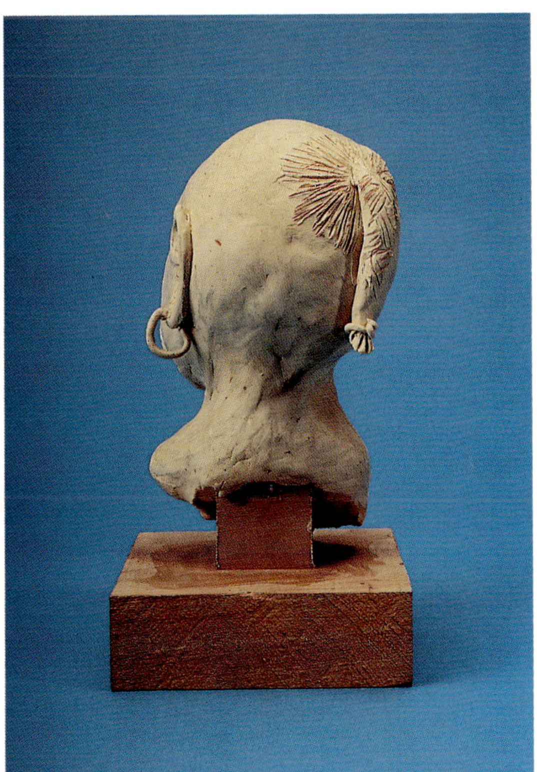

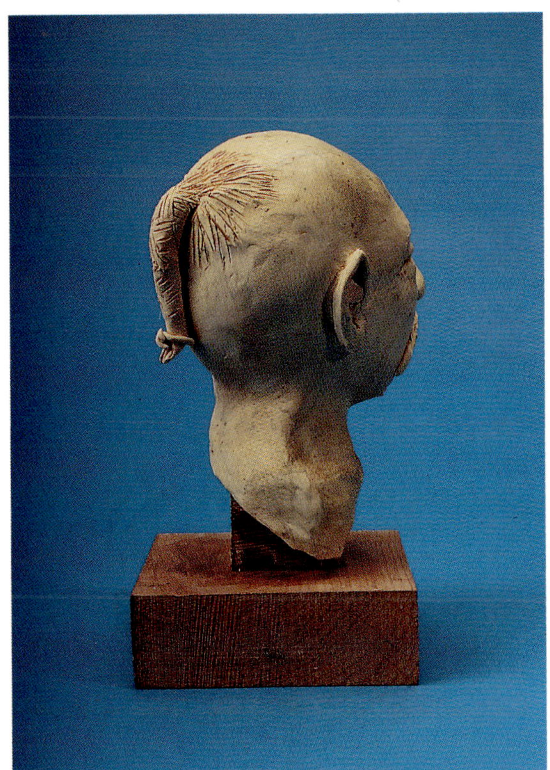

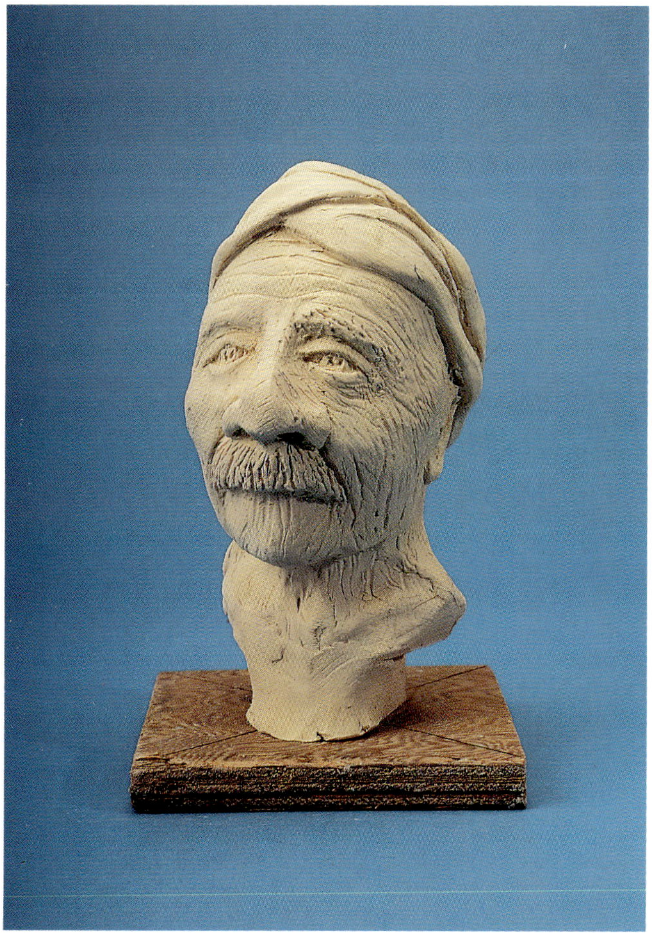
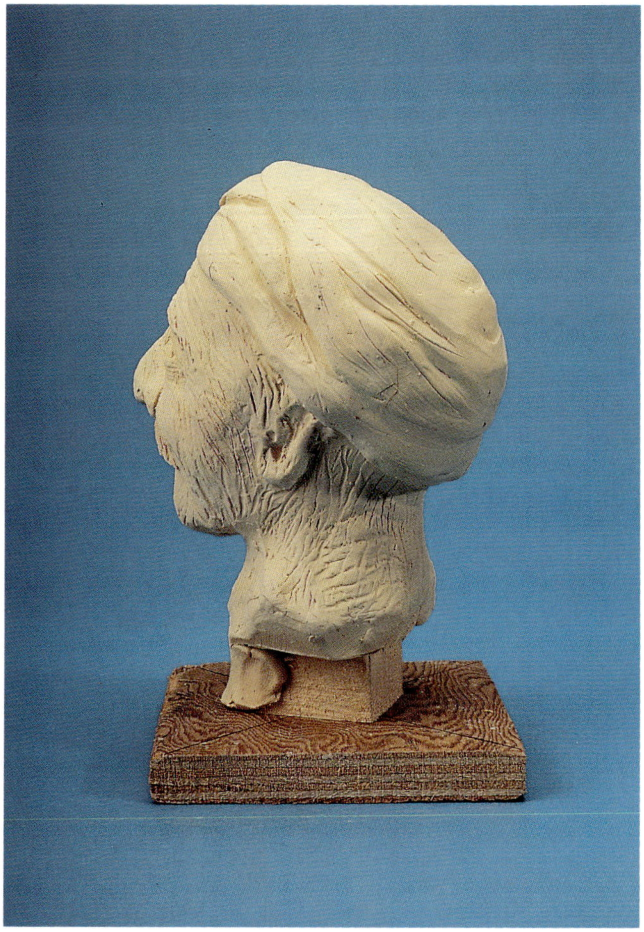
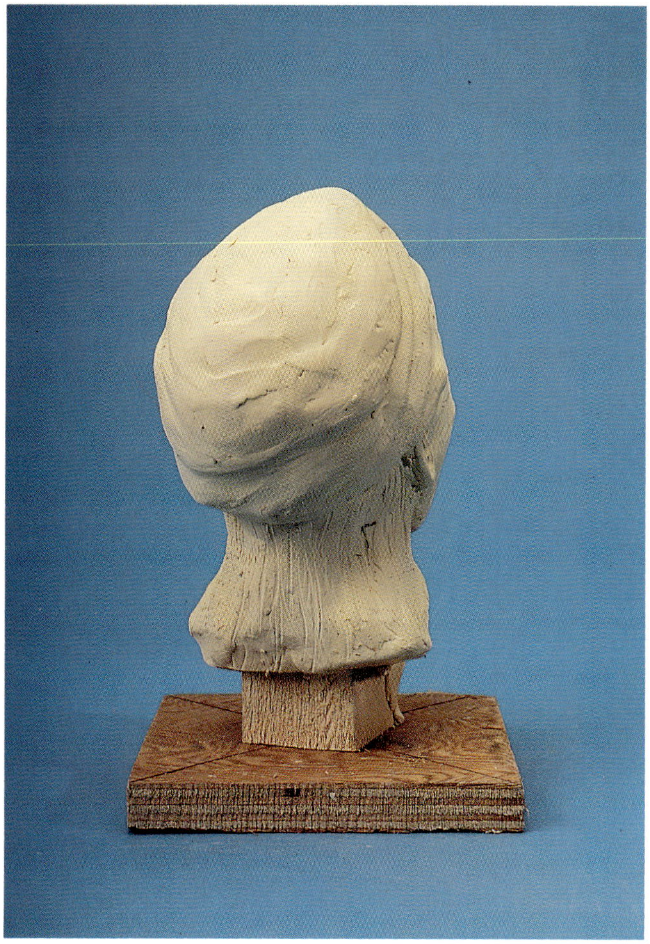
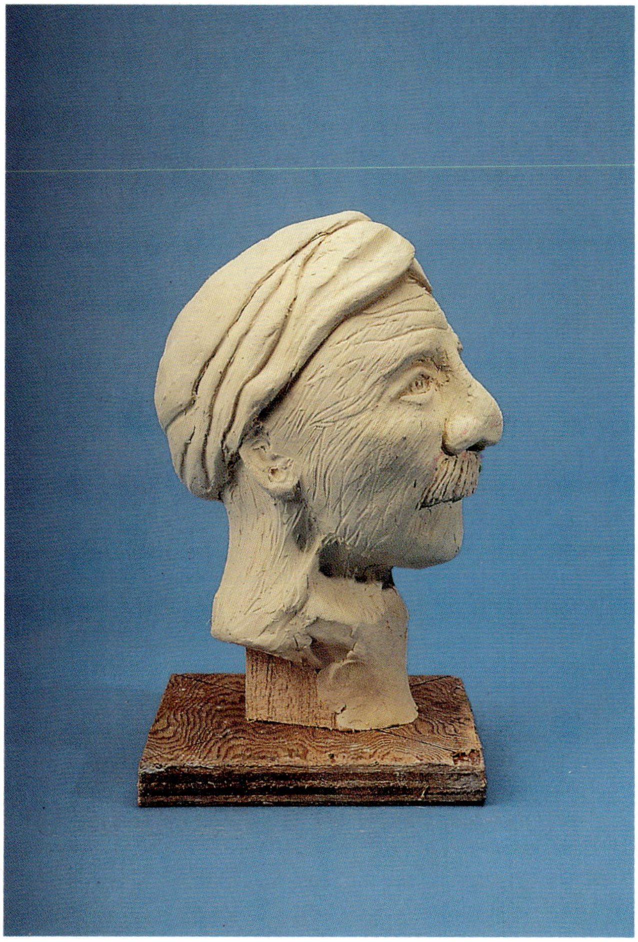

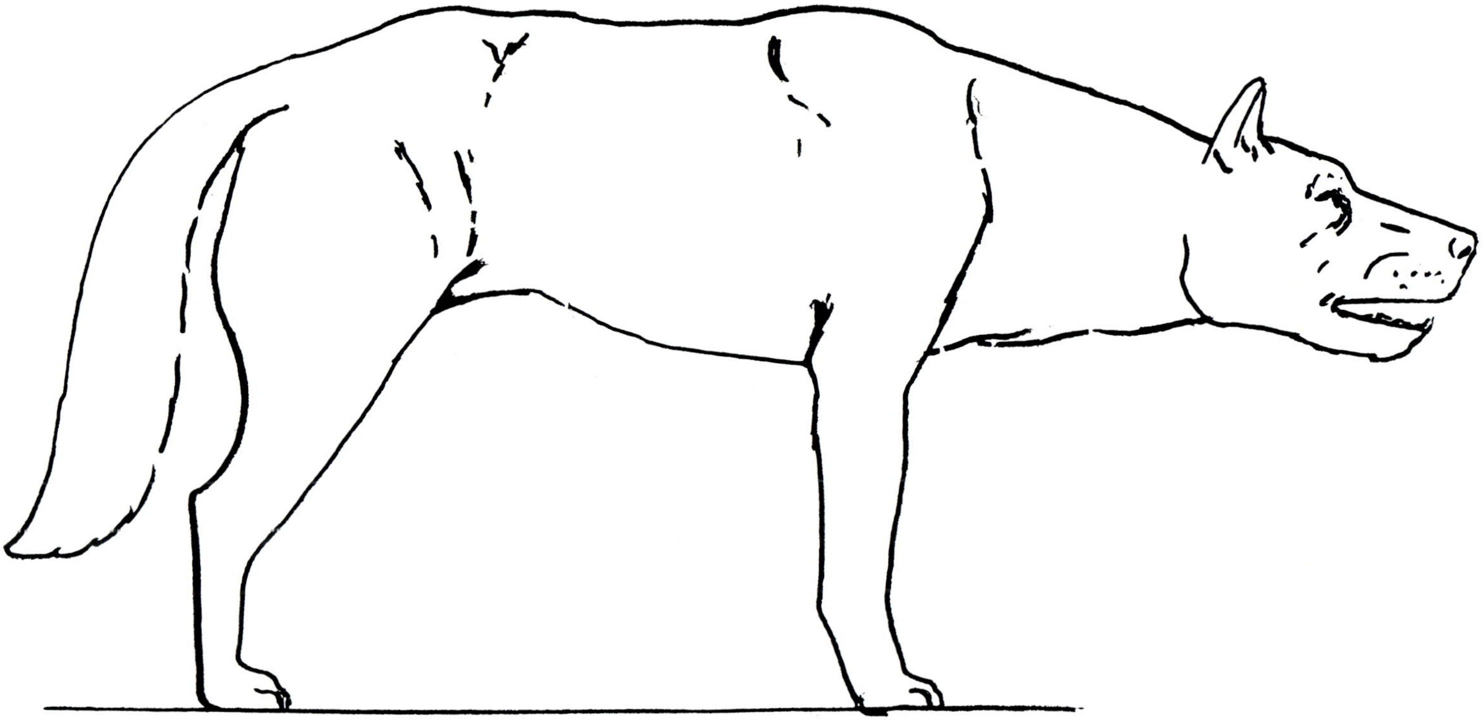

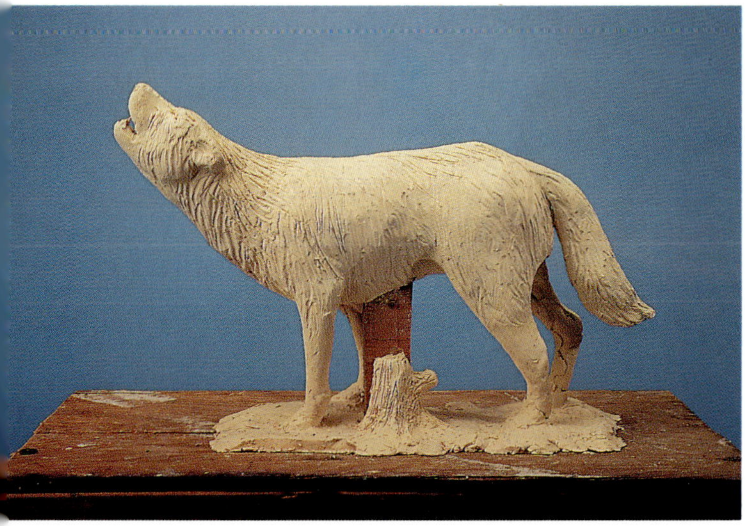

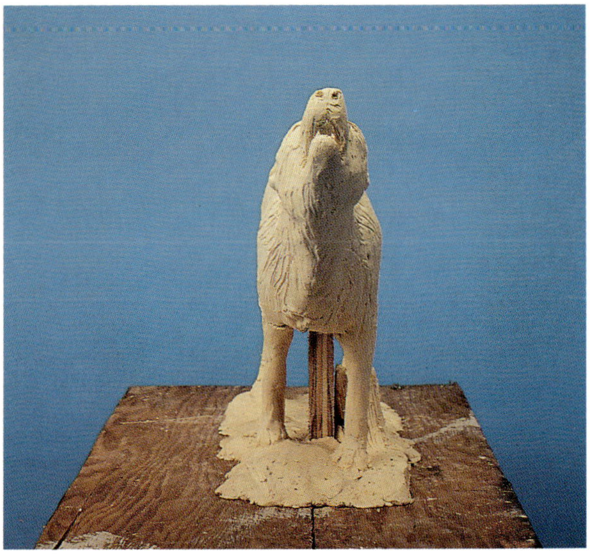

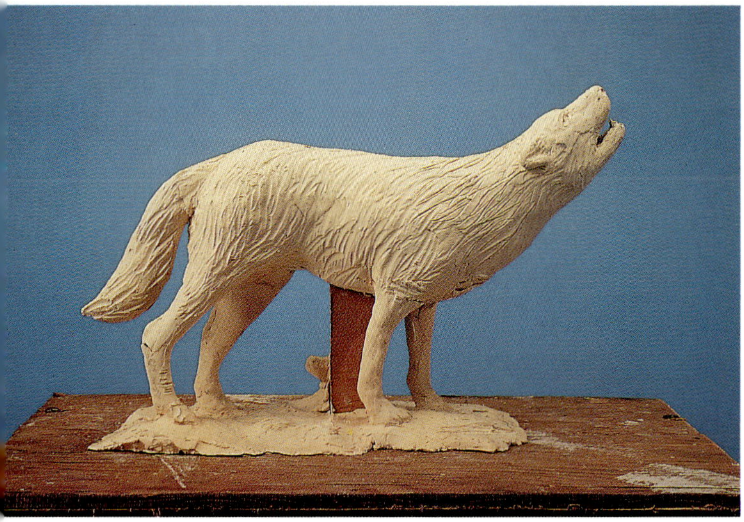

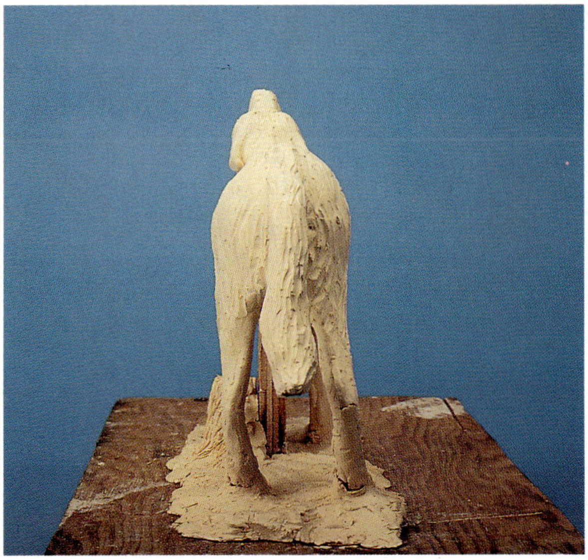

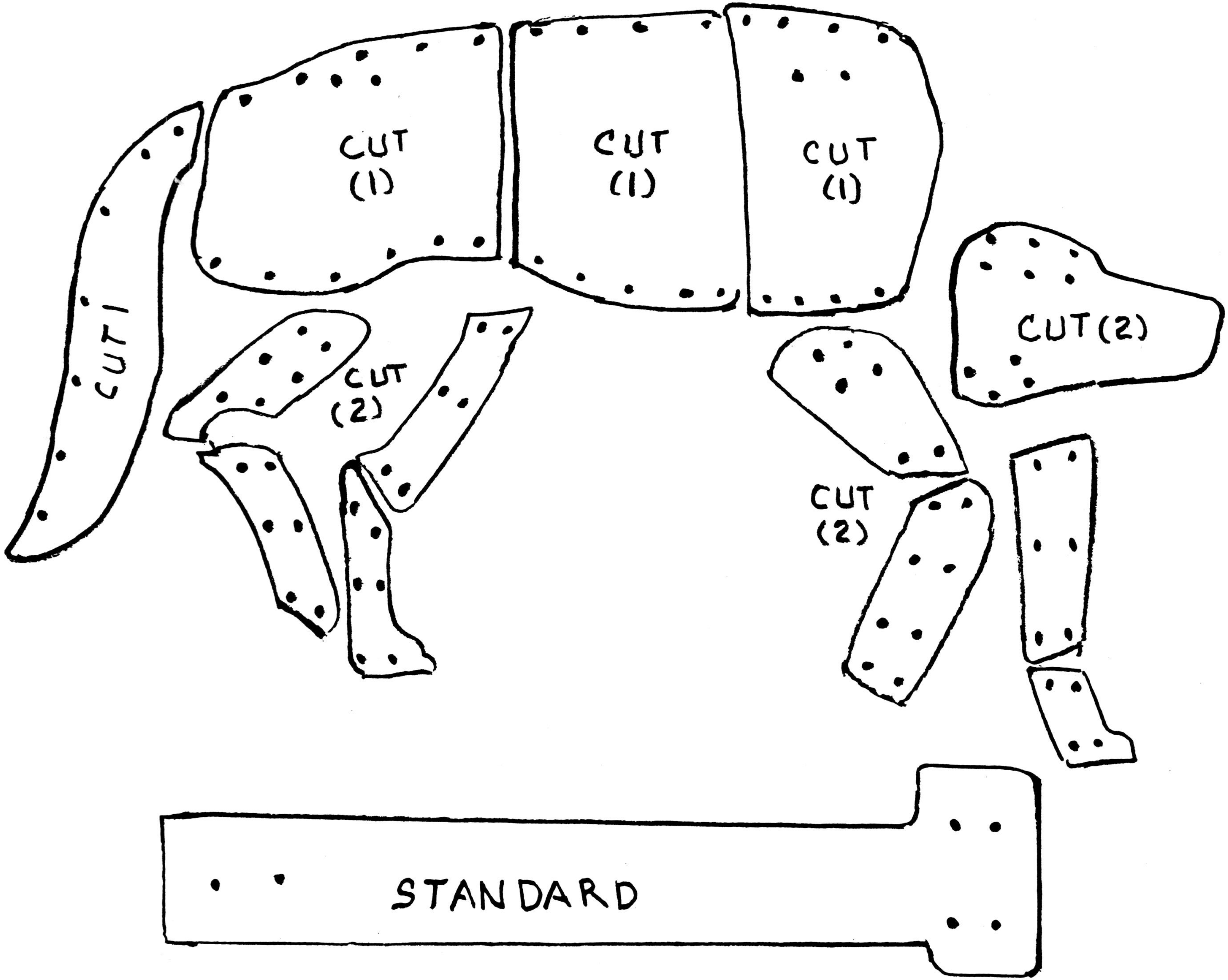
CUT (1)
CUT (1)
CUT (1)
CUT(2)
CUT 1
CUT (2)
CUT (2)
STANDARD